THE LIFE WE LONGED FOR

Danchi Housing and the Middle Class Dream in Postwar Japan

**Weatherhead
East Asian Institute**

Studies of the Weatherhead East Asian Institute,
Columbia University

The Studies of the Weatherhead East Asian Institute of Columbia University were inaugurated in 1962 to bring to a wider public the results of significant new research on modern and contemporary East Asia.

LAURA NEITZEL

THE LIFE WE LONGED FOR

Danchi Housing and the Middle Class Dream in Postwar Japan

MerwinAsia

Portland, Maine

MerwinAsia
59 West St., Unit 3W
Portland, ME 04102
USA

Copyright © 2016 by MerwinAsia

www.merwinasia.com

Distributed by the University of Hawai'i Press

Library of Congress Control Number: 2015947026

ISBN 978-1-937385-86-6 (Hardcover)
ISBN 978-1-937385-87-3 (Paperback)

Printed in the United States of America

The paper used in this publication meets the minimum
requirements of the American National Standard for
Information Services—Permanence of Paper for Printed
Library Materials, ANSI/NISO Z39/48-1992

Cover and interior design by Lucian Burg, LU Design Studios,
Portland, ME
www.ludesignstudios.com

For my parents

Jan and Hal Neitzel

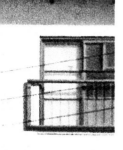

CONTENTS

Acknowledgments

The word "acknowledgment" is inadequate to express the gratitude I feel to the many people who have supported and encouraged me through the process of researching and writing this book. This would be a lesser book and I a lesser person without them.

Three great teachers and scholars have guided me over the years. Elizabeth Tsunoda first ignited my passion for history. Her confidence in me, which far exceeded my faith in myself, provided the courage to pursue doctoral studies. From the very inception of this project Harry Harootunian has been ever generous with his time, insights, and guidance. His work has inspired me and his friendship has been a great gift. My deepest gratitude belongs to Carol Gluck who has exercised a profound influence on me as a historian and teacher. Her lessons resonate each time I strive to illustrate the relevance of the past to my students; and even more so as I seek to mentor and support them as they pursue their individual paths. My highest aspiration is to be to my students what Carol Gluck has been to me.

Over the course of my graduate and professional career, I have been blessed with the friendship of several amazing women. Spending Friday nights in the library with Jody van der Goes, walking and talking the streets of New York with Nerina Rustomji, sipping whiskey with Ann Stinson, holding late night kitchen seminars with Janet Poole, and traveling the world with Barbara Jones have nourished mind and soul and helped advance my thinking on this and other scholarly and life projects.

Many other scholars have contributed directly or indirectly to the evolution of this book, including Betsy Blackmar, Kim Brandt, Ann Douglas, Darryl Flaherty, Ken Kawashima, Marvin Marcus, Ken Tadashi Oshima, Greg Pflugfelder, Jordan Sand, Henry Smith, Anders Stephanson, Umemori Naoyuki, and Gwendolyn Wright. Nishida Yoshiaki, Kudō Akira, Harada Sumitaka, and Kase Kazutoshi of the Institute for Social Science at Tokyo University offered invaluable support and advice during initial research. I am grateful to Kuriyagawa Ichirō and others at the Urban Development Corporation in Tokyo (now the Urban Renaissance Agency) for providing vital information about the early Japan Housing Corporation and opening their archives for my research.

The students of Kim Brandt and Harry Harootunian's Columbia University graduate seminar on postwar Japan provided helpful comments and questions on an earlier draft of the manuscript. Chapter One benefited from the insights of members of the University Seminar on Modern Japan, particularly from those of discussant Darryl Flaherty. I am thankful to an anonymous reviewer who offered valuable suggestions for clarification and improvement. I am especially grateful to Amy Conte for her patient and thorough reading of the manuscript in its final stages. Her insightful comments improved the book significantly.

Research for this project was possible thanks to a multi-year Fellowship from the Graduate School of Arts and Sciences at Columbia University, a Fulbright Graduate Research Fellowship, a Junior Japan Fellowship, and the Expanding East Asian Studies Postdoctoral Fellowship. The University Seminars at Columbia University provided generous support for the publication of the book and for this I am deeply thankful.

Without the advocacy of Columbia University's Weatherhead East Asian Institute and the support of MerwinAsia this book may never have come to print. I am deeply grateful to Carol Gluck, Kim Brandt, Dan Rivero, and Ross Yelsey at Weatherhead for standing behind me and this project. It is a great honor to have this book included among the Studies of the Weatherhead East Asian Institute. Working with Doug Merwin on the publication of the book was a true pleasure. More than he knows, I appreciate his kindly guidance throughout the process, not to mention his sound editorial advice. Finally, I am grateful to Lucian Burg for the lovely design of the cover and interior of the book.

I have found a warm professional home at Brookdale Community College and am indebted to many colleagues there, including Yoshiko Hurley who offered vital assistance as I pursued photo permissions and Ethel Brandon and Jeanne Vloyanetes who located sources for me. I am fortunate to be part of a community of History colleagues who inspire me and make going to work a joy.

The greatest debts I owe to my family. To my sisters Lea Crawford and Amy Conte and their families, Steve, Taylor, Casey, Richard, Claire, and Hal I owe love and gratitude for believing in me, always. This book would still be on my "to do" list if not for the love and boundless support of my husband Tom Albunio. He introduced beautiful daughters and grandsons into my world and filled our home with garden flowers and simmering pots of tomato sauce. I thank him, especially, for giving me the life I always longed for.

I dedicate the book to my parents who encouraged me to pursue my passions even when they led me far from family. My mother created a beautiful and loving home for us, and helped me discover that the greatest joy of travel is returning home. In large ways and small, she continues to teach me about resilience and courage. My father was my collaborator and editor from the time I began to write and with his vast library of books was my "Google" before there was such a thing. Although he passed away before the book was published, his influence is evident on each and every page.

Introduction

Everyone's everyone's everyone's home,
Our, our, our Housing Corporation.
Voices you can hear, hear, hear,
Voices, voices, voices, lively voices,
To the east, to the west, to the south, to the north,
In a song brimming with expanding hope.

Chorus of the "Japan Housing Corporation Song"[1]

The age of the *danchi*

Japan's urban peripheries are dotted with apartment blocks known to all as "*danchi*." Consisting of older buildings of four- or five stories as well as newer high rises of ten-plus floors, they are clustered by the dozens in urban communities and suburban "new towns," the largest of which house many thousands of people within a single complex. With numbers inscribed on their exterior walls to distinguish one building from the other, the ferro-concrete *danchi* convey a drab sameness relieved only by the colorful laundry and bedding which invariably hang airing from their balconies. Since the 1950s when they were first constructed on a large scale by the state-sponsored Japan Housing Corporation (JHC), millions of Japanese people have lived in *danchi* apartments either temporarily or long-term but, in the words of one observer, "even if you never lived in one, they are part of the landscape."[2] They have been part of the infrastructure of post-war Japan and a backdrop to people's everyday lives. (see figures 1 and 2)

From the perspective of the early twenty-first century, it can be difficult to imagine that these standardized concrete buildings, in their homogeneous groupings, were ever considered desirable places to live. Many of those built in the 1950s and 1960s have not aged well, with decaying playground equipment,

---

1. Lyrics by Satō Hachirō. Song reproduced in *Danchi biyori* (Tokyo: Albatros, 2008).
2. Ibid.

rusting railings and mailboxes, and pathways overgrown with weeds. Newer *danchi* communities built in the 1970s or 1980s and located in far distant suburbs are stark reminders of the tremendous compromises people were required to make in order to live and work at a time when land prices were exploding and the economy was bubbling. Yet to people of certain generations, particularly those who raised families or grew up during what came to be called "the era of high-speed economic growth" (mid-1950s–early 1970s), the *danchi* tend to spark memories and nostalgia. Almost invariably, "It was the life we longed for" (*akogareta seikatsu*) is the wistful comment about the *danchi* of the 1950s and 1960s. It was this "longing" and a desire to understand its significance which was the impetus for this book.

At first glance, the reasons for such "longing" are easy to comprehend. The Japan Housing Corporation was established in 1955 to address the nation's continuing housing crisis in the wake of World War II. While examples of state-initiated collective housing predated the establishment of the JHC, as did use of the word "*danchi*" to refer to collective housing built "on one grouping of land" (*ichidan no tochi ni*), it would be the JHC that would give both the term and the *danchi* apartment a bright new image.[3] Apartments were designed to appeal to the JHC's target constituency, the aspiring middle-class families that government officials believed would rebuild Japan. Their concrete construction was widely touted and had great appeal after the aerial bombings of World War II had reduced wooden homes to ash. Apartments were equipped with electricity, private baths, flush toilets, steel doors with locks, and modern "dining kitchens." In an extremely tight housing market, income-eligible people had to win a competitive lottery to secure an apartment, and in the early years, living in the *danchi* was the prerogative of relatively affluent white-collar families of the "new middle class." As copious studies and exposés of *danchi* life made clear, these families were well ahead of the national curve in the acquisition of refrigerators, televisions, washing machines, and other objects of consumer desire in the late 1950s and early 1960s. At a time when urban housing markets were still marked by dire shortages and most people endured abysmal living standards, it is not surprising that *danchi* life entered the social imaginary as something to envy.

And the appeal of the *danchi* transcended their modern amenities and the lifestyles of their inhabitants. Their interior designs were born of the idealism of the early postwar period. Architects and social engineers viewed the prewar

---

3.   The most notable precursor to JHC *danchi* were the Dōjunkai Apartments built in 1920s. The word "*danchi*," like all Japanese nouns, functions as both the singular and plural. I follow Japanese usage and use the same word for both.

"family system" as a conservative force which had supported the nation's misguided war effort, and they sought to reform the postwar family through a reorganization of living space. Many of their ideas took built form in the *danchi* interior, which merged prewar conceptions of "cultured living" with postwar aspirations to elevate the status of the housewife, separate young married couples from the pressures of the extended family, democratize relationships among family members, and promote "privacy" among individual family members and between the family and community. The *danchi* nuclear family was envisioned as the antithesis of the "feudal" extended family and the impersonal *danchi* community a welcome departure from the intrusions and surveillance of the village community of wartime Japan.

Yet in other ways, memories of "longing" for *danchi* life are more complex. By the mid-1970s, the majority of Japanese people owned the consumer items associated with a *danchi* lifestyle. And because the JHC was a major innovator in construction methods and housing design, many of the floor plans, construction techniques, and fixtures it developed for the *danchi* became standard in housing both public and private. Most significant among these were the "nDK" (number of rooms plus dining kitchen) and "nLDK" (number of rooms plus living room and dining kitchen) as ways of configuring and designating interior space which were developed for the *danchi* and later became standard in much of Japanese housing. Thus, even if people did not live in *danchi* apartments, many had dining kitchens, stainless steel sinks, and pre-cast concrete walls inspired by them.

Moreover, in the economic crisis of the early 1970s, as many people began to note the human and environmental costs of high-speed economic growth, the JHC *danchi* came under severe criticism for promoting urban sprawl, driving up land prices, and homogenizing living space. Yet even in the midst of critiques of what, in many ways, had become their *own* everyday lives, people continued to evoke the *danchi* as "the life we longed for." In other words, people nostalgically recalled "longing" for the *danchi* lifestyle more than they did the experience of actually achieving it. Svetlana Boym, in her work on nostalgia, suggests that "at first glance, nostalgia is a longing for a place, but actually it is a yearning for a different time."[4] This certainly holds true of "longing" for the life of the *danchi*. The *danchi* evoke a space and a lifestyle, but much more than that, they evoke an age.[5]

4. Svetlana Boym, *The Future of Nostalgia* (Basic Books, 2001, xv).
5. A dialogue between economist Hara Takeshi and novelist Shigematsu Kiyoshi in a book titled *The Era of the Danchi* (Danchi no jidai) (Tokyo: Shinchosha, 2010) conveys their recollections growing up during the era of high-speed growth. Hara

So a book about the *danchi* is about a physical space, a place for living, but it is equally about "a different time," the era of high-speed economic growth. The nearly two decades between the mid-1950s and the early 1970s would witness the transformation of everyday life in Japan. Double-digit national growth, full employment, and rapidly rising personal incomes would transform workplaces, homes, lifestyles, and urban infrastructures. Physical traces of the war would be paved over and its memories fade in the frenetic pace of economic growth. These years would also be marked by high-stakes conflict between capital and labor, political protest over Japan's postwar relationship with the United States, and student protests in the context of the global 1960s. The years of "high-speed economic growth," were a time of possibility, energy, and contention over the meanings of postwar change. Everyday life was "filled with the future," to borrow a concept of Harry Harootunian, when the meanings of postwar life were in flux.[6]

Yet these decades would eventually be foundational of a certain vision of everyday life—one apparent, among other places, in the lifestyle of the *danchi*. Media and government designations of the young nuclear families in their bright, modern *danchi* apartments as "vanguards" of postwar change would have their effects, helping to "fix meanings"[7] and reestablish normative ideals of the postwar home and family. As one of the earliest and most visible examples of postwar prosperity, the *danchi* would play an important role in redefining the parameters of middle-class aspirations for home and family life. But perhaps more important, after decades of war and hardship, the upwardly mobile, middle-class family living a comfortable, middle-class lifestyle presented an alluring vision of life getting better, of a future better than the present. It would be in this sense that the "*danchi* vanguard" would have its greatest impact. It was none other than the middle-class dream of an ever-improving-life that would become the true locus of people's longing; a middle-class dream that continues to entice and disappoint to this day.

The *danchi* in global context

The age of the *danchi* was a global age, one shared by industrialized nations

grew up in the *danchi* and wrote the novel *Takiyama komyūn 1974* (Kodansha bunko, 2010) on his boyhood experiences there.

6.   Harootunian's copious work on the meanings of everyday life suggests that the temporality of the everyday is one which has not yet been coopted by narratives of development and is therefore filled with great potential for rupture from the past. See "Shadowing History: National narratives and the persistence of the everyday," in *Cultural Studies* 18: 2/3 (March/May 2004), 181-200.

7.   Ibid., 181.

emerging from World War II. *Danchi* were ubiquitous on Japan's postwar urban landscape but so were remarkably similar housing projects in cities from
Moscow to Chicago, Brasília to Shanghai, Paris to East Berlin. Born of the international movement of the interwar period and merging the concerns of social
reformers, government bureaucrats, and architects, mass housing projects were
conceived as an answer to myriad problems of modern, industrialized societies:
how to house large numbers of people converging on cities, how to lessen class
disparities which threatened social order, how to promote a modern, hygienic
lifestyle among new city dwellers, and, perhaps most interesting to the architects
who designed them, how to apply methods of mass production to the construction of housing. Mass housing, argued historian Florian Urban, emerged as a
"strategy for modernization" and came to "stand rhetorically for progress and
prosperity."[8]

The years following World War II would become the high point of mass
housing projects as a necessary response to dire shortages resulting from the
war. Across Europe and Asia, urban infrastructures were destroyed in the aerial
bombing campaigns of the war, leaving millions homeless and destitute. Even
places untouched by battle, such as the continental United States and South
America, experienced tremendous housing shortages as postwar populations
soared and cities grew. Compelled by such shortages and fueled by the reformist
zeal of postwar governments confident of their abilities to solve the problems
of their societies, mass housing projects were embraced around the world as an
expedient and revolutionary way to rebuild after the war.[9]

Although architects participated in a global discourse on mass housing
design and the inspiration for "seemingly universal tower blocks" was similar
across nations, as Urban pointed out, "the mass-produced offspring of the so-
called international style was . . . never truly international."[10] The exact shapes,
target constituencies, and, most importantly, the meanings associated with mass
housing differed from nation to nation. In the United States, projects such as
Chicago's Robert Taylor Homes were built in the name of clearing slums and
reforming urban blight.[11] In France, "concrete cordons" of massive housing

---

8. Florian Urban, *Tower and Slab: Histories of Global Mass Housing* (New York:
    Routledge, 2012), 3.

9. On mid-century "high modernism" see James Scott, *Seeing Like a State: How
    Certain Schemes to Improve the Human Condition have Failed* (New Haven: Yale
    University Press, 1998).

10. Urban, 2.

11. Urban and Arnold Hirsch describe how, in fact, they functioned to reinforce racial

estates encircling major cities such as Paris became part of an infrastructure of decolonization as immigrants from the nation's former colonies took up residence in the distant suburbs.[12] If in second world East Berlin mass housing was "tied to the narrative of socialist advancement," in third world Brazil it was constructed in the name of national progress and of moving beyond the class divisions of the nation's colonial past.[13] In the end, each nation had its own mass housing story.

In Japan, that story would focus not on housing and reforming the urban poor but on rebuilding and expanding the middle class. Housing emerged as a concern of the Japanese nation-state in the late nineteenth century when industrialization brought with it the growth of urban slums. During the boom years of World War I when urban housing shortages resulted in rent gouging and disruptive landlord-tenant disputes, housing was identified as one of the many "social problems" plaguing major cities. However, the tremendous challenges of mobilizing for World War II would transform the nature of the "housing problem" in the eyes of the state. As shortages of "clothing, food, and housing" (*i-shoku-jū*) imperiled the war effort, these came to be considered national resources to be mobilized and "the people" (*kokumin*), not the urban poor, the proper focus of housing and other welfare-related policies. The institutional foundations of the JHC and other postwar housing policies were rooted in this history. In the late 1940s and early 1950, as the nation mobilized not for war but for economic recovery and growth, those deemed the most productive members of society would be the primary focus of housing policy. Unlike many European nations whose housing policies after World War II sought to promote egalitarian social welfare, "Japanese governments have never set out to expand the social housing sector," asserted housing scholars Hirayama Yosuke and Richard Ronald, "nor accepted the concept of universal citizenship rights to housing."[14]

Above all else, the focus of Japan's postwar housing policy has been the promotion of homeownership. In a nation where renting was the majority

---

segregation and created "second ghettoes" themselves. Urban, pp. 19-31, and Arnold R. Hirsch, *Making the Second Ghetto: Race and Housing in Chicago, 1940-1960* (Chicago: The University of Chicago Press, 1998).

12. Urban, pp. 37-57, and Kristin Ross, *Fast Cars, Clean Bodies: Decolonization and the Reordering of French Culture* (Cambridge, MA: The MIT Press, 1995).

13. Urban, 69 and 79-99.

14. Yosuke Hirayama and Richard Ronald, "Introduction: Does the housing system matter?" in Yosuke Hirayama and Richard Ronald, ed., *Housing and Social Transition in Japan* (New York: Routledge, 2007), 2.

experience prior to World War II, especially in urban areas, this was an aspiration which had to be "nurtured" by state and society "on both ideological and pragmatic grounds."[15] Even rental *danchi* apartments played an important role within a broader array of postwar housing policies focused on this goal. Institutionally, both the JHC and other public housing agencies were intended as stopgap measures with mandates to supply housing until the private market, devastated by war, was able to recover. Rental *danchi* housing was also meant to be a temporary measure for individual families—a stopover on the path to homeownership. The *danchi* helped establish the new objective of homeownership in other ways as well. As a celebrated example of postwar, middle-class life filled with shiny consumer goods, the *danchi* helped establish the comfortable, domestic sphere as an object of people's aspirations. Perhaps the greatest significance of *danchi* living, at least in theory, was as practice for the lifestyle of "my home" (*mai hōmu*) as it was invoked in the 1970s.

With its focus on nurturing the middle class, Japan's postwar housing policy participated in yet another transnational story of the post-World War II era: the "great middle-class expansion."[16] Emerging from depression and war, policymakers in many countries, particularly Allied nations, sought to forge new social contracts dedicated to reducing the gaps between the wealthiest and poorest members of their societies and to growing the middle. While policies differed from nation to nation—focusing on "facilitating access to the market" in the United States or on "institutionalizing social protection" as in many Western European nations—the concept that a strong middle class was a necessary component of a democratic, capitalist society became one of the ideological foundations of the postwar world.[17] This premise was readily embraced in defeated nations such as Japan and Germany, where older power elites lost legitimacy, at least for a time, and the destruction of war helped to level class inequality. Olivier Zunz wrote, "In the span of one postwar generation in Japan, and other parts of Asia, in Western Europe, and in North America, people of widely different cultural and national traditions, as well as of different wealth, status, and power, including workers, came to see themselves as belonging to a

15. Ann Waswo, *Housing in Postwar Japan: A Social History* (New York: RoutledgeCurzon, 2002), 92.

16. Oliver Zunz, "Introduction: Social Contracts Under Stress," in Oliver Zunz, Leonard Schoppa, and Nobuhiro Hiwatari, ed., *Social Contracts Under Stress: The Middle Classes of America, Europe, and Japan at the Turn of the Century* (New York: Russell Sage Foundation, 2002), 3.

17. Ibid., 2.

broad middle class in a society that was predominantly middle class."[18]

The concept of "middle class" can be difficult to pin down because both its use in social discourse and the ways people apply this term to their own lives are more often about aspirations and perceptions than about the objective reality of socio-economic hierarchies. To borrow Andrew Gordon's phrase, middle class is a "shifting cultural construct," a nexus of discourses from above and below on society and people's perceptions of their places within it.[19] While the history of Japan's modern middle class can be traced to the late nineteenth century, the years following World War II brought a "revolution in the self-perception of Japanese people" as a sense of membership in the middle class shifted from a "minority to a majority experience."[20] To an extent not seen in other industrialized nations, Japan experienced a "blurring of the collar line," as Zunz noted, and "by the 1960s, it hardly seemed possible to identify a separate Japanese working class."[21] Many factors help to explain this shift in self identification, including the very nature of Japan's postwar social contract, forged in the era of high- speed growth, in which workers abandoned militant labor actions in exchange for job security and access to the comforts of middle-class life.[22] The *danchi* certainly played a role in this "blurring of the collar line." As an image of comfortable life at a time of great discord, their inhabitants appeared as, in the words of critic Tada Michitarō, "the vanguard for the dream of the middle-classification of the entire country."[23]

In the 1950s and 1960s, the sudden availability and affordability of consumer durables such as refrigerators, televisions, and washing machines would contribute to "middle-classification" as more people began to acquire objects and lifestyles long associated with the "middle class." What in Japan was labeled the "revolution of everyday life" was yet another shared story of the postwar and in many ways, the most significant. Many large-scale factors help explain the mass diffusion of consumer goods into homes around the developed capitalist world after World War II, including pent-up demand after years of depression and war, over two decades of sustained economic growth and full-employment,

---

18. Ibid., 3.
19. Andrew Gordon, "The Short Happy Life of the Japanese Middle Class," in Olivier Zunz, Leonard Schoppa, and Nobuhiro Hiwatari, 110.
20. Ibid.
21. Zunz, 7.
22. Andrew Gordon, *The Wages of Affluence: Labor and Management in Postwar Japan* (Cambridge, MA: Harvard University Press, 1998).
23. Tada Michitarō, "Tsukiai no arachi, danchi seikatsu," *Fujin kōron* (February 1961): 71.

the resumption of international trade, and the conversion of production for the battlefield to production for the home. As Konrad Jarausch and Michael Geyer noted in their work on postwar Germany, "Much as cataclysmic violence forged the short twentieth century, a revolution of consumption marked its *longue durée*," suggesting that the true "subject" of the twentieth century was "the consumer, as opposed to the soldier."[24]

In dominant historical narratives of Japanese history since the end of World War II, the transformation of daily life resulting from the mass consumption of mass-produced consumer goods appears as an almost natural phenomenon. Distinct from the first half of the twentieth century, which was dominated by overseas expansionism and the acquisition of colonial empire, Japan's postwar "economic nationalism" evoked energies now turned toward peaceful development. In this narrative, things play a large role—whether the transistor radios, Toyotas, and Sony Walkmans that became synonymous with "Made in Japan" in export markets, or the refrigerators, washing machines, electric rice cookers, and televisions that "revolutionized" everyday life in Japan itself. Indeed, as Marilyn Ivy has noted, one could almost tell Japan's postwar history "according to electric appliances."[25] They construct a progressive chronology across the decades, a succession of desires fulfilled in the 1950s, 1960s, and 1970s.

When families were acquiring refrigerators, televisions, washing machines, private baths, and other goods, the consumer revolution was highly noteworthy. As housing scholar Yamaguchi Masatomo noted, "in 1955, almost no one owned these things. But by 1973 almost everyone did. And these were things that transformed people's lives . . ."[26] They resulted in the rearrangement of interior living space, changes in household labor, the privatization of activities that were previously communal, and, consequently, the transfiguration of relationships within families and communities. Perhaps most significantly, these transformations contributed to a sense of finally moving beyond a recent past marked by war, deprivation, and hunger. Indeed, the impact of "the rather sudden

---

24. Konrad H. Jarausch and Michael Geyer, *Shattered Past: Reconstructing German Histories* (Princeton: Princeton University Press, 2003), 269.

25. Marilyn Ivy, "Formations of Mass Culture," in Andrew Gordon, ed., *Postwar Japan as History* (Berkeley: University of California Press, 1993), 249.

26. In 1955 less than ten percent of Japanese people owned washing machines, electric fans, rice cookers, televisions, refrigerators, and other electrical appliances, while in 1973, over eighty percent of the people owned them. Kō do seichō kangaeru kai., ed., *Kōdo seichōto nihonjin: part II katei-hen: kazoku no seikatsu no monogatari* (Tokyo: Nihon edeitā sukūru shuppanbu, 1985), 66.

descent of a number of large appliances into households ruined by war cannot possibly be underestimated," noted Jarausch and Geyer.[27] This was perhaps particularly true in Germany and Japan, where total defeat and occupation created a crisis of meaning in the years following the war and where, to an extent not seen in other places, consumption helped to provide new "meaning and orientation" to postwar life.[28]

The postwar histories of mass housing, middle-class expansion, and consumer revolution would play out differently from nation to nation, creating their own expectations, anxieties, and disappointments. In Japan, they would intersect at the middle-class *danchi*, and perhaps this helps to explain why, in the context of high-speed economic growth, the *danchi* became such prominent signifiers of postwar change. Yet in many ways, the life people came to long for in Japan— one of access to a comfortable middle-class life of expanding prosperity—was one people of many nations came to expect in the boom years following World War II. It was the life *we* longed for during the "age of the *danchi*."

Danchi and the problem of everyday life

The romance with mass housing would end, and this, too, would be a global story. "Its ubiquity notwithstanding," noted Urban, "no urban form in history has roused such controversy." [29] Some of the controversy stemmed from the very nature of large-scale, mass-produced housing which threatened to homogenize cityscapes, disrupt more naturally forming communities, and create monotonous interiors. But most critiques focused on the failed social agendas of state-sponsored projects which sought to rewire and reform family and community behavior through architecture. The economic crisis of the 1970s would bring disillusionment with the mass solutions of the early postwar years and, as Andreas Huyssen wrote, "rather than standing as harbingers and promises of the new life, modernist housing projects became symbols of alienation and dehumanization . . ."[30]

---

27. Jarausch and Geyer, 308.
28. Ibid., 313.
29. Urban, 1.
30. Andreas Huyssen, "Mapping the Postmodern," in *New German Critique* 33 (Fall 1984): 14. See too Fredric Jameson, "The Politics of Theory: Ideological Positions in the Postmodern Debate," in the same issue, and David Harvey, *The Condition of Postmodernity: An Enquiry into the Origins of Cultural Change*, (Cambridge, MA: Blackwell, 1990), 36-39, for similar critiques of mass housing. To Huyssen and others, the critique of modernist mass planning was central to the emergence of a

Appraisals of the *danchi* resonated with this global discourse as critics in the 1970s accused them of colonizing the landscape and standardizing living space. Even at the height of their popularity in the late 1950s and early 1960s, assessments of *danchi* life were often negative, with stereotypical portrayals of cookie-cutter lives and social conformity in worlds of spatial homogeneity and temporal synchronicity. Elite critics feared that the people were being duped by false promises of transformative consumption; their tiny living spaces filled with mass-produced objects that threatened to crowd them out of house and home and drain meaning from their lives. Films and novels set in the *danchi* typically included the requisite scene of husbands departing for work at the same time, wearing identical business suits, carrying identical briefcases, their wives cheerfully seeing them off wearing identically crisp dresses. Such depictions reflected anxieties about consumption-driven middle-class life common in many advanced nations after the war.

Yet evaluations of *danchi* life were also part of a longer national discourse on everyday life, one which spoke to Japan's experience of modernity since the late nineteenth century. Changes in everyday life which accompanied the rapid modernization of the state and economy after the Meiji Restoration were often understood as the ineluctable infusion of Western influences into the home. This interpretation of change as the "Westernization" and after World War II, the "Americanization" of everyday life created many problems—including a sense of temporal and spatial unevenness in the home, a feeling of "the jarring coexistence of several pasts and the present in the now of everydayness."[31] From the nineteenth century forward, this problem obsessed reformers and critics who bemoaned people living "double lives" in hybrid spaces that included chairs and *tatami* mats, sofas and *shoji* screens, business suits and *kimono*. Prior to World War II, these discussions often focused on the homes of the small but influential urban middle class, whose desire to accumulate the "cultural capital" key to demonstrating their middle-class identities often made their homes notable examples of the "double life."[32] Reconciling perceived temporal and spatial imbalances within the home would be one of the primary agendas of postwar architects and housing officials.

"post" modern critique of modernity.

31. Harry Harootunian, *Overcome by Modernity: History, Culture, and Community in Interwar Japan* (Princeton: Princeton University Press, 2000), xvii.

32. See Jordan Sand, *House and Home in Modern Japan: Architecture, Domestic Space, and Bourgeois Culture, 1880–1930* (Cambridge, MA: Harvard University Asia Center, 2003), for extensive discussion of the "double life" in the prewar middle-class home.

The equation of modernity with "Westernization" also created a fundamental dilemma—a feeling that Japan was perpetually "behind" and "catching up" but, at the same time, that modernity brought with it the loss of "tradition" and older ways.[33] Defeat in World War II and Japan's subsequent occupation compounded this sense of "backwardness" and created a perception that the nation that had taken a wrong turn in its pursuit of modernity. While no area of life was spared examination in the days following the end of the war, architects tended to turn their attentions to what they called the "feudal" home, arguing that the very structure of the traditional Japanese home perpetuated authoritarianism and paternalism in the family. In the 1950s and 1960s, the *danchi* lifestyle was proffered as the antithesis of the "feudal home" and as evidence that when it came to housing conditions and living standards Japan was back on track and "catching up." Just as important, the structures of the *danchi* family and community were considered proof that Japanese society was "modernizing." The family was nuclearizing and relations with the community and workplace were rational, impersonal, and contractual rather than "traditional" and ascriptive—following the prescription for modernity according to the Parsonian model of the day. The modern *danchi* space was the alleged progenitor of the modern postwar home and family.

One reason standards of everyday life were perpetually "behind" and unable to "catch up," according to critics, was that the Japanese people were continuously exhorted to sacrifice their daily lives to larger causes, particularly to the projects of the state. After the Meiji Restoration, the modern nation-state had pursued a "rich nation, strong army" but critics noted that the majority of people had remained poor, their living standards stuck in a bygone age, or only partially modernized—examples of the ultimate "double life." World War II, a foolhardy war which left millions homeless and hungry, was the ultimate proof of the people's sacrifice. Architects and reformers exhorted people to reclaim their everyday lives for themselves and pursue private lives separate from the projects of the state. In the words of sociologist Minami Hiroshi, "we [developed] a consciousness of a right to everyday life (*seikatsu-ken*) . . . a consciousness of

33. Harootunian, *Overcome by Modernity*, xvi. Harootunian sees this belief that "true time was kept by the modern West" as one of the foundational dilemmas of modern Japan, as well as of other non-Western nations. He historicizes this concept while critiquing it, insisting on "co-eval modernity" which "shared the same historical temporality of modernity . . . found elsewhere in Europe and the United States." xvi.

rights born of the opposition between politics and everyday life."[34]

By the late 1960s, this fundamental critique would be rearticulated in discussions of "my home-ism" (*mai homushugi*) as critics feared that the pursuit of the domestic comforts of hearth and home had absorbed and diffused the political energies of the early postwar. More fundamentally, they noted, achieving middle-class life in "my home" required a new set of sacrifices, now to the corporation, sacrifices that did not necessarily pay off in a more comfortable life. For by the 1970s, the fundamental critique of the *danchi* as "too small, too far, too expensive" was one that could be applied to urban housing conditions in general. The "rabbit hutch" pejorative which many Japanese began using to describe their own homes, suggested that living standards were still substandard in international comparison. Although the "Japanese miracle" had allowed the nation to "catch up" with, even surpass other nations in international trade, when it came to housing and living conditions, Japan still lagged behind. Critics suggested that these two phenomena were not unrelated: the "rabbit hutch" had, in a sense, helped make the "miracle" happen. Daily life was the sacrifice the people had made—again— but this time for economic nationalism. Caught up in such debates, the *danchi* were both structure and construct, both a real space for living and discursive site for analyzing middle-class life. Their story is thus central to both the celebratory and critical history and historiography of postwar Japan.

The chapters of this book trace a rough chronology of the *danchi,* starting with the early postwar when many of the ideals that would inspire the *danchi* interior space were articulated by reformers and architects, and moving to the "era of high-speed growth" when these ideas would take built form and the *danchi* would become a "vanguard" of postwar change. The final chapter touches on two other important moments in the *danchi* chronology—the economic crisis of the 1970s which would bring an end to the romance with the *danchi* as people assessed the high costs of high-speed growth, and the turn of the twenty-first century when a resurgence of interest in the *danchi* of the 1950s and 1960s would evoke nostalgia for the optimism and hopefulness of that earlier age. Throughout, the book seeks to place the *danchi* in global context of the 1950s through the 1970s, years that would witness both the apex and nadir of global mass housing. It also places the story in trans-war perspective and suggests that although the *danchi* lifestyle was envisioned as a complete departure from the nation's militaristic past, it was, in fact, built upon solid prewar and wartime foundations.

Each chapter also explores a different aspect of the *danchi* story, drawing on the writings of architects and reformers; works on housing policy and urban

---

34. Minami Hiroshi, *Zoku: Shōwa bunka* (Tokyo: Keisō shobō, 1990), 11.

planning; studies of the home, family, consumption, and middle-class life; as well as fiction and films set in the *danchi*. By bringing together diverse fields of study, the book sheds new light on many of our key understandings of postwar Japan. For example, many have explored the ideology of the "mass middle class" prevalent since the 1960s, but this study suggests that the standardization of living space, first achieved in the *danchi*, was key to this perception of a universal middle class. Housing scholars have described the creation of a "homeownership society" after World War II, but this study helps us understand *why* so many made this their "middle-class dream." Sociologists of the postwar family have described the concept of normative "life stages" that shaped many people's expectations of their lives. This study suggests that there was a key spatial element to these "stages" that led ever further into the suburbs to the *danchi*, and eventually, to "my home." The *danchi* serve as a concrete site, literally, for exploring issues central to the social, cultural, and intellectual history of postwar Japan.

The book is not, however, an ethnography of *danchi* life. One challenge of this project was to avoid reproducing the very logics and ideologies it sought to analyze. *Danchi* inhabitants were favorite informants for sociologists and anthropologists who considered them examples of an advanced lifestyle and used them as guinea pigs to monitor the effects of "modernization" on Japanese society in general. I did not follow in their footsteps and seek out current or former *danchi* inhabitants to interview. Although their voices can be discerned in the many surveys and studies described here, I was most interested in the agendas of the architects, social scientists, cultural critics, and others who placed the *danchi* in their spotlights. My goal was to historicize and understand why the *danchi* and their inhabitants were invested with such ongoing social and cultural significance.

The *danchi* provide a spatial, social, and ideological site to analyze postwar Japan precisely because of the hopes and desires invested in them by so many different people: by architects who saw in their designs solutions to the "problems" of the Japanese home and family in the wake of the war, by the state which touted them as a "vanguard" of a revolution in consumerism, by manufacturers and advertisers who saw them as a "showcase" for their wares, and by individuals who envisioned in their private, appliance-filled interiors the possibility of a better future. While the history of the *danchi* is one that is particular to Japan, the expectations born of the boom years following World War II resonate across national boundaries. Even as our headlines predict the demise of a middle-class dream which promises lives better than those of our parents, the "longings" born of that time still matter. For it is against them that we continue to measure our hopes for the future and disillusionments with the present.

THE LIFE WE LONGED FOR

Danchi Housing and the Middle Class
Dream in Postwar Japan

Chapter One

THE REVOLUTION OF EVERYDAY LIFE

One object at a time, the barracks will begin to be filled with household goods [again] but I pray that people will not forget what they are experiencing now as they endeavor to reconstruct their daily lives in the midst of difficulty, and take much joy from the fact that in the end, their lives, their everyday lives, will be what they built themselves.

Kon Wajirō, 1945[1]

The Politics of Loss

In the early 1960s, in the midst of the high-speed economic growth that would mark the next decade, the phrase "revolution of everyday life" was commonly invoked to describe changes transforming the Japanese home. Popularized by the government's 1960 White Paper on National Life, the term was used to describe the impact of people's increased acquisition of off-the-rack clothing, instant foods, and, most importantly, new appliances such as washing machines, rice cookers, and refrigerators. Emphasizing the transformative power of these new consumer goods, the White Paper noted, "one might call this a 'consumer revolution' but the tremendous changes in our daily lives are such that this can be considered a fundamental 'revolution of everyday life' (*seikatsu kakumei*)."[2] This announcement, like the declaration five years earlier that it was "no longer the postwar" (*mohaya sengo dewa nai*), has become a familiar benchmark in periodizations of Japan's history since 1945. If the statement, "it is no longer the postwar" declared the possibility of shifting focus from immediate survival to a future-oriented quest for "modernization," the latter phrase offered a vision of

---

1. In Kon Wajirō, *Seikatsugaku—Kon Wajirōshū dai 5 maki* (Tokyo: Domesu shuppan, 1971), 200.
2. Keizai kikaku chō, *Kokumin seikatsu hakusho, Shōwa 35-nen* (Tokyo: Okurashō insatsu kyoku, 1961), ii.

that future in the making.

This was not a vision of Japan's future that appealed to all. To many critics in the early 1960s, the new consumption appeared less a revolution in the making than a revolution derailed. The government's announcement of the "revolution of everyday life" came at the end of a series of events of the late 1950s and early 1960s that, in retrospect, marked a high point of political activism. The year-long strike at the Miike Coal Mine, which ended in defeat for labor in 1960, was the last of the militant strikes that punctuated the early postwar years. Labor historians argue that, for better or worse, it marked the beginning of a new, more conciliatory phase of postwar industrial relations.[3] Massive demonstrations against the renewal of the U.S.-Japan Security Treaty brought over 100,000 people to the streets in the summer of 1960 but the fervor and scale of these demonstrations were not matched again. The following autumn, as Prime Minister Ikeda Hayato announced his "income doubling" initiative and later as the government predicted a "revolution of everyday life," it seemed to many critics that the pursuit of consumption had won out over the desire for political transformation that seemed so possible in the chaotic days following the end of the war. A narrative of political energies rechanneled and neutralized by a quest for the comforts of "my home" would become one of the entrenched narratives of the postwar era. It seemed that people had retreated from the streets and picket lines for the routine of work and the comfort and security of their private lives.[4]

Yet the phrase "revolution of everyday life" had its origins not in the emerging affluence of the early 1960s but in the uncertain desperation following the end of World War II. Kon Wajirō warned in a 1947 essay that the "revolution of daily life" could not happen unless "politics and daily life become entirely one," suggesting not a dichotomous relationship between private life and political activism but the confluence of the two.[5] Eight years of total war, the last of which was marked by nightly bombing campaigns over Japan's major cities, left the country starving and destitute. Surviving day-to-day proved a daunting

---

3. See Andrew Gordon, *The Wages of Affluence: Labor and Management in Postwar Japan* (Cambridge, MA: Harvard University Press, 1998).

4. One of the earliest examples of this interpretation of the private as apolitical can be found in the debate between Maruyama Masao and Yoshimoto Takaaki, "8/15 and 5/19" and "The End of Fictitious System," in Wm. Theodore deBary, Carol Gluck, Arthur Tiedeman, ed., *Sources of Japanese Tradition, Volume II* (New York: Columbia University Press, 2005), 1094-1100.

5. Kon Wajirō, "Seikatsu no kakumei," in *Seikatsu-gaku: Kon Wajirō shū dai 5 maki* (Tokyo: Domesu shuppan, 1971), 50.

challenge in an environment where money had lost its value, the rations system was inefficient and inadequate, and people were thrown into the survival-of-the-fittest environment of the black market. For most Japanese, the struggle simply to secure food, clothing, and shelter dominated the months, often years after the end of the war. Hunger sparked grass-roots activism, and throughout the difficult years of 1945 and 1946 there were numerous mass demonstrations for food and shelter.[6] To people living through the early postwar, consumption was far from apolitical—it was the political issue that mattered the most.

It was from the intersection of desperation for survival and desire for a different future that the phrase "revolution of everyday life" was born. The destruction of the wartime state created a "rare moment of flux," John Dower has noted, when "millions began to consider what it might mean to create private life free from the dictates of the state. . . . People were acutely aware of the need to reinvent their own lives."[7] This re-envisioning produced damning critiques of the wartime state. Critics suggested that the devastation of the war revealed how much the common Japanese people had been required to sacrifice for the sake of the nation. Architect Nishiyama Uzō declared that the war had laid bare trends evident since Japan began its campaign of rapid modernization in the nineteenth century. Achieving a "rich nation and strong army" had required perpetual sacrifice from the Japanese people, and their current homelessness and destitution were the ultimate evidence of this.[8] Now was the time, Nishiyama insisted, for people to overcome their passivity in the face of demands from the state and become "subjects" of their own daily lives.[9] In the words of sociologist Minami Hiroshi, "Betrayed by the nation-state (*kokka ni uragirare*) and reduced to the direst distress, people's sense of value turned, overnight, from orientation toward the public [good] to individual self-sufficiency."[10]

To many architects, it was in housing standards that the state's suppression of daily life was the most evident. Housing, architect Tange Kenzō noted in a 1949 publication, had suffered "chronic illness" throughout Japan's modern history and this illness had now been made "acute" by the housing shortage caused by

6.   John Dower, *Embracing Defeat: Japan in the Wake of World War II* (New York: W.W. Norton & Company, Inc., 1991), 96.

7.   Ibid., 121.

8.   Nishiyama Uzō, *Nihon no jūtaku mondai* (Tokyo: Iwanami shinsho, 1952), 151.

9.   Nishiyama Uzō, *Kore kara no sumai: jōyōshiki no hanashi* (Tokyo: Sagami shobō, 1947), 249.

10. Minami Hiroshi, *Zoku: Shōwa bunka* (Tokyo: Keisō shobō, 1990), 9.

the war.[11] In fact, the housing shortage following World War II reached crisis proportions. Over half of homes in urban areas and one-fifth nationwide were lost to bombings or the creation of air-raid defenses. Over 750,000 homes were destroyed in Tokyo alone.[12] Compounding the shortage caused by the bombing campaigns over 215 of Japan's cities were years of under-building during the war and the repatriation of millions of soldiers and civilians from battlefields and empire after its end. This left the country with an estimated shortage of 4.2 million housing units in late 1945—a third of Japan's housing stock. For years after the war, people in urban areas could be found living in converted bomb shelters, trains, and buses, and hastily constructed barracks and shantytowns. Newspapers reported creative housing solutions such as that of a teacher who lived in his classroom, teaching by day and sleeping on his desk at night or the man who "lived like a dog," literally in a doghouse.[13] Even after the worst shantytowns had been cleared away in the 1950s, overcrowding and difficult living conditions continued for many more years. As Ann Waswo stated, "The housing crisis (*jūtaku nan*) was a central feature of daily life for over two decades for millions of Japanese."[14]

As pressing as the housing shortage, Nishiyama and other architects argued, was the problem of housing quality. "Our houses of today took shape for the most part during the three hundred years of the Tokugawa period, during which time the people were kept ignorant," Maekawa Kunio noted in 1948, "and [this mode of design] has continued since the Meiji period with its policies of military government that kept the people poor."[15] To architects such as Maekawa and Nishiyama, sub-standard, outdated housing was the ultimate indicator of the people's sacrifice on behalf of the nation.

Daily life (*seikatsu*)—defined in Japan as the material and temporal realm of "clothing, food, and housing" (*i-shoku-jū*)—thus emerged as a subject of extensive debate and reorganization in the aftermath of World War II. In the

---

11. Tange Kenzō, "Konnichi no jūtaku no jōkyō, Kensetsushō, ed., *Ashita no jūtaku to toshi*, (Tokyo: Shōkokusha, 1949), 83. Nishiyama makes a similar point in *Nihon no jūtaku mondai*, 57-58.

12. André Sorensen, *The Making of Urban Japan: Cities and planning from Edo to the twenty-first century* (New York: Routledge, 2004), 159.

13. "Tsukue no ue ni neoki," *Asahi Shimbun*, February 17, 1948.

14. Ann Waswo, *Housing in Postwar Japan: A Social History* (New York: RoutledgeCurzon, 2002), 2.

15. Jonathan M. Reynolds, *Maekawa Kunio and the Emergence of Japanese Modernist Architecture* (Berkeley: University of California Press, 2001), 142.

process, the issue of everyday life became central to one of the foundational narratives of postwar Japan that suggested that the Japanese people themselves had been the ultimate victims of the nation's expansionist and militarist aims. Michael Wildt has noted a similar trend in Germany in the desperate days after the war when "[people's] main concern was not to shed their guilt but to make their way in a 'society under rubble.'"[16] Of Japan, John Dower has noted, "The misery at hand was more immediate and palpable than accounts of devastation that the imperial forces had wreaked on strangers in foreign lands."[17] Historians of both Germany and Japan have suggested that this victim mentality fostered long-term forgetfulness of wartime atrocities committed in the name of the Führer and the Emperor. The desperation of the early postwar was the crucible in which this victim mentality developed, often displacing memories of the war itself. Yet as important as it is to understand how suffering promoted forgetting is the issue of how it shaped remembering. In the case of Japan, the critical focus on the sacrifice of the people contributed not only to condemnation of the wartime regime, but also invited a reevaluation of the nation's entire modern experience since the Meiji Restoration of the nineteenth century. As Carol Gluck has noted, ". . . because people saw the war as a judgment on a longer history, the question immediately became the nature of Japan's modernity, and also of the pre-modern that preceded and was responsible for it. These two linked narratives, one of the war, the other of the modern, comprised the main historical agenda, newly construed from the vantage point of 1945."[18]

To reformers, daily life was one area in which the "problematic" nature of Japan's modernity was most evident—with profound implications for the nation. To many critics, Japan's housing crisis was an indicator of an even larger problem: a crisis of the home and family. Japan's "household system," which vested male household heads with broad authority over their families and was ideologically associated with the emperor-centered "family nation," lost legitimacy with defeat. In the revised postwar Civil Code, it was disenfranchised altogether as household heads were stripped of power over decisions pertaining to the extended family and the principle of equal inheritance was established in law. Architectural

16. Michael Wildt, "Continuities and Discontinuities of Consumer Mentality in West Germany in the 1950s," in Richard Bessel and Dirk Schumann, ed., *Life After Death: Approaches to the Cultural and Social History of Europe During the 1940s and 1950s* (Cambridge: Cambridge University Press, 2003), 212.

17. Dower, 119.

18. Carol Gluck, "The Past in the Present," in Andrew Gordon ed., *Postwar Japan as History* (Berkeley: University of California Press, 1993), 64.

concerns with housing thus overlapped with legal debates over the status of the family after the war. Architects insisted that Japan's outmoded home was a bastion of the "household system" and therefore also culpable for the national tragedy of militarism and war. In its very structure and layout of rooms, architects suggested, the Japanese home perpetuated the power of the household head. Thus it was not enough to codify democratic family relationships in law, they also had to be inscribed in living space. The "revolution of everyday life" called for by architects and social reformers sought to restructure the house and, by extension, the relationships within.

Here we examine the "revolution of everyday life" as it was envisioned by Japanese architects and reformers at the end of the war. This is a story in which the U.S.-led Occupation played a surprisingly small role. The Occupation was little interested in the everyday lives of the Japanese people. Popular memory focuses on the resentment people felt when, in the midst of the devastating housing crisis, the Occupation commandeered the best and often only remaining housing for its own personnel.[19] And besides disbanding the Jūtaku Eidan, Japan's wartime housing authority, for being an "instrument of militarism," the Occupation largely left housing policy to Japanese authorities. As Carola Hein noted, "Facilitating the physical rebuilding of Japan's cities was not a concern of the occupiers who considered the hardship of the population to be a proper punishment for the wars of aggression that the Japanese military had waged on its neighbors from 1931, and on the United States from 1941."[20]

Perhaps more surprising is the fact that early postwar reformers did not envision Japan's new home and family life in American terms. The "revolution of everyday life" was not aimed at achieving American-style commodity culture but at transforming human relationships. In the early 1960s, as we have seen, the phrase "revolution of everyday life" would be appropriated to describe the influx of commodities transforming daily life, and the United States would figure as a constant reference against which Japan's rising living standards were measured. But in the mid- and late 1940s, reformers warned against becoming a "cultural colony" of the United States. As Nishiyama warned, the new Japan was to take care not simply to "imitate the refrigerator and television culture of the United States."[21]

---

19. Dower, 115.
20. Carola Hein, "Rebuilding Japanese Cities After 1945," in Carola Hein, Jeffry Diefendorf, and Ishida Yorifusa, ed., *Rebuilding Urban Japan After 1945*, (New York: Palgrave Macmillan, 2003), 2.
21. Nishiyama Uzō, *Kore kara no sumai*, 249-50.

Like many other reformers after World War II, architects saw the end of the war as an opportunity to rebuild Japan from scratch. During this "time of flux" a future radically different from the past seemed possible. "Before our very eyes," Nishiyama exhorted, "the hope-filled, glittering job of creating a new style of living awaits the blow of our pickaxes."[22] Yet history did not stop and start over again in August of 1945, and we now recognize the extent to which Japan was rebuilt on a deep foundation of trans-war continuities. The Occupation carried out the majority of its mandates through preexisting bureaucratic structures. The Emperor, although no longer the locus of sovereignty, was reinvested as the "symbol of the Nation and Unity of the People." Conservative politics and politicians were resurrected as Occupation priorities shifted with the deepening of the Cold War. Postwar housing policy, too, was built on prewar and wartime precedents; and many of the visions that sought to reshape postwar home life drew on the agendas of reformers of the 1920s. All of these continuities would have their own effects on postwar understandings of home and family. Yet early postwar reformers did not see these continuities and eventualities. In the rubble, they saw the chance to build a different type of home and family.

At a time of great flux, architects and reformers saw themselves as social engineers confronting the task of affixing new meanings to living space and to family relationships. Through their discussions of daily life in the home, architects joined in some of the great social debates of their time: How to eliminate patriarchy and promote the dignity of women, how to protect individual privacy and create a realm of everyday life separate from the projects of the state, how to create a new democratic family and by extension a democratic society.[23] Many of their ideas were eventually rendered spatially in the form of new plans for living space, including the design of the *danchi* interior. Theirs was the original vision of the "revolution in everyday life," and their debates can be read as the early intellectual history of the *danchi*.

House Divided

Debates over the postwar home emerged as the architectural profession engaged in self-critique after the war. Like members of most professions in the early postwar, architects began evaluating how they had been complicit with the aims of

---

22. Ibid., 6.
23. Discussions of "subjectivity" in daily life in many ways mirrored the wider debates on "human agency and active subjectivity" described in J. Victor Koschmann, *Revolution and Subjectivity in Postwar Japan* (Chicago: The University of Chicago Press), 1996.

the wartime state. As in Germany in the 1930s and 1940s, architects had been subject to pressures to produce designs that celebrated the nation. Jonathan Reynolds points out in his work on Maekawa Kunio, "In the political climate of the 1940s it became impossible to participate in architectural discourse without conceding to certain nationalistic demands . . ."[24] In the end, Reynolds argues, official pressures placed on Japanese architects were less severe than those experienced by many of their Europen counterparts. "The Japanese government did not carry out a unified national building program or establish an officially sanctioned architectural style in the manner of Nazi Germany . . ."[25] Yet the perception among many modernist architects after the war was that architecture in Japan had compromised its core values and been uniquely "distorted and abnormal." As Hamaguchi Ryūichi noted in the introduction of his 1947 modernist manifesto, *Humanist Architecture,* "We cannot deny the fact that modern architecture, like all of Japan, was distorted by the power [of the state] and began to follow a pitiful path out of step with the progress of the world."[26]

In such a climate of critique, many architects turned to the project of designing housing for ordinary people as a primary mandate. Reynolds notes that Maekawa and other architects, "shared a belief that with the fall of the military, far-reaching changes were possible; they mustered their rhetorical powers to advance a vision of 'architecture for the people' in a democratic society."[27] The desperate housing shortage in the aftermath of the war perhaps made housing an obvious goal. Architects noted that Japan's housing crisis paralleled the devastation in Europe after World War I that had helped inspire the modernist housing movement there. But designing "architecture for the people," or in the words of Hamaguchi, "humanist architecture," was also seen as a way to redeem the profession that had gone astray during the war. Architects

---

24. Reynolds, 134.

25. Ibid., 119.

26. Hamaguchi Ryūichi, *Hyūmanizumu no kenchiku* (Tokyo: Kenchiku jyānaru, 1995), foreward. Many architects were complicit with the wartime state to varying degrees. Nishiyama Uzō was employed by the state housing authority, the Jūtaku Eidan, during the war. Maekawa Kunio submitted designs for nationalistic projects such as the "Memorial Hall to the Founding of the Nation" in 1937, for war memorials, and, most controversially, for the "Japan-Thailand Cultural Center" in 1944. He also served as a juror for the competition for the "Greater Co-Prosperity Sphere Memorial Hall" which was won by Tange Kenzō. In the end, none of these projects was constructed. See Reynolds, 118-134.

27. Reynolds, 136.

saw the reorientation of postwar concerns toward "the people" as a corrective to prewar emphasis "too closely bound to the demands of the government."[28] Thus many young architects embraced designing housing as "the starting point for postwar architecture."[29] As one architect subsequently recalled of the early postwar years, "It was a time when housing was to change architecture. It was as if housing would bring a revolution."[30]

Nishiyama Uzō's concern with housing "for the people" originated before the war when he was a graduate student studying architecture at Kyoto University. He attributed his interest in urban, working-class housing to the deplorable housing conditions he saw every day walking to and from campus and to the "negative example" of his professors who seemed oblivious to this situation and taught only classical architectural styles. Housing conditions were deplorable, in Nishiyama's estimation, because no one had scientifically analyzed how to design a small house specifically for the urban working class. Their design and construction were "left to the carpenters" and considered outside the domain of formal architectural study.[31] Nishiyama's graduation thesis called for architects to "scientificize design" (*keikaku no "kagakuka"*). If architects could discern the logic and basic principles governing people's use of living space, they would be able to design a home suitable to the urban Japanese family.[32] Nishiyama is widely credited with the foundational thinking and research that led to the establishment of recommended housing standards in Japan. It was to his research that many young architects turned after the war as they endeavored to design "housing for the people."[33]

Many architects in postwar Japan, like their counterparts around the world, were inspired by the ideals of "functionalism." With origins in the modernist movement of the 1920s, functionalism sought to create housing appropriate to the industrial age by using science and technology to reduce living space to its most elemental functions—treating the "home as a machine," as Le Corbusier

---

28. Ibid., 137.
29. Funō Shūji commentary in Hamaguchi Ryūichi, *Hyūmanizumu no kenchiku: sairon*" (Tokyo: Kenchiku kaikan), 1994, 26.
30. Miyawaki Mayumi, "nLDK igo," *Kenchiku zasshi: tokushū yuragi no naka no kazoku to nLDK*, No. 1371, Vol. 110 (April 1995): 24.
31. See interview with Ōmoto Keino in *Shōgen: Nihon no jūtaku seisaku* (Tokyo: Nihon hyōronsha, 1991), 562-63.
32. Ibid.
33. See Suzuki Shigebumi, *Suzuki Shigebumi jūkyo ronshū: sumai no keikaku, sumai no bunka* (Tokyo: Shōkokusha, 1988).

suggested. In Japan, the renewed appeal of functionalism after the war was in part due to its claims to an "international style" that transcended national conventions. Designing living space in accordance with the basic, seemingly universal functions of people's daily lives held the promise of overcoming the nation, and was thus the ideal architectural mode at this moment of postwar critique. As Hamaguchi Ryūichi noted in his *Humanist Architecture*, "Functionalism does not care whether there is historical continuity between the architecture of our age and the architecture of the previous age. It cares only that the architecture of our age is [appropriate to] the people of our age . . ."[34] Functionalism thus held tremendous appeal to architects eager to overcome Japan's recent past. Years later Hamaguchi reminisced, ""It was a rose-colored time when it wasn't questioned that humanism and functionalism were tied together.""[35] Functionalism seemed to enable archtects to "overcome nationality" (*kokuseki o koete*) and accordingly produce a style for the people, not the state.[36]

Adding to the postwar appeal of functionalism was the fact that it seemed the very antithesis of "traditional" Japanese living space that was designed to be multi-functional with rooms that could be converted from eating to sleeping to entertaining. Nishiyama in fact made a career of opposing the idea of "convertibility" (*tenyōsei*). This fundamental premise of traditional Japanese architecture, he claimed, justified and perpetuated undersized and inadequate housing by suggesting that people could do more with less space.[37] One of Nishiyama's ongoing concerns was with the size of housing, and during his tenure with the wartime housing authority, the Jūtaku Eidan, he continually pushed for housing standards that mandated larger minimum dwelling sizes. Nishiyama later claimed that this was his form of resistance against the state which continually reduced minimum housing standards during the war.[38]

The wide-open space of the "Japanese" home with only sliding screens dividing the rooms also suggested a vision of family life that postwar reformers found problematic. In 1935, Watsuji Tetsurō, in his famous book on climate and culture, propounded one of the most famous idealizations of this Japanese home by claiming that the home without interior walls, doors, or locks to divide its inner space mirrored a division-less family in which the unity of the whole

---

34. Hamaguchi, *Hyūmanizumu no kenchiku*, 107.
35. Hamaguchi, *Hyūmanizum no kenchiku: sairon*, 15.
36. Ibid., 84.
37. Nishiyama Uzō, *Jūtaku keikaku, Nishiyama Uzō chosaku shū 1* (Tokyo: Keisō shobō, 1967), 9.
38. See interview with Ōmoto Keino in *Shōgen: Nihon no jūtaku seisaku*, 569-73.

took precedence over its individual members. Watsuji claimed that the Japanese home did not share the divisions that marked capitalist society or, indeed, homes in other capitalist countries of Europe or the United States, thus remaining "a tiny centre of unity in the middle of the wide world."[39] This characterization made Watsuji's home an ideal model for Japan's emperor-centered "family state" during the war.[40] As Harry Harootunian has observed of Watsuji's writings, "The survival of the Japanese home, and all its associations, merely meant that the past still existed in the present and that the Japanese had made no disruptive break with it in their pursuit of capitalist modernity."[41]

The history of the modern Japanese home was of course much more complicated. Modernity shaped and reshaped housing as well as people's sensibilities about lifestyles and "dwelling."[42] The home emerged as a contested site and locus of debates about the very nature of modernity in Japan. It was in and through the home that issues of tradition versus modernity often manifested themselves most visibly, especially as people began acquiring Western furniture and other objects in the years following the Meiji Restoration. Many middle- and upper-class homes were characterized by what critics called the "double life" (*nijū seikatsu*) where rooms furnished with sofa, table, and chairs lay next to ones with *tatami* flooring and *futon* bedding. From the nineteenth century on, writers and reformers wrote about the problem of the "double life," or "floor-sitting versus chair-sitting" as it was sometimes called, with some advocating one over the other and others seeking to strike the proper balance between the two.[43] Campaigns for the "rationalization of the home" often aimed at eliminating the problems produced by this mixture of "Japanese" and "Western" elements.

And far from evidencing a division-less society, by the early twentieth century, the home had become the ultimate marker of class distinction. For the aspiring middle class, the home became a stage for the cultivation and performance of

---

39. Watsuji Tetsurō, *Climate and Culture: A Philosophical Study*, translation of *Fudō* by Geoffrey Bownas (Tokyo: The Hokuseido Press), 1961, 165.

40. Ibid.

41. Harry Harootunian, *Overcome by Modernity: History, Culture, and Community in Interwar Japan* (Princeton: Princeton University Press, 2000), 266.

42. Jordan Sand, *House and Home in Modern Japan: Architecture, Domestic Space, and Bourgeois Culture, 1880-1930* (Cambridge, MA: Harvard University Asia Center, 2003).

43. For a historical treatment of the "double life" in the home from the Meiji period until after World War II, see Sawada Tomoko, *Yuka-za, isu-za: kikyo yōshiki ni miru nihon jūtaku interia-shi* (Tokyo: Sumai no toshokan shuppan-kyoku, 1995).

a lifestyle that identified them as bourgeois. Certainly not separate from the world of capitalist commodification, by the 1920s the home itself had become the ultimate object for acquisition. Homeownership, still a minority experience in prewar Japan, was the ultimate emblem of class position.[44] Thus the home was not hermetically sealed from the intrusions of the modern world as Watsuji suggested. It was utterly interpenetrated with the divisions of capitalist society; a site where the contradictions inherent in modern life were often the most visible.

Yet the undifferentiated, convertible space of the idealized "Japanese home" became the foil to postwar architects who saw in it the spatial manifestation of patriarchal society. The wide-open spaces of the home, they claimed, perpetuated the "household system" by giving unlimited visual control not only to the household head but also to the infamous mother-in-law who engaged in "bride bullying" (yome ijime) to make new daughters-in-law conform to the expectations of the household. In the Japanese home, legal scholar Kawashima Takeyoshi complained, "Everyone knows everyone else's movements and emotions and matches theirs to them. Conformity is expected."[45]

Whereas Watsuji had celebrated a "Japanese home" that demonstrated the unity of family and nation, postwar reformers called for its division and separation to promote the sovereignty of the nuclear family unit. In his first book after the war, The Home of the Future, Nishiyama argued that the starting place for the democratization of the home lay in spatially circumscribing the power of the household head by promoting the privacy of individual family members. Young married couples should move out and establish their own "units of livelihood" (seikatsu tan'i).[46] And it was not enough for nuclear families to separate themselves from their extended families and establish independent households. Separations were also necessary within the homes of nuclear families to promote new types of relationships between the family and community, husband and wife, and parents and children. Postwar reformers called for walls to separate not only the family from outside influences but also family members from one another. This individualization of privacy extended to all but the conjugal couple which, ideally, was to share a new intimacy in marriage based not on the mediation of the traditional matchmaker, but on love.[47] The creation of private space was necessary to cultivate the individualism that would be the foundation of postwar democracy. In the "new Japan" envisioned by postwar architects, the

44. Sand, 294-98.
45. Kawashima Takeyoshi, Kekkon (Tokyo: Iwanami shoten, 1954), 86.
46. Nishiyama Uzō, Kore kara no sumai (Tokyo: Sagami shobō, 1947), 125.
47. Kawashima, Kekkon, 213.

house was literally to be divided: the extended family dispersed, single-family homes built, walls and doors erected, and the meddling community shut out. The "home of the future" required erecting the very barriers within the home that were denied by Watsuji. As architectural critic Funo Shūji wrote years later, "The postwar house attempted to promote the ideal of the postwar family— the independence of the [nuclear] family, and the independence of individuals within the family—and it divided space accordingly."[48]

The nuclear family thus became the prototype of the ideal postwar family. Yet the romance with the nuclear family was not new to the postwar. In the early twentieth century, the urban nuclear family (*katei*) had emerged in discourse as the "modern" other to the "traditional," rural extended family (*ie*).[49] This dichotomization of "modern" nuclear family versus "traditional" extended family hid the fact that in reality, both were integral parts of the same household system since the Meiji era. As Nishikawa Yūko claims, the "dual system" of extended plus nuclear family "had certain advantages to a nation belatedly entering the system of nation-states."[50] The system of primogeniture prevented the dispersion of capital needed for industrialization while non-inheriting sons and daughters provided an endless source of cheap labor for urban factories. The extended family also provided a social insurance system when non-inheriting sons, still legally part of the extended family, required refuge from the fluctuations of the capitalist economy. And contrary to postwar critiques that associated only the extended family with wartime patriotism, both the nuclear family and the household were mobilized to support the war effort. "*Katei aikoku*" ([nuclear] family patriotism), "*katei hōkoku*," (family service to the state), and "*katei tonarigumi*" (family neighborhood associations) had all been invoked in the name of the war.[51] Upholding the nuclear family as the model of enlightened, modern family life and the cornerstone of postwar peace thus required some historical forgetfulness. The concept of the extended family, Nishikawa suggests, was in effect sacrificed after the war, "allowing the nuclear family to survive."[52]

Likewise, the impulse to insulate the nuclear family from the outside world

---

48. Funo Shūji, *Suramu to usagi goya* (Tokyo: Seikyūsha, 1985), 264.
49. Jordan Sand, "At Home in the Meiji Period: Inventing Japanese Domesticity," in Stephen Vlastos, ed., *Mirror of Modernity: Invented Traditions of Modern Japan* (Berkeley: University of California Press, 1998), 191-207.
50. Nishikawa Yūko, "The Changing Form of Dwellings and the Establishment of the *Katei* (Home) in Modern Japan," *Nichibei josei jānaru* 8 (1995): 33.
51. Ibid., 31.
52. Ibid.

had its roots in the prewar era. As Jordan Sand demonstrated, since the early twentieth century, reformers were concerned with creating a bounded, private living space for the middle class family. In the prewar bourgeois home, emphasis had been placed on establishing separations between the urban middle class family and outsiders, particularly domestic help and urban masses that might contaminate the home now subject to ever more rigorous standards of hygiene. As Sand notes, "The household was posed against its neighbors and guests, and the family against its servants."[53] After 1945, as wartime "neighborhood associations" came under attack as agents of surveillance and enforcers of conformity during the war, the effort to quarantine the nuclear family from urban contaminants was re-envisioned as a postwar project to shut out the pernicious ideological pressures of the community.

Walls separating family members suggested a realignment of definitions of public and private. Whereas Watsuji had suggested that the line between public and private was demarcated at the gate of the house, making the family one against the community (and, by implication, the nation one against the world), Nishiyama felt the line dividing public and private should run through the center of the home itself. He insisted that the home should no longer be considered a private sanctuary that situated itself versus the outside world but should constitute a combination of public and private space. He saw the home as a space for "communitarian private life" (kyōdōteki shiseikatsu); a hybrid space mixing public and private functions.[54] The bedroom would be the space of private life while the dining room and living room were to be "public" spaces within the private home. These public spaces were not to be shared with people outside one's family like the tatami-matted formal room (zashiki) of the past. Rather, the "public life within the home" (ie no uchi no ōyake seikatsu) was to be exercised by the family itself; children would learn civic virtues at the kitchen table.[55]

Japan's "home of the future" thus required a fundamental realignment of living space. A house newly divided, it sought to rewire family relationships while protecting "the people" from the intrusions of the community and the state. Yet the reforms sought by architects had physical requirements that simply were not feasible in the years immediately after the war. While their vision required a proliferation of single family homes and within those homes, more space to accommodate private rooms, in the late 1940s, multiple generations living under one roof or even in one room was much more typical, especially in cities.

---

53. Sand, 43.
54. Nishiyama Uzō, Kore kara no sumai, 72.
55. Ibid., 72, 109.

While the architectural solutions to Japan's housing problem might take time to achieve, Nishiyama suggested, it was not too soon to begin practicing "ways of dwelling" (*sumikata*) that would be the foundation of the postwar home. In the future, individuals would have their own private rooms. For now, they would have to learn to "knock."[56]

The "Feudal Home"

To reformers, the problem with the Japanese home was not simply spatial but also temporal. Like Watsuji, early postwar reformers viewed the home as a remnant of the past still existing in the present. But whereas Watsuji celebrated this fact, postwar reformers suggested that this temporal unevenness hindered Japan's ability to progress. The word used to describe this temporal backwardness was "feudal." This pejorative was ubiquitous in the early postwar. Many critics, such as Nishiyama, used it to refer to elements hindering the even unfolding of the Marxist stages of history.[57] Others utilized it in a more generalized sense to criticize any- and everything related to "traditional" Japan. In critiques of home and everyday life it invoked a sense of uneven temporality—of the past coexisting with and creating problems in the present.

In *The Home of the Future*, Nishiyama emphasized that the small urban house and lifestyle were not "traditional" but themselves products of capitalist development. The expansion of cities that accompanied the growth of capitalism resulted in the construction of large numbers of small dwellings for rent to the new and often migrant urban population. Because of size restrictions and rising land prices, carpenters cut corners by eliminating the "*doma*," a space that was essential in farmhouses. The *doma*, a large room with a dirt floor, was the part of the house used for work, cooking, and other functions that required standing. Chores and other functions requiring sitting or reclining were done in the other rooms covered with *tatami* flooring. By cutting off the *doma*, Nishiyama insisted, the urban home had been "crippled" and its inhabitants forced to accomplish all functions of the home sitting on the floor.[58] Although it was the conditions of capitalist development that had resulted in this altered living space, Nishiyama argued that the ambitions of the state that had forced people to sacrifice all to building a "rich nation and strong army" froze any further development of urban living space. It became, in effect, a "semi-feudal remnant" in the midst of a

---

56. Ibid., 136.
57. See interview with Ōmoto Keino, 568.
58. Nishiyama, *Kore kara no sumai*, 22-26.

developing and differentiating capitalist society.[59]

Nishiyama's evidence of temporal unevenness at the heart of the Japanese home came from a series of "surveys of how people live" (*sumikata chōsa*) that he conducted during his tenure with the Jūtaku Eidan during the war. His surveys focused on the homes of poor working class families in Kyoto that consisted, typically, of one six-*tatami* mat room and one 4.5 *tatami*-mat room with cooking facilities situated off the back of the home. While these small living spaces were designed to be convertible and multi-functional, Nishiyama's discovery was that families did not convert their living spaces from daytime to nighttime uses. They tended to designate the room closest to the kitchen as eating space and when bedtime came, rather than clearing it away and spreading futon bedding there, the whole family—parents and children together—would pile into the second and most often only other room to sleep.[60] His surveys proved to Nishiyama that although living spaces did not reflect it, the Japanese urban working class was developing historically, "moving in the direction of separation by function (*kinō bunka*) *not* toward convertability."[61] In other words, urban families—who already lived "modern" lives as they divided their lives functionally between home and workplace—also assigned specific functions to specific rooms. In essence, they were modern people who were forced to live in "feudal" homes. Echoing Le Corbusier who after World War I noted that modern workers were forced to live in dwellings no longer "adapted to their needs,"[62] Nishiyama concluded that the "shape of [people's] lives" (*seikatsu no kata*) had been transformed by capitalist modernity, but the "shape of their homes" (*jūtaku no kata*) had not.[63] Architect and designer Hamaguchi Miho, who noticed a similar disjunction between the way people lived and the historical origins of their living spaces, equated this mismatch to "storing new wine in old wine sacks."[64]

What Nishiyama found most worrisome about his findings was that by not converting eating spaces to sleeping spaces, people perpetuated the worrisome

59. In his interview with Ōmoto Keino, Nishiyama claimed that he used the term "semi-feudal" in the way implied by Kōza-ha Marxists. Ōmoto, 568.
60. For a concise, third-person description of Nishiyama's experiments, see Suzuki Shigebumi. *Suzuki Shigabumi jūkyo ronshū: sumai no keikaku: sumai no bunka* (Tokyo: Shōkokusha, 1988), 18-28.
61. Nishiyama Uzō, *Kore kara no sumai*, 166.
62. Le Corbusier, *Towards a New Architecture* (New York: Dover Publications, Inc., 1986), 269.
63. Nishiyama, *Kore kara no sumai*, 241-49.
64. Hamaguchi Miho, *Nihon jūtaku no hōkensei* (Tokyo: Sagami shobō, 1950), 107.

practice of intergenerational co-sleeping. Although the tradition of co-sleeping had a long history in Japan in dwellings large and small, Nishiyama was alarmed at families sleeping together in the same room and was thoroughly committed to modern Western notions that children and adults should be separated at night for reasons of hygiene, sexual morality, and personal privacy.[65] Nishiyama also believed that over time, all other functions of the home—including cooking, eating, and caring for children—would be socialized, leaving sleeping as the primary function of the urban home. Thus, providing proper sleeping conditions was the lowest minimum standard for the urban home, one that was undermined by the mistaken belief that people "converted" their living space from function to function.[66] So from his surveys Nishiyama drew his "first principle" of housing design: that to discourage intergenerational co-sleeping and provide adequate space for parents and children to sleep separately, even the smallest of dwellings should promote the "separation of eating and sleeping" (*shokushin bunri*). After the war, designing living spaces that upheld this principle became an important quest of young architects.[67] As we will see in Chapter Two, it was the creation of the "dining kitchen" for the *danchi* that finally solved this fundamental housing problem. Accordingly, in the estimation of architectural historian Fujimori Terunobu, "no phrase has had a more decisive influence on modern Japanese housing history than . . . 'the separation of eating and sleeping.'"[68]

Hamaguchi Miho, in her seminal 1953 text *The Feudalism of the Japanese Home*, focused on a different set of problems produced by the "stunted" development of the home. Unlike Nishiyama, who was interested in the homes of the urban working class, Hamaguchi's focus was the middle-class home. She claimed that the home of the urban salaried worker assumed "feudal" hierarchies that no longer pertained in the urban setting but whose persistence created all sorts of problems—especially for women. Her critique participated in a sizeable early postwar discourse about the position of women in Japanese society. To many—from Occupation reformers to Japanese critics—their enfranchisement was considered the starting point for the democratization of home and society. To Hamaguchi, simply changing the legal rights of women was not enough to elevate their position in Japanese society. The rigid hierarchies that subordinated

---

65. For a history of "co-sleeping" in Japan and Europe and an analysis of how Victorian principles influenced reformers such as Nishiyama, see Waswo, 67-69.

66. Nishiyama Uzō, *Jūtaku Keikaku*, 404.

67. See Suzuki Shigebumi.

68. Fujimori Terunobu, "Dainingu ki'chin tanjōki: gakumon mo mare ni katsu," *Jūtaku tokushū* (April 1988): 103.

women were inscribed in and perpetuated by living space. Improving women's status thus required eliminating "feudalism" from the home.

Hamaguchi's first concern was the urban kitchen. Typically a dingy room situated off the back of the house to prevent smoke and cooking smells from permeating the rest of the home, the kitchen, Hamaguchi argued, was the most ignoble room of the house. The fact that neither guests nor the "man of the house" ever set foot there and that cooking and eating were done in separate rooms were Hamaguchi's evidence of the "lowly position" of the kitchen within a presumed hierarchy of rooms. In the past, Hamaguchi argued, it was natural that spaces for cooking and eating would be separated and that the former, primarily occupied by servants, would assume a lower position. This configuration was also still acceptable in the countryside because the historical role of peasants as servants to the samurai class made the kitchen a natural gathering place for farming families. The problem was that the social composition of the urban family did not match the class assumptions of its living space. Servants and maids had become rare, especially since the end of the war. Now it was the same person—the housewife—both preparing and sharing in the consumption of the food, but these two functions were still separated spatially owing to the outmoded values of the space. The current system equated the housewife with a servant and the ignoble position of the kitchen perpetuated the lowly position of the wife in the family. Space should be brought into alignment with the current social system, Hamaguchi argued. "We can say that the house is 'natural' when the human composition and the composition of living space are in agreement."[69]

Another set of "feudal" assumptions still permeating the urban home concerned the position of the household within the community. Here Hamaguchi tapped into prewar and wartime critiques that denounced "wasteful" household traditions such as seasonal gift-giving and costly weddings and funerals undertaken, critics claimed, to maintain a household's standing in the community. Hamaguchi argued that this wastefulness extended to the very spatial configuration of the home. In the countryside, several rooms were dedicated to "formal" (kakushiki) purposes such as receiving guests. The problem with this practice, Hamaguchi noted, was that families dedicated the best rooms of the house to such "formal" purposes, leaving the less desirable rooms to serve as "functional" rooms used by the family. The comfort of individual family members was thus sacrificed to maintaining the social standing of the extended family. These rooms also commanded different levels of respect. The formal areas (associated primarily with men) were held in higher esteem than

69. Hamaguchi, 33-35.

the functional rooms such as the kitchen (associated primarily with women). Contrasting a "functional standard of living" with a "formal standard of living," Hamaguchi contended, ". . . in one the denominator is human beings; in the other the household."[70]

Again, the coexistence of two spatial ideals—functional and formal —created yet a different and more problematic effect in the urban home. Because of the larger size of homes in the countryside, Hamaguchi argued, these two principles coexisted side by side but completely separately: there were rooms meant for use by the family and rooms reserved for guests. In smaller apartments and homes in the city, however, the two spatial ideals were merged in the same room. To Hamaguchi, this hybrid space represented a Japanese society caught between feudalism and modernity.[71] It also resulted in extra work for the housewife as it was her job to convert space from formal to functional uses, again work that was once undertaken by servants. The result, observed Maekawa Kunio, was a housewife who aged before her time: ". . . it is not inconceivable that in this kind of house, the winds of feudal patriarchy are exhaled by the domineering husband as he reclines in a lordly fashion. Meanwhile, the wife does not have a moment's rest from morning until night and rapidly grows older, becoming an old woman by the age of forty."[72]

The concern with women's labor expressed by both Hamaguchi and Maekawa was one that would dominate discussions of the postwar home and family. Indeed, many of the home appliances that people began acquiring in the late 1950s and 1960s were celebrated for "liberating" housewives from the drudgery of housework. Yet discussions of women's labor drew on a set of concerns dating from the war that linked the problem of women and housework to the reproduction of race and nation. Postwar discussions of women's labor in the home often drew on the ideas of Kagoyama Takashi, a researcher of social policy during the war. Kagoyama wrote *The Composition of the Lives of the Japanese People* in the early 1940s when the daily lives and livelihoods of the people—their *seikatsu*—had become a major concern of the state in its efforts to mobilize the resources of society for war. Everyday life (*nichijō seikatsu*) as defined by Kagoyama was a temporal category: the "twenty-four hour, one-day unit." In modern industrial society, he argued, this one-day unit was divided among three functions—labor, rest, and sleep—and was the basic temporal unit for the consumption and reproduction of labor power. Kagoyama challenged the common viewpoint that labor, situated in the workplace, was productive while rest and sleep, situated in

70. Ibid., 60.
71. Ibid., 106.
72. Quoted in Reynolds, 142.

the home, were consumptive. Using labor power as his unit of analysis, he turned this interpretation on its head and insisted: "In 'productive' life (*seisan seikatsu*) things are produced but labor power is consumed. In 'consumptive' life (*shōhi seikatsu*) things are consumed but labor power reproduced. Therefore, from the viewpoint of labor power, productive life is consumptive and consumptive life is productive."[73] To Kagoyama, the home was not a separate sphere, divorced from the workplace. Rather, work and non-work were "two sides of a single economic life."[74] Daily life was none other than a closed system for the metabolism and reproduction of energy to be devoted to labor.[75]

After the war, Nishiyama, Hamaguchi, and others utilized Kagoyama's theories to insist that the primary function of the home itself was as a space of rest and the reproduction of labor power. But within Kagoyama's theory, women's labor presented a problem. Kagoyama assumed that it was male labor that was consumed in the workplace and whose reproduction was the primary function of the home. Much female labor power, on the contrary, was expended in the home on behalf of reproducing the labor power of others, not to mention the literal reproduction of labor power for the next generation. Whereas for men, two of the three categories of work, rest, and sleep were accomplished within the home, for many women, all three took place there. The reproduction of female labor power was therefore much more difficult, temporally and spatially.[76] Postwar

73. Kagoyama Takashi, *Kokumin seikatsu no kōzō* (1943), reprinted in Ishikawa Hiroyoshi, comp., *Yoka goraku kenkyū kiso bunkenshū*. Vol. 22 (Tokyo: Daikūsha, 1990), 24.

74. Ibid., 22.

75. Just as Nishiyama claimed that his campaign to increase minimum housing sizes while working for the Jūtaku Eidan was a form of wartime resistance, Kagoyama's insistence that even in the midst of total war, labor power could not expand endlessly without adequate time to "reproduce" itself through rest and sleep was also interpreted later as an act of resistance against the state during the war. See Terade Kōji, *Seikatsu bunka-ron e no shōtai* (Tokyo: Kōbundō, 1994), 122.

76. Kon Wajirō, also utilizing the basic theories of Kagoyama, argued that the requirements for the reproduction of labor also differed according to social class. Laborers who worked with their bodies needed wide-open rooms with little furniture or ornamentation so that they could sleep without obstruction. Those who labored with their minds, however, required a more complex space—with gardens or home decorations to gaze upon—in order to rest their mind and reproduce their labor for the following day. Likening the laborer to a car that required gasoline (food) and oil (life in the home) to run, Kon insisted that "the more elaborate the machine, the higher quality of oil required." The complexity

studies of the home insisted that while the home needed to be reconfigured to promote rest, it also needed to be rationalized to accommodate women's labor and create time for its reproduction.

Once again it was functionalism that would help to accomplish these goals, according to Hamaguchi. In an essay titled "The time of daily life, the space of daily life" (*Seikatsu jikan to seikatsu kūkan*), Hamaguchi utilized Kagoyama's theory to argue once again that converting rooms from function to function or from functional to formal purposes was not only inefficient but also created work for the housewife and consumed her precious time. Western-style homes that assigned "one time to one space" (the bedroom at bedtime, for instance) were more efficient than Japanese houses in which one space served multiple functions in one day. Assigning specific functions to specific rooms would increase the efficiency of the home and reduce women's labor.[77] Nishiyama, equally concerned with women's labor, suggested a different solution: the socialization of housework. He suggested that Japan continue practices started during the war when, out of necessity, many communities had collaborated on household chores such as cooking, laundry, and child-care.[78] Whether by the division of space by function or the socialization of housework, Hamaguchi and Nishiyama sought to reduce the home to its most basic function in industrial society: a space of rest for both men and women.

Implicit in the writings of both Nishiyama and Hamaguchi was the assumption that dividing space by function was more advanced and "modern" than converting from one function to another. They also assumed a developmental trajectory from the rural home built for the extended family still, they implied, residing in the past, to the urban home of the nuclear family, already residing in the modern present. In their quest to bring space and time into alignment, at least in the city, they sought to expunge the past dwelling in the present. In the context of the early postwar, this was a past they judged problematic and expendable, one to be designed out of the postwar Japanese home.

Architects' efforts were riddled with contradictions. Even as they exhorted "the people" to become "subjects" of their own daily lives, architects envisioned themselves as social engineers entrusted with a mandate to formulate a new

---

of living space was thus commensurate with the complexity of work. Kon Wajirō, *Seikatsugaku: Kon Wajirō shū*, Volume 5 (Tokyo: Domesu Shuppan, 1971), 143-148.

77. Hamaguchi Miho, "Seikatsu jikan, seikatsu kūkan," in Kenchikugaku taikei henshū iin, ed., *Kenchikugaku taikei: jūkyo-ron I* (Tokyo: Shōkokusha, 1954), 285-371.

78. Nishiyama, *Kore kara no sumai*, 160-69.

blueprint for the home and family. Nishiyama Uzō seemed to recognize this contradiction and argued that in the current housing crisis, a home designed to individual preference was a luxury that only the very wealthy could afford. While "the energy to realize the improvement and rationalization of housing must come from the people's awakening desire for it," argued Nishiyama, it was still the role of architects to design housing "forms" (*kata*) that could be mass-produced for widespread construction and the role of the state to ensure their "rational distribution."[79] People could exercise their own subjectivity within these housing "forms" through their "way of dwelling" (*sumikata*) which, presumably, respected the new spatial divisions within the house: by function, between generations, and between the "public" and "private" spaces of the home.[80]

More paradoxical was that even as architects blamed the prewar and wartime state for suppressing the living standards of "the people" and "distorting" the architectural profession, many looked to the postwar state to alleviate the housing crisis after 1945. In its attempts to mobilize for total war, the state had expanded its reach into the realm of everyday life and this, ironically, expanded people's expectations of it after the war. In fact, the state was the only agency with the means and organizational capacity to address the housing crisis after the war and, as we will see in the next chapter, the devastation of World War II created the conditions for the proliferation of state-sponsored mass housing around the world. Postwar housing authorities turned to architects such as Nishyama, Maekawa, and Hamaguchi Miho to lend their expertise to help solve the housing crisis. And to many architects, struggling like everyone else to survive after the war, commissions offered by state housing authorities were often the best jobs in town. They offered opportunities for architects to realize their visions of "housing for the people." In the end, many of the reformist visions of architects took built form courtesy of the government—as we will see in the next chapter, the *danchi* built by the Japan Housing Corporation are the best example of this. The "revolution of everyday life" would lose its subversive potential as "housing for the people" became projects of the state.

Yet many of the ideas that emerged from these early postwar discussions would have profound and lasting impacts on postwar architecture. Nishiyama's insistence that eating and sleeping be separated was one of the fundamental ideals underlying the design of the *danchi* interior, as was Hamaguchi Miho's campaign to bring the kitchen to the center of the home. As the basis of a reformed postwar home, these visions would become fundamental to revised notions of the middle-class family and the middle-class home.

---

79. Ibid., 250-52.
80. Ibid.

Chapter Two

BUILDING THE POSTWAR MIDDLE CLASS

Disregard the poor? I guess that's true. At any rate, with an overall housing shortage, it was a question of where to start building. If we had set aside those who would contribute to Japan's recovery and assisted only those who would be baggage in those efforts, Japan could not be rebuilt. We [made policies] to support the families who would help rebuild Japan in the future.

Housing Official, Kawashima Hiroshi[1]

Back to the Future

The year 1955 was an important landmark in the history of postwar Japan. At the time, but more so retrospectively, the year seemed to mark the dividing line between the early years of hardship after World War II and the period of "high-speed economic growth" that characterized the 1960s and early 1970s. That year was first identified as a turning point by a now-famous economic White Paper that announced that as of that year Japan was "no longer postwar." Economic recovery from the war had been accomplished, and it was now time for the nation to set its sights on "modernization."[2] Looking back, we identify 1955 as the year in which the conservative political party that was to dominate Japanese politics until the 1990s was consolidated. So significant has the year been to understanding postwar politics that the unique balance between the conservative Liberal Democratic Party (LDP) majority and its small but boisterous socialist opposition which defined politics during those decades, was eventually labeled simply the "1955 system." In cultural and social histories, too, 1955 often represents "the dividing line between the postwar and the post-postwar" after which people's lives began to be rapidly and ineluctably transformed by the consumption

---

1. Interview with Ōmoto Keinō in *Shōgen: nihon no jūtaku seisaku* (Tokyo: Nihon hyōronsha, 1991), 275-276.
2. *Shōwa sanjū-ichi nendo keizai hakusho* (Tokyo: Keizai kikakuchō, 1956), 42.

of mass-produced goods for the home.[3] Not unlike 1948 in annals of West German history, when currency reform seemed to mark "the return of prosperity in collective memory," 1955 seemed to herald the possibility of moving beyond the day-to-day survival mode of the first postwar decade and focusing on the future. [4]

It also brought the establishment of the Japan Housing Corporation (JHC), the state-sponsored housing agency charged with building mass housing complexes called *danchi* for urban middle-class families.[5] Even ten years after the end of the war, Japan suffered a shortage of nearly three million housing units, affecting over sixteen percent of urban households. The amount of housing space per person, at 3.4 *tatami* mats per person, was still lower than its 1941 ratio of 3.8 per person. And the rental market, devastated by wartime regulations, stood at a mere thirty percent of urban housing compared with seventy-six percent in 1941.[6] The shortage resulting from war was compounded by housing demands created by recovery. Economic growth, jump-started by the Korean War, brought tremendous influxes of people into urban areas where rising land prices greatly aggravated efforts to house them. In Tokyo alone, between 1950 and 1955, the population had increased by almost two million people, bringing it to the unprecedented number of 8.04 million.[7] An explosion in land prices further complicated matters. In 1950, prices for residential land in Japan's six major metropolitan areas were 174 percent of what they had been in 1936; by

3. Marilyn Ivy, "Formations of Mass Culture," in Andrew Gordon, ed., *Postwar Japan as History* (Berkeley: University of California Press, 1993), 247.
4. Michael Wildt, "Continuities and Discontinuities of Consumer Mentality in West Germany in the 1950s," in Richard Bessel and Dirk Schumann, ed., *Life After Death: Approaches to a Cultural and Social History of Europe During the 1940s and 1950s* (Cambridge: Cambridge University Press, 2003), 211.
5. The precise origins of the word "*danchi*" are not clear. The word was used periodically previous to the establishment of the JHC to refer to collective housing projects built on single sites, but it was the JHC that made "*danchi*" a household word. Subsequently, it was used to refer to collective housing in general but with the JHC model as the image of *danchi* life. The JHC, in other words, *danchi*-fied the *danchi*. The word "*danchi*" is the contraction of two words: grouping (*dan*) and land (*chi*). One of the clauses of the law that created the JHC stipulated: "The housing the JHC builds shall be collective housing built *on one grouping of land*" (*ichidan no tochi ni*). It is the land aspect of the *danchi* that is emphasized in its name.
6. *Shōwa 31-nendo keizai hakusho*, 284.
7. Sanuki Toshio, *Seichō suru toshi, suitai suru toshi* (Tokyo: Jiji tsōshinsha, 1983), 36.

1955 they stood at 527 percent.[8] The "housing problem," now as much that of a "modernizing" as a "recovering" Japan, thus became a pressing issue for political parties on both the left and right in the mid-1950s. Prime Minister Hatoyama Ichirō, the man who eventually presided over the union of the conservative Liberal and Democratic Parties to form the LDP in late 1955, came to power vowing to "expand housing policy." He promised to solve Japan's housing crisis in ten years and, in a famous pronouncement, to increase housing stocks by 420,000 units within ten years.[9] The JHC was established in July of 1955 to help fulfill this goal. Its establishment was thus an integral part of the 1955 political consolidation.

The JHC is dealt with only briefly in studies of postwar housing policy, perhaps due to the fact that its total contribution to Japan's postwar housing stock would be relatively insignificant compared to that of the private sector and other types of public housing. Between 1945 and 1998, fifty-one million housing units were built in Japan. Of these, approximately fifty-four percent were built with private funds. Of the remaining forty-six percent built with public funds, only three percent were built by the JHC and its successor institutions.[10] Yet the long-term contributions of the JHC *danchi* would lie elsewhere. With the *danchi*, the JHC created and promoted a specific configuration of urban, everyday life that became a prototype of middle-class life. It became a test bed for the development of housing technology and played a pioneering role in the standardization and modernization of interior living space. Built on urban peripheries, JHC mass housing hastened the shift of urban populations away from city centers and out into rapidly developing suburbs. No less than the highways and other massive construction projects that transformed the face of postwar Japan, large suburban enclaves of middle-class *danchi* projects became part of the infrastructure for high-speed economic growth.

The *danchi* became not only a physical prototype of postwar everyday life but an ideological one, as well. Apartments were promoted by architects and social engineers as innovative living spaces that would help bring to fruition their early postwar visions of reformed postwar families and communities. With modern kitchens, private baths, and steel doors that locked out intrusive neighbors; and inhabited by families that, unlike most at the time, could afford refrigerators,

---

8. Jūtaku kin'yū kōko, *Shiryō de miru nihon no jūtaku mondai* (Tokyo: Jūtaku kin'yū kōko, 1980), 40.

9. *Kensetsushō jūgo nen shoshi* (Tokyo: Kensetsu kōhō kyōgikai, 1963), 190.

10. Building Center of Japan, ed., *A Quick Look at Housing in Japan* (Tokyo: The Building Center of Japan, 1998), 23.

washing machines, electric rice cookers, and other objects of desire, the *danchi* entered the postwar social imaginary as a "life to long for" (*akogareta seikatsu*).[11] This phrase suggested that the vast majority of Japanese people did not live *danchi* lifestyles at the time. Yet, the *danchi* became a powerful vision of an attainable middle-class lifestyle and, as such, became embedded in the 1955 narrative in fundamental ways. *Danchi* life, like the year 1955 itself, seemed to represent the "bright life" of rising prosperity after years of deprivation and hardship. In both individual narratives of people making good and securing *danchi* apartments, and national narratives of Japan's rising standard of living, the *danchi* offered concrete proof that Japan was "no longer postwar."

The "Golden Age" of Mass Housing

The *danchi* became emblematic of the "bright life" of the post-postwar, but the institutional foundations and priorities of the JHC were rooted firmly in the experiences of mobilization, war, and recovery. Around the world, the housing crisis resulting from World War II created an unprecedented role for states to provide housing and ushered in a golden age of state-sponsored housing both quantitatively and qualitatively. This golden age, from 1945 through the early 1970s, was one born of necessity. A United Nations report, published in 1949 and focusing on seventeen Western European nations, estimated that cumulatively they suffered a shortage of over fourteen million housing units, or about one-fifth of their prewar housing stock.[12] The war also left twenty-five million Russians and twenty million Germans homeless.[13] With this magnitude of devastation, in most nations, only governments had the resources and organizational capacities to address the problem. Qualitatively, too, in the decade or so after the war, many governments were the main source of housing innovation, due once again to the magnitude of the crisis. The demand for large amounts of hous-

11. According to the White Paper on National Life for 1960, a comparative study of *danchi* residents and people living in Tokyo indicated that seventy-six percent of *danchi* residents owned washing machines compared to 49.2 percent of Tokyoites. For rice cookers, the percentages were fifty-six versus 25.1 percent, refrigerators: 20.5 versus 13.7 percent, electric and gas stoves: 63.2 versus 37.1 percent, televisions: 61.1 versus 60.6 percent. *Shōwa sanjū-go nendo kokumin seikatsu hakusho* (Tokyo: Keizai kikakuchō, 1960), 144.

12. Michael Harloe, *The People's Home? Social Rented Housing in Europe and America* (Cambridge, MA: Blackwell Publishers, 1995), 256.

13. Tony Judt, *Postwar: A History of Europe Since 1945* (New York: The Penguin Press, 2005), 16-17.

ing as quickly as possible created pressure to rationalize designs and modernize building techniques. Housing became a "plannable instrument" and therefore a "testbed for innovations in housing techniques."[14] As Florian Urban noted, "In light of a shortage that was enhanced by the destruction of the Second World War, state-subsidized mass housing came to be universally accepted as the most efficient answer to the challenges posed by social plight: it became synonymous with modernization."[15]

As in Europe, Japan's golden age of state-sponsored housing had a long prehistory. From the early years of Meiji, the conditions of urban housing and growth of slums that accompanied capitalist industrialization drew state concern, but it was not until the industrial boom times of World War I, when urban housing shortages led to price gouging and extensive landlord-tenant disputes, that urban housing came to be considered a "social problem" worthy of systematic focus and policymaking. This focus was intensified after the 1923 Great Kantō Earthquake created a dire housing shortage in Tokyo and Yokohama.[16] Yet the immediate and

---

14. Harloe, 264.
15. Florian Urban, *Tower and Slab: Histories of Global Mass Housing* (New York: Routledge, 2012), 13.
16. There is debate among housing scholars as to how to periodize the history of Japan's housing policy. Honma Yoshihito has classified 1918 the "first year of housing policy in Japan" for it was the year that a survey committee was organized within the Relief Section of the Home Ministry in order to compile proposals addressing Japan's various social problems, including the problem of housing. Among these was a "Plan for the Improvement of Small Housing" (*Shōjūtaku kairyō yōkō*) published in 1919. Policies resulting from this plan included indirect state support in the form of low interest loans to public corporations building housing for low-income families and to unions of private, middle-class home owners constructing housing for themselves. After the Great Kantō Earthquake in 1923, efforts to house the middle class were redirected into the Dōjunkai housing projects, the state's first attempt to guide housing directly. The Dōjunkai was eventually dissolved into the wartime housing authority, the Jūtaku Eidan. Other scholars such as Ōmoto Keino suggest the indirect policies of the interwar period were a "prehistory" to the more integrated and direct housing policy that began as Japan mobilized for war in the 1930s and 1940s. I share this latter viewpoint. Honma Yoshihito, *Naimushō jūtaku seisaku no kyōjun* (Tokyo: Ochanomizu shobō, 1988). For Ōmoto's periodization and discussion of the history of housing policy in Japan, see Ōmoto Keino, 849-867. Also, for an interesting analysis of how government-sponsored housing surveys can be read to understand the gradual expansion and generalization of governmental concern with the "housing

most important prehistory of postwar housing policy came from the experience of mobilizing for war in the 1930s and 1940s. It was then that conceptions of the "housing problem," previously considered one of the many "social problems" afflicting specific urban populations, was transformed into a more generalized concern for the welfare and, more importantly, fighting capacity of the people at large. The 1938 creation of a Welfare Ministry concerned exclusively with the conditions, amounts and distribution of food, clothing and housing—now considered national resources to be mobilized for the "total war" effort—marked a new phase in the evolution of welfare policy in Japan. As Gregory Kasza has argued, while there was much social policy pertaining to welfare before the war, it was mobilization for war more than anything else that led to the establishment of a modern welfare regime in Japan.[17]

As part of its mandate to increase the quantity and quality of "people's housing" (*kokumin jūtaku*), in 1941 the Welfare Ministry created Japan's first full-fledged housing agency, the Housing Authority, or Jūtaku Eidan. With deepening shortages of basic building materials and the passage of a rent control law which froze rents at August 1938 levels, private builders increasingly lost the incentive and ability to build housing, and the state took over the direct construction and allocation of housing. The Housing Authority was established with a budget of 1.1 billion yen and the goal of building 300,000 housing units in five years. In addition to addressing the growing housing shortage, it also concerned itself with determining minimum housing standards. The emphasis in this case was on the word *minimum*. The mandate of the Welfare Ministry was to determine the minimum amounts of food, clothing, and housing necessary to guarantee the reproduction of labor. In 1941, it commissioned a committee of architects, among them Nishiyama Uzō, to come up with housing standards for Japan. The committee created several housing designs and proposals but, in the end, its overly ambitious plans were used only for reference. The Housing Authority published its own set of standards in March of 1941, establishing six basic housing sizes ranging from thirty to eighty square meters and stipulating "principles" about the standardization of housing measurements, materials, light and ventilation requirements, and toilet and kitchen facilities. Although these principles were not legally mandated or enforced, this was the first time the

---

problem," see Kawai Takao, ed., *Kindai nihon shakai chōsashi III*, (Tokyo: Keio tsūshin, 1989).

17. See Gregory J. Kasza, "War and Welfare Policy in Japan," *The Journal of Asian Studies* 61.2 (May 2002): 417-435.

Japanese state promoted housing standards.[18]

In terms of results, the wartime Housing Authority's attempts to provide housing were an abysmal failure. During the war, it managed to build only 95,000 of its proposed housing units and those that it did build were of questionable quality.[19] Shortages of laborers to cut down trees and build houses, of trucks to transport wood from forests to construction sites, and of basic supplies such as nails and fuel to fire roofing tiles brought housing construction almost to a standstill. Housing objectives were often undermined by other war-related projects. At the same time that the Housing Authority was struggling to acquire construction materials and increase housing stock, other state authorities such as the police were knocking down urban housing to create firebreaks. The Housing Authority often resorted to utilizing materials from these knocked-down houses to build new ones, so that the state was "building with one hand and destroying . . . with the other."[20] Attempts to guarantee quality were equally unsuccessful. As building materials became scarce, the Housing Authority twice reduced its minimum standard size: from nine to seven *tsubo* (29.7 to 23.1 square meters) in 1942 and from seven to 6.25 *tsubo* (20.6 square meters) in 1944.21 Ichiura Ken, who occupied various positions in the Housing Authority between 1941 and 1945 recalled:

> We would knock down [a house] because it was going to get destroyed in an air raid. We'd clear a hundred meters on each side of the Tokaido line, or we'd take down houses where city plan[ners] were going to build roads. In the end, we had such a shortage of materials that we would use the old materials to build houses. And each house got smaller. That was our job at the Housing Authority. We had a standard plan but the General Staff Headquarters would tell us to cut corners.[22]

Yet the legacy of wartime housing policy lay not in these failures but in how it transformed the relationship between the state and the housing problem. It established housing as a national resource and the general population, "the

---

18. Both the recommendations of the Japan Architectural Society (*Nihon kenchiku gakkai*) and the Welfare Ministry's planning standards with revisions are published in Nishiyama Uzō, *Jūtaku keikaku: Nishiyama Uzō chosaku-shū* (Tokyo: Keisō shobō, 1967), 584-598 and 599-617.

19. Kasza, 426.

20 Interview with wartime housing engineer Hayakawa Fumio in Ōmoto Keino, 93.

21. One *tsubo* equals 3.3 square meters or 35.54 square feet.

22. Interview with Ōmoto Keino, in ibid., 101.

people" (*kokumin*), as the objects of housing policy. Housing would no longer be conceptualized as a "social" problem" but as a problem of the nation. Thus it is no surprise that after the war promoting "the formation of a social mainstream"[23] would become the overarching priority of housing policy.

The experiences of mobilization and war also poised the state to become the first responder to the housing crisis after World War II. In 1945, the War Rehabilitation Board, charged with rebuilding Japan's war-torn cities, estimated that one of every five homes had been destroyed. The destruction was greatest in urban areas which had been the targets of concentrated air raids and where rental housing markets, long the mainstay of urban housing, had been devastated by wartime and early postwar restrictions on construction and rent levels.[24] For the first several years after the war, the state attempted to address the housing crisis with a series of emergency stopgap measures. Besides building barracks and other temporary housing, it placed people without housing in homes with "excess capacity," [25] placed restrictions on building types and sizes, and attempted to control migration into cities of one-hundred thousand or more by restricting residence to people who could prove that they had a job and place to live—a measure that was much publicized but difficult to enforce. Even with such measures in place, the housing crisis was visibly dire in the early years after the war, becoming yet another vital necessity sold on the black market, with

23. Hirayama Yosuke, "Housing policy and social inequality in Japan, in Misa Izuhara, ed., *Comparing Social Policies: Exploring new perspectives in Britain and Japan* (Bristol: Policy Press, 2003), 151.

24. Whereas before the war 70 percent of all urban housing had been rented, in 1948, this figure was 46.5 percent. The percentage continued to drop until the discontinuation of building restrictions after 1951. In Tokyo, in 1950, 35.6 percent of housing was for rent and in 1951, 29.8 percent. Martin Pawley has argued that similar rent controls instituted in Europe during World War I made a postwar housing shortage virtually inevitable. Restricting rents, he observed, "sacrificed long-term market stability for short-term relief." This argument can certainly be made of Japan after World War II. The disincentives to build for the rental market during and after the war greatly aggravated the housing shortage and slowed recovery efforts. Statistics from Harada Sumitaka, "Sengo jūtaku hōsei no seiritsu katei," in *Fukushi kokka-6*, Tokyo daigaku shakai kagaku kenkyūjo "fukushi kokka" kenkyūkai *Fukushi kokka-6* ed. (Tokyo: Tokyo daigaku shuppan-kai, 1985), 340. On Europe, see Martin Pawley, *Architecture verus Housing*, (New York: Praeger Publishers, 1971), 21-22.

25. Designated as homes with over eight rooms or forty-two tatami mats.

rapacious landlords even renting *tatami* mats individually.[26] As noted in Chapter One, the Occupation took little direct interest in the housing crisis and what influence it did have was the byproduct of directives with other objectives. In 1947 it dismantled the Housing Authority, claiming it was an "instrument of militarism." The infamous inflation control measures instituted under the "Dodge Line"[27] in 1949 drastically curtailed the reconstruction ambitions of the War Rehabilitation Board. And the Occupation greatly exacerbated the housing crisis by diverting materials and labor to the construction of "dependents housing" for SCAP personnel although, ironically, many builders learned modern construction techniques in the process of building housing for Occupation authorities.[28]

The systematization of postwar housing policy began in 1950 with the establishment of the Housing Loan Corporation (HLC). The HLC was charged with providing low-interest loans to individuals building homes for their own occupancy or to organizations building housing for their employees and was considered the first of "three pillars" of postwar housing policy. The second pillar, Public Housing, was established the following year with the passage of the Public Housing Law which mandated nationally funded but locally-administered public housing authorities to construct two varieties of rental housing: "type one" apartments for people with low to mid-level incomes and "type two" apartments for those with low incomes. When the Japan Housing Corporation was established in 1955, it was presented to the Japanese public as the completion of an as-yet insufficient array of housing institutions. It was established in the name of building housing for middle-income families whose needs were not being met by the other two housing agencies, which catered to the relatively wealthy and the relatively poor, respectively. It was dubbed the third and final pillar of housing policy and charged with constructing housing

---

26. Ann Waswo, *Housing in Postwar Japan: A Social History* (New York: RoutledgeCurzon, 2002), 50.

27. Instituted by Detroit banker Joseph Dodge as Occupation priorities shifted toward Japan's economic rehabilitation with the start of the Cold War, the "Dodge Line" sought to decrease inflation by balancing the budget and curtailing public spending. It also instituted a 360 yen to the dollar exchange rate to make Japanese exports more competitive in international markets.

28. Nishiyama Uzō, *Nihon no sumai* (Tokyo: Keisō shobō, 1976), 212. For the recollections of various housing officials during the Occupation, see interviews with Ōmoto Keino, *Shōgen: Nihon no jūtaku seisaku* (Tokyo: Nihon kōron-sha, 1991), chapters 6-12.

for Japan's forgotten middle class.

Ostensibly, the "three pillars" provided for people of all socio-economic circumstances. From the time of the establishment of Public Housing in 1951, however, it became clear that postwar housing policy would be driven by national, not egalitarian, social imperatives. This became evident when jurisdiction over housing was transferred from the Welfare Ministry to the Construction Ministry after a turf battle over the control of Public Housing. Both ministries submitted public housing bills to the Diet in 1951, each with a different focus. The Welfare Ministry bill sought to provide housing for the most destitute, with rents adjusted according to ability to pay and priority assigned according to need. The Construction Ministry bill, which prevailed in the end, took as its mandate the provision of housing to the workers who would rebuild Japan rather than those who, in the words of career bureaucrat Kawashima Hiroshi, would be "baggage" in these efforts.[29] Rents would be subsidized, but only those who could afford them were allowed to enter the lottery competition to receive public housing. The Construction Ministry also administered the JHC, whose target constituency typically had incomes *above* the middle-level range. In the words of Ann Waswo, it was made clear from the beginning that "the Construction Ministry was in the business of housing provision, not livelihood assistance to families in distressed circumstances."[30] Not surprisingly, a primary criticism of both wartime and postwar housing policy has been that it placed state imperatives over social welfare or, more precisely, imagined social welfare in terms of state goals. This was no less true of efforts to mobilize for war in the 1930s and 1940s than it was of efforts to mobilize for economic growth in the 1950s and 1960s.

Even in the direst days after the war, at no time did the amount of publicly financed or constructed housing exceed that built by the private sector.[31] And compared to many European nations, the Japanese state sponsored the construction of considerably less housing. Even during the peak decade of 1950–59, the share of social rental housing to total new housing construction

---

29. Interview with Ōmoto Keino in *Shōgen*, 275-76.

30. Ann Waswo, "Urban Housing Policy in 20th-Century Japan," *ISS Discussion Paper Series No. F-82* (Tokyo: University of Tokyo Institute of Social Science), 17.

31. In 1945, the public sector built or financed 105,067 housing units; the private sector 130,733. In 1950, public 120,481, private 216,819; in 1955, public 152,392 (including 20,000 housing units built by the JHC), private 249,747; and in 1960, public 218,963 (30,000 JHC) and private 392,303. *Kensetsushō jūgo nen shoshi*, 192.

in Japan was 18.4 percent, compared to 45.8 percent in West Germany and 64 percent in England and Wales.[32] In the case of Japan, housing policy would reorganize itself around one over-arching principle: the promotion of homeownership. The first housing pillar, the Housing Loan Corporation, was key to making this goal a reality as the state "supported private home loans over any substantial social housing system, and by doing so . . . directly subsidized and [was] central to, the financial maintenance of the homeownership system."[33] Statistics tell of the success of this policy: prior to 1945, over seventy percent of housing in urban areas was rented; by 1955, sixty-four percent of housing was privately owned.[34] Yet to the architects of Japan's housing policy, the other two pillars of housing policy also played a role in the cultivation of homeownership. Meant to be less hierarchical than sequential, public housing and JHC rental housing were meant to be "*tsunagi*" or temporary stopgap measures, both for individual families and as publicly funded programs. It was believed that state-built and managed housing would not be necessary in Japan after five or ten years, by which time the private market would have recovered.[35]

The three sequential pillars also suggested a merging of urban spatial and individual life trajectories through the logic of "*sumikae*" or moving house. Ideally, over the course of a career, one moved from public housing or a one-room wooden apartment building in the inner city, to the *danchi* in the suburbs, and finally on to "my home," perhaps financed by the Housing Loan Corporation, farther still from the city center. Housing scholar Hirayama Yosuke noted, "This system defined how a life course should develop in the

32. Iwao Sato, "Welfare regime theories and the Japanese housing system," in Hirayama Yosuke and Richard Ronald, ed., *Housing and Social Transition in Japan* (New York: Routledge, 2007), 78.

33. In 1998 homeownership rate was sixty-three percent. Richard Ronald, "Home Ownership, Ideology, and Diversity: Re-evaluating Concepts of Housing Ideology in the Case of Japan," in *Housing, Theory, and Society*, 2004; 21: 56.

34. Ibid., 55.

35. Harada, 351. Although both Public Housing and the JHC (renamed the Housing and Urban Development Corporation in 1981, the Urban Development Corporation in 1999, and the Urban Renaissance Agency in 2004, each time with amended mandates) are still in existence, critics of Japan's postwar housing policy often cite the temporary intentions of their architects as proof of an overall housing policy that encourages homeownership above all else.

social mainstream and required people to climb up a 'housing ladder' by self-reliance."[36]

The function of the *danchi* and of public housing in general, then, "was as a bridge and transitional phase on the way to homeownership."[37] Even within the *danchi*, one was expected to move from one apartment size to the next as the family grew. As *danchi* resident and economist Hara Takeshi noted, ". . . the JHC provided different types of housing to coordinate with the evolution [of the family] from newlyweds, to the birth of one child, to the birth of a second child, with 1DK, 2DK, 3K, 3DK, etc."[38] Of course, in reality it did not always work out this way. A 1966 report on a *danchi* complex in Osaka noted that sixty percent of original inhabitants who had arrived in 1956 still lived there ten years later.[39] By the mid-1970s, it became evident that some families did not move on at all, spending a lifetime in the *danchi* even with second generations reportedly establishing themselves there.[40] Yet it is important to note how the concept of a "housing ladder" promoted and perpetuated the notion of life stages unfolding naturally over space and time, an idea that would become one of the most powerful constructs in postwar Japan.

The needs of special populations fell outside the province of the "three pillars." The most destitute had to seek other types of aid and income assistance from the Welfare Ministry. Financial assistance often did not bring incomes up to the level that would make recipients eligible to enter public housing. The Welfare Ministry maintained jurisdiction over housing for repatriates from overseas colonies, the "*hikiagesha*," and the Construction Ministry created separate housing programs for *burakumin*, the former outcaste group. Korean residents in Japan were ineligible for public housing of any type until the 1980s.[41] These "marginal" populations often ended up living in dilapidated housing in

---

36. Hirayama "Housing policy and social inequality in Japan,"158.

37. Funo Shūji, *Suramu to usagi goya* (Tokyo: Seikyūsha, 1985), 264.

38. Hara Takeshi and Shigematsu Kiyoshi, *Danchi no jidai* (Tokyo: Shinchosha, 2010), 99.

39. Reported in Christie Kiefer, "Personality and Social Change in a Japanese Danchi" (Ph.D. Diss., University of California, Berkeley), 203.

40. Anne E. Imamura, *Urban Japanese Housewives: At Home and in the Community* (Honolulu: University of Hawaii Press, 1987), 53. The exodus to the suburbs did not always occur, either, especially after the late 1960s when "mansions" (*manshon*)—essentially condominiums for sale in center cities—became a viable alternative to buying a home in the suburbs. See, too, Hara and Shigematsu, 101.

41. Hirayama, 160-162.

specific neighborhoods that defined them as "distinctive socio-spaces outside the housing ladder system."[42]

Even considering these limitations, it is still appropriate to refer to the era between 1945 and the 1970s as the "golden age" of public mass housing in Japan. This was particularly true for the Japan Housing Corporation, whose construction and land development efforts increased steadily over these years, peaking at 85,000 housing units built in 1971 alone. The JHC was responsible for housing innovations such as the dining kitchen, stainless steel sinks, pre-cast concrete construction, and other improvements that were also diffused into the private sector. It was building for a new generation of modern, middle-class families who were envisioned as the hope of the postwar future. Built upon the past, the *danchi* faced the future.

Making a Middle-Class Constituency

The creation of a "third pillar" of housing policy was justified in the name of constructing housing for a forgotten middle class not covered by other housing initiatives. Yet the discussions that led to the establishment of the JHC suggest that this "middle class" was less forgotten than found for the purpose of creating the institution. Harada Sumitaka, in a rereading of the Diet proceedings that preceded the establishment of the JHC, challenged the view of the "third pillar" as the completion of an incomplete array of housing options. The establishment of the JHC, he argued, in fact created a "crack" in an already-complete set of housing policies.[43] In order to create a constituency that justified the establishment of a new housing corporation, requirements for loan eligibility from the Housing Loan Corporation were raised and for Public Housing eligibility lowered, cutting a middle swath of eligibility for JHC housing. This led to fundamental changes in Public Housing. In the year the JHC was established, both the number and size of "type one" apartments for those with higher incomes, were greatly decreased in order to push people from the upper limits of Public Housing into JHC housing. The number of "type two" apartments was increased accordingly, designating low-income families the primary target of Public Housing.[44] In this way, the creation of the JHC resulted in the "welfarization" of Public Housing.

It also required the "middle-classification" of the *danchi*. "*Danchi*"—both the word and the housing type—existed before the JHC's establishment. The

---

42. Ibid.

43. Harada, 364-65.

44. Kōei jūtaku nijū nenshi kankō iinkai ed., *Kōei jūtaku nijū nenshi* (Tokyo: Nihon jūtaku kyōkai, 1973), 151.

word referred generally to collective housing projects built on single sites, and it certainly did *not* convey an image of modern living. It was the JHC that gave the *danchi* a bright, middle-class image by merging prewar conceptions of middle-class values with postwar visions of a reformed postwar family and community. It did this very purposefully to attract prospective residents to its housing.

The JHC was a low-cost means of increasing Japan's housing stock. Besides building on relatively inexpensive land outside city centers, the JHC was also roughly fifty percent financed with private capital, mostly from insurance companies. In this way, noted Waswo, "additional housing in the form of JHC *danchi* could be built and the state could pay the interest differentials owed to the corporation's lenders without a noticeable increase in public spending."[45] And unlike Public Housing, JHC rents were not subsidized—making its apartments expensive to rent by the standards of the day. Rents were almost twice as high as in other public housing and residents were required to have monthly incomes over five times the rent, making the income qualifications for living in the *danchi* "an insurmountable barrier to most of the employed population."[46] So what was a cheap way for the state to increase housing stocks translated into housing that was both expensive and inconveniently located for potential residents. As Harada argued, the attributes that eventually expressed the fundamental critique of JHC housing, "too small, too far, too expensive" were built into its very conception.[47]

In the mid-1950s, even in the midst of the ongoing housing crisis, the location and cost of JHC housing created real concerns about *who* would choose to live in expensive apartment housing a forty- or fifty-minute commute from the city. Nishiyama Uzō, in a 1956 roundtable discussion published in the JHC's in-house magazine, *Ienami*, noted that those who could afford JHC rents were not typically the kind of people who rented housing. The JHC might succeed in renting its apartments during the present dire housing shortage but, Nishiyama warned, it would experience vacancies later unless it carefully defined its "target class." The type of people who could afford JHC housing, he noted, had "different demands," and it was up to the JHC to enhance the attractiveness of JHC versus Public Housing.[48] Guaranteeing a constituency for its housing, in other words, also required the middle-classification of the *danchi* living space through the promotion of attributes long associated with the new middle-class:

45. Waswo, "Urban Housing Policy in 20th-Century Japan," 21.

46. Waswo, *Housing in Postwar Japan*, 76.

47. Harada, 368.

48. *Ienami*, February, 1956.

family-oriented life, "rational" and modern living habits, fixation on educational and occupational achievements, the housewife as professional manager of the home, specific consumption habits, and a life-spatial trajectory away from cities into the suburbs, all repackaged in the name of postwar reforms.

The official ten-year history of the JHC described this process as "Public Housing plus alpha" (*Kōei + arufa*) for, ironically, the original JHC apartment layout was but a slightly amended version of a design created for a "type one" Public Housing apartment in 1951. The "alpha" consisted of an extra *tsubo* (3.306 square meters) of space, a shiny, stainless-steel sink in the kitchen, a private bath and flush toilet, metal doors that locked, and the renaming of the eat-in kitchen (already a part of the 1951 design) with the modern English name, "dining kitchen" (abbreviated "DK").[49] Building on received notions of middle-classness, the *danchi*'s "special features" were meant to appeal to a specific middle-class sensibility or, more fundamentally, to a notion that middle-class families possessed, in the words of the ten-year history of the JHC, a "modern consciousness of how to live" and therefore required a living space with more modern amenities.[50] But over time, these features came to define *danchi* life itself, which in turn, helped redefine notions of what it meant to live a middle-class life. Individual features of the *danchi*—the "dining kitchen," the locking steel door, concrete walls, private bath, bedroom, and balcony—became symbolic of various attributes of postwar middle-class life.

The most celebrated among the *danchi* innovations was the "dining kitchen." Prior to the DK, cooking and dining spaces were separate. The DK was a kitchen in which people both cooked and ate, generally at tables and chairs rather than seated at low tables on the floor. The JHC created the DK as part of an effort to modernize public housing and make it attractive to its target "middle-class" constituency. Yet the DK eventually became standard in housing both public and private and the room around which postwar interior space was organized. The acronyms "nDK," meaning "*n*umber of rooms plus *d*ining *k*itchen," and eventually "nLDK" (*n*umber of rooms plus *l*iving room and *d*ining *k*itchen) became standard ways of conceptualizing and describing housing plans. The creation of the JHC in 1955 is therefore treated in architectural histories as a turning point of major consequence. "The DK," insisted architectural historian

---

49. The basic public housing units were twelve *tsubo* in size; the first JHC apartments were thirteen (making them approximately forty-three square meters / 463 square feet in size). Nihon jūtaku kōdan jū nenshi kankō iinkai, ed., *Nihon jūtaku kōdan jū nenshi* (Tokyo: Nihon jōtaku kôdan), 136.

50. Ibid., 138.

Fujimori Terunobu, "was the greatest gift of architectural planning to postwar housing."[51]

A focus on the kitchen was not new. From the late nineteenth century, rethinking the space of the home had been part of remaking the urban family to suit the changing requirements of industrial capitalism. Jordan Sand has described how, starting in the Meiji period, reformers attempted to reform the family by reorganizing living space, "join[ing]" the family "in a normative way to the space of the home."[52] The family in question belonged to the new, urban, putative middle class and was defined against the patriarchal, extended "family system" of the countryside. Although, as Nishikawa Yūko has argued, these two ways of organizing family life composed an interdependent and complimentary "dual system," they were often delineated as opposites in the discourse on the urban middle class.[53] Some of the attributes that characterized the "modern" nuclear "hōmu," or "katei" as reformers called it, in contradistinction with the "traditional" extended "family system" of the "ie," were family bonds based on mutual affection rather than inheritance and succession, the primacy of the "family circle," a redefinition of the relationship between the home and the outside world, and a new managerial role for the housewife within the home. The kitchen and dining room—still separate spaces—played into each of these projects. Overseeing, "rationalizing," and improving the hygienic conditions of the kitchen were projects that sought to establish the middle-class housewife as a domestic manager. A normative discourse encouraging families to place primacy on the family-centered parts of the house versus the "public" spaces of the entryway or receiving room also emphasized the kitchen and dining areas. The ultimate expression of modern family life was to be the shared meal taken at the same table rather than from individual dining trays—making the dining room and table the stage for the "performance" of modern family life.[54]

Discussions of the kitchen after the war assumed many of these earlier ideals but rearticulated them in the language of postwar reform. Architect Hamaguchi

51. Fujimori Terunobu, "Dainingu ki'chin tanjōki: gakumon mo mare in katsu," *Jūtaku tokushū* (April 1988): 102.

52. Jordan Sand, "At Home in the Meiji Period," in Stephen Vlastos, ed., *Mirror of Modernity: Invented Traditions of Modern Japan* (Berkeley: University of California Press, 1998), 207.

53. Nishikawa Yūko, "The Changing Form of Dwellings and the Establishment of the *Katei* (Home) in Modern Japan," *U.S.-Japan Women's Journal* (*Nichibei josei jānaru*) 8 (1995): 3-36.

54. Sand, 197-201.

Miho, like reformers before her, argued for the rationalization and modernization of the kitchen, but now in the name of democratizing the postwar Japanese home and ridding it of "feudalism"—the codeword and pejorative in the early postwar for almost anything referring to prewar and wartime Japan. Her famous 1950 book, *The Feudalism of the Japanese Home*, argued that the lowly condition of the urban kitchen indicated the perpetuation of various "feudal" hierarchies in postwar Japan.[55] Drawing the kitchen to the middle of the home and making it a bright and cheerful space where the family and neighbors could gather was the key to eliminating the "feudal" home of the past and democratizing the family. Hamaguchi's interest in reforming the kitchen was not merely academic. She occasionally served as an advisor to the JHC and is credited with designing the shiny stainless steel sink unit that became the hallmark of the DK.

The DK design was steeped in long-held assumptions such as these but it also had a direct prehistory concerned less with middle-class lifestyles than with working-class morality. In the words of Suzuki Shigebumi, the architect who created the eat-in kitchen for the 51C Public Housing design in 1951 which became the prototype for the DK, the primary function of the DK was to "bring order to the smallest of dwellings" (*kyokushō jūtaku no chitsujoka*).[56] What was *dis*orderly about small dwellings was not how and where people cooked and ate, but how and where they slept. Suzuki and his colleagues at the University of Tokyo were highly influenced by the wartime research of Nishiyama Uzō which revealed that contrary to notions of Japanese living space being entirely convertible urban families in small dwellings tended to dedicate one room to eating and, instead of also utilizing it to sleep, would all pile into another shared room to sleep.[57] Thus the separation of sleeping space by generation and between adolescent children of opposite sexes was the primary "problem" that needed solving with a new housing design. Indeed, Nishiyama called this the "first principle" of housing.

Suzuki came up with a design that finally forced people to uphold these separations, and his revelation led to the creation of the DK. His first discovery, building on Nishiyama's work, was that the actual layout of rooms had a large influence on how space was used. In surveys of two-room apartments consisting of one six-*tatami* room, one 4.5-*tatami* room and a kitchen conducted in Tokyo, Kawasaki, and Yokohama, Suzuki discovered that the placement of

---

55. See Chapter One for a detailed discussion of this work.
56. Suzuki Shigebumi, *Sumai no keikaku, sumai no bunka* (Tokyo: Shōkokusha, 1988), 27.
57. See Chapter One.

rooms relative to the kitchen influenced sleeping and eating arrangements. If the kitchen was situated next to the smaller, 4.5-mat room, people behaved in the way that Nishiyama's research indicated. They tended to use that room exclusively for eating and then all pile into the larger, six-mat room to sleep. If, however, the kitchen was placed next to the larger, six-mat room, the family had no choice but to convert its use from eating to sleeping at bedtime since the 4.5 mat room would not accommodate enough people. Thus, Suzuki concluded, the latter design was much more conducive to the separation of eating and sleeping. Best of all, however, would be if apartments had three rooms—a suggestion that "social conditions" would not yet allow for public housing.[58]

Suzuki's solution to this problem and the basis of the famous "51C Plan" for Public Housing was, in effect, to add a small amount of space to the kitchen, making it into a room where the family could eat. The problem of *separating* sleeping spaces could be solved by *combining* cooking and eating spaces. The original 51C Plan also placed walls between the six- and 4.5-mat rooms to promote privacy but with the effect, later surveys revealed, of defeating the larger purpose. The walls meant that depending on the season, one room became much colder or hotter than the other, so families tended to sleep in the more comfortable room, switching by season.[59] The walls were later replaced with sliding doors. (see figure 3)

It was Suzuki's "eat-in kitchen" which he designed for the Public Housing 51C that was picked up by the JHC several years later, modernized, and renamed the "DK."[60] Yet this original goal of "bringing order to the smallest dwelling" by separating eating and sleeping has long been forgotten even as most homes continue to include a "dining kitchen." As Nishiyama said in a 1988 interview, "It was a measure for the impoverished classes during an impoverished time. It is not strange that the designers of today do not know the real meaning of the 'separation of eating and sleeping.'"[61] The humble origins of the space that came to epitomize the modern postwar home have long since been forgotten.

The DK-ization of everyday life

The idea of eating in the kitchen was a novel one and not without its problems. Most kitchens were dank, dark, and dirty—not the kind of places where one would like to linger over a meal. Its modern name notwithstanding, the first din-

58. Suzuki, 23.
59. Ibid., 25.
60. Ibid., 78.
61. Quoted in Fujimori, "Dainingu ki'chin tanjōki," 103.

ing kitchen was not much of an improvement. "Before the stainless steel sink was put in, the DK was a horrible place," recalled Hamaguchi Miho. "The goal was to bring the K [kitchen] up to the standard of the D or the LD [living/ dining room] but what happened was that the D and LD became like the filthy K."[62] One problem was that people tended to eat on the floor of the DK, using low tables or heated *kotatsu* tables, also low to the floor. Another was that the equipment in the kitchen, particularly the sink made of concrete, was cold and uninviting. The JHC made the early decision to equip every apartment with a kitchen table that required the family to eat sitting on chairs. The inclusion of the table—bolted to the floor—was also meant to insure that people actually dined in the dining kitchen.[63] (see figure 4) In addition to providing a table, the JHC commissioned Hamaguchi to redesign and "beautify" the sink.[64] According to Honjō Masahiko, JHC director of design at the time, it was believed that the sink would "make" the DK.

The kitchen sink has its own history, one that tells much about shifting visions of home, family life, and the pursuit of "modern living." Its development followed two trajectories: from a workspace used while sitting on the floor to one used while standing, and from a space that was hidden to one that was visible.[65] The transformation from sitting to standing was a project of kitchen reformers of the interwar period seeking to rationalize the kitchen workspace and improve its standards of hygiene by raising surfaces and equipment from the floor. In the Taishō period, department store displays of modern life featured the "*bunka nagashi*" or "culture sink" to go along with the modern "culture house" of the day.[66] The JHC kitchen already assumed that the users would be standing, but the most important objective of the JHC was to create a "kitchen that could be seen."[67] It was Hamaguchi's new sink that finally achieved

62. Quoted in Fujimori Terunobu, *Shōwa jūtaku monogatari* (Tokyo: Shin kenchikusha, 1990), 307.

63. *Nihon jūtaku kōdan jū-nenshi*, 137. The JHC eventually phased out this practice as people became used to tables and chairs and were better able to afford them for their homes. It phased them out first in major cities such as Tokyo and Osaka and later in smaller regional cities such as Fukuoka where, it was believed, a "time gap" perpetuated outmoded sleeping and dining habits for longer.

64. Ibid., 303.

65. Amano Masako and Sakurai Atsushi, *Mono to onna no sengo shi* (Tokyo: Yūshindō, 1992), 151.

66. Ibid., 156.

67. Suzuki, 26.

this objective. It was made of stainless steel that brightened the kitchen with its gleaming surfaces. Its rational "point system" design provided a complete workstation with spaces for installing gas burners and cutting and preparing food. In the opinions of many, including the *danchi* housewives surveyed at the time, it was the stainless steel sink that gave the DK its allure. "To the housewife in charge of the kitchen," noted the JHC's inhouse magazine, "the [stainless steel sink] is an object of longing . . . a sink that isn't stainless isn't even a sink."[68] Fujimori recalls, "It was the age when to polish the sink until it sparkled was the pride of the *danchi* housewife."[69]

Not only was the DK with its shiny sink now a kitchen that "could be seen," it was one that the JHC was eager to show. Many of its promotional photos were taken in the kitchen and showed young couples sharing a meal or neighbor women gathered over tea in the clean, brightly lit DK. (see figure 5) Indeed, the kitchen was one of the most highly visible spaces in Japan of the late 1950s and 1960s. It was a favorite topic in women's magazines, and a popular setting for television documentaries and home dramas.[70] The kitchen was also a common target for appliance manufacturers seeking to sell their wares. Whether the goal was to fill JHC housing or to sell refrigerators and toasters, all suggested that the kitchen was where postwar Japan was being remade: the family "democratized," the housewife "liberated" from the drudgery of housework, and everyday life filled with the rice cookers, refrigerators, blenders, toasters, and washing machines as the emblems of Japan's daily-improving everyday life. "Brightening the kitchen," concluded Hamaguchi, "gave birth to a modern home suitable to the new age."[71]

To Hamaguchi Miho's husband, modernist architect Hamaguchi Ryūichi, the "new age" signified a new phase in the history of architecture in Japan. The stainless steel sink finally fulfilled one of the primary objectives of modernist architecture: to use industrial methods to build for the industrial age. Until the stainless steel sink, Hamaguchi claimed, Japanese modernism was "handmade." Previous to Hamaguchi Miho's design for the JHC, stainless steel had been used for kitchen sinks in some private homes but at great expense. The earliest prototypes of the JHC sink, produced by a company called Sun Wave, were

68. "Sutenresu nagashi no ryōsan kōjō," *Ienami* (JHC's inhouse magazine) (March 1963): 42.

69. Fujimori, *Shōwa jūtaku monogatari*, 309.

70. JHC apartments often appeared in television specials dedicated to "apartment living" or Japan's changing lifestyle. These are chronicled in the JHC's *Ienami*.

71. Quoted in Fujimori, *Shōwa jūtaku monogatari*, 307.

hand-fitted, took two to three hours to attach, and cost a prohibitive 30,000 yen apiece. Kanō Hisaakira, the first president of the JHC, placed an order for 10,000 units under the condition they be produced at the cost 10,000 yen each. Sun Wave was able to meet both output and cost demands by stamping out the units in single sheets, one every forty seconds.[72] The economy of scale achieved in the process of mass-producing sinks for the JHC's DK made the sink affordable for use in other housing, and it eventually became a standard fixture in postwar housing. "With the sink," commented Hamaguchi Ryūichi, "I thought, 'We've done it. Japan, too.'"[73]

The diffusion of JHC technology to the private sector was not limited to the sink. Construction techniques developed by the JHC—such as the method of pre-casting concrete walls in a factory then transporting them to construction sites for assembly (*PC-kōhō*)—were widely adopted by private builders.[74] Other items developed for the *danchi* such as cylinder locks, Western-style flush toilets,[75] window frames, exhaust fans, and shelving became standard-issue in much postwar housing. Developers and construction agencies trusted the so-called "standardized items for collective housing" developed for the JHC (labeled "*k.j. buhin*"—*kôkyô jûtaku hyôjun kikaku buhin*) and utilized them in their projects. Toilet manufacturer Toto credits the establishment of the JHC with the diffusion and subsequent popularity of the Western-style flush

72. "Sutenresu nagashi no ryōsan kōjō," 42-43.
73. Quoted in Fujimori, *Shōwa jūtaku monogatari*, 310.
74. The development of the "PC-construction technique" in the mid-1960s was in response to a shortage of skilled construction workers resulting from the expansive construction in and around Tokyo in preparation for the 1964 Tokyo Olympics. Manufacturing walls in a factory cut down on the need for skilled labor. *Nihon ni okeru shūgō jūtaku no fukyū katei*, 179-81. According to Ann Waswo, the adoption of JHC construction technology was instrumental in driving small construction companies out of business in the 1960s and 1970s and in the consolidation of a group of large construction companies that subsequently dominated the industry. See Waswo, *Housing in Postwar Japan*, 98.
75. *Danchi* built in the Kansai area utilized Western-style toilets from the JHC's inception in 1955. It was not until 1960 that they were used throughout JHC housing. Housing & Urban Development Corporation, *'Ing Report: Searching for a new conversation with the times: Changes and related technological development in housing facilities built by the Housing & Urban Development Corporation* (Tokyo: Building Technology Laboratory, Housing & Urban Development Corporation, April 1997), 13.

toilet in private homes,[76] and by 1975, twenty years after the establishment of the JHC, nearly seventy-five percent of Japanese kitchens had stainless steel sinks. By 1982, the percentage was close to eighty-six percent.[77] It is thus not surprising that the *danchi* were eventually blamed for what one author labeled the "DK-ization" (*DK-ka*) and "*k.j. buhin*-ization" (*kj buhin-ka*) of Japanese living space.[78]

These phrases imply more than the standardization of space and diffusion of household equipment. The "2DK" in many ways became synonymous with postwar everyday life. The author of a retrospective in 2001 described the 2DK as "the lifestyle that symbolized postwar Japan."[79] Sociologist Minami Hiroshi described the *danchi* as the "model" of the postwar "Japanese-style modern lifestyle" (*Nihon-gata kindai seikatsu yōshiki*).[80] These statements suggest that the significance of *danchi* life amounted to more than the sum of its modern parts. The *danchi* represented rising levels of mass prosperity, and a new way of organizing family and community life. "Envied" and beyond most people's reach in the late 1950s, for better and worse, the "2DK lifestyle" eventually became something many people called their own.

Outward Bound: The Suburbanization of Postwar Japan

The JHC created a prototype of middle-class life that was also suburban. As land in urban areas became prohibitively expensive, it began to seek inexpensive land outside of city centers to build its large projects, something it was able to do since, unlike locally administered Public Housing projects, its jurisdiction transcended municipal boundaries. This allowed it to build housing for the urban, white-collar workforce in prefectures surrounding large cities, where the huge expanses of land necessary to construct massive housing projects were still available and relatively inexpensive. One of the primary mandates of the JHC, along with providing housing, was to develop land or, more literally, "produce residential land" (*takuchi no seizō*) and "build towns" (*machizukuri*). In fact, the JHC did not locate its projects *in* the suburbs, it manufactured suburban communities from whole cloth. Early JHC projects were often located in what was still the middle of the coun-

76. Kurita Yasuo and Toriumi Shigeru, *Sōgō jūsetsu kiki e tenkai suru: Tōtō* (Tokyo: Asahi sonorama, 1981), 82.

77. Yamada Kōichi et al., ed., *Monogatari / mono no kenchiku-shi: daidokoro no hanashi* (Tokyo: Kashima shuppankai, 1995), 93.

78. Honma Yoshihito, *Mai hōmu gēmu* (Tokyo: Ōtsuki shoten , 1980), 102.

79. Aoki Toshiya, *Saigen Shōwa 30 nendai: danchi 2DK no kurashi* (Tokyo: Kawade shobō shinsha, 2001), 4.

80. Minami Hiroshi, *Zoku: Shōwa bunka, 1945-1989* (Tokyo: Keisōshobō, 1990), 27.

tryside and therefore required the creation of extensive physical and social infrastructures to support them: transportation networks, electricity, water, stores, schools, parks, post offices, and branches of the local police, fire station and city hall. (see figure 6) Different in appearance and substance from the suburbs of postwar America, the *danchi* suburbs were not neat rows of privately owned residential homes trimmed with orderly lawns and quiet streets. They were blocks of urban rental apartment buildings brought to the countryside. Aerial shots of the early *danchi* projects—a favorite angle of promotional photographs—show them as concrete islands of urbanity surrounded by oceans of rice paddies. (see figure 7) It was as if observers could not grasp the magnificence of the *danchi* from the ground. In February of 1960, Senri New Town in Osaka hired a helicopter to take residents up to see what their new home looked like from the air. One housewife reportedly observed that Senri looked like a "town from a fairytale."[81]

Many towns associated the beginning of their transformation into "bedroom towns" with the arrival of the first JHC apartment complex. In *Suburban City: The Postwar Social History of a Regional City,* author Suzuki Hitoshi detailed the changes he had witnessed since the war in his hometown of Kashiwa in Chiba Prefecture outside Tokyo. In a process he called "residential-ization" (*jūtaku-ka*), Suzuki described the incremental transformation of farms and former military installations into housing tracts, a process that began on a small, piece-meal scale just several years after the war. What Suzuki labeled Kashiwa's "*danchi*-ization" (*danchi-ka*) occurred in three phases with the arrival of three successively larger projects. Arakōyama Danchi, consisting of 114 units, began taking residents in November 1956, Hikarigaoka Danchi, with 974 units, opened in March 1957, and Toyoshiki Danchi, consisting of 4,666 units, opened in April 1964. In Suzuki's estimation, it was the arrival of these *danchi*, particularly Hikarigaoka and Toyoshiki, that "triggered" the transformation of Kashiwa into a "bed town" of Tokyo commuters.[82] The three projects added greatly to Kashiwa's population. Assuming that each unit accommodated the average *danchi* family of 3.4 people, the construction of these three projects increased Kashiwa's population by nearly twenty thousand.[83] Suzuki's *Suburban City* is a product of the early 1970s when many people were beginning to take stock of the problems

81. *Ienami*, March 1960.
82. Suzuki Hitoshi, *Kinkō toshi: aru chihōtoshi no sengo shakai-shi* (Tokyo: Nihon keizai shimbun-sha, 1973), 19.
83. Suzuki did not note Kashiwa's population in the 1950s but wrote that in 1972 it was 180,819 people, making the *danchi* population a significant proportion of the population. Ibid.

that had accompanied high-speed economic growth. Accordingly, it focused on the losses and dislocations that had accompanied the town's transformation: growing crime, a shrinking sense of community spirit and identity, and the loss of local businesses to the incursion of chain markets and department stores. But Suzuki's project also sought to chronicle the tremendous changes he had witnessed in his own life, changes he observed through the transformation of Kashiwa.[84]

The JHC's move to develop regions outside city centers occurred on the cusp of a vast demographic shift of people into the developing suburbs. After World War II, Japan became a predominantly urban country. In 1950, thirty-eight percent of the people in Japan lived in cities. By 1970, the urban population had increased to seventy-two percent.[85] In major urban areas such as Tokyo, Osaka and Nagoya, the growth was explosive. In the thirty-five years between 1945 and 1980, over 19.3 million people moved into the Tokyo metropolitan region alone. Sixty percent of this growth occurred between 1955 and 1975, the years of "high-speed growth."[86] These statistics of high-speed urbanization conceal an inner dynamic of suburbanization within urban regions. Although in the decade or so immediately following the end of World War II population flowed predominantly to city centers, by the mid- and late-1950s, it began to turn outward toward the suburbs. New population in Tokyo proper peaked in 1957 with 246,000 new residents but began a steady decline in subsequent years. And starting in the mid-1950s, peak population growth in the Tokyo region shifted ten kilometers farther from the center city every five years. This meant that by the mid-1970s, highest population growth occurred fifty to sixty kilometers from the city.[87] By 1990, forty-one million people—one third of Japan's entire population—lived in the suburbs of Japan's three largest cities.[88] The JHC both rode this demographic wave and hastened its advance by pulling housing ever further from city centers, with the infrastructure and train lines to support it right behind.[89]

---

84. Ibid., 2.
85. Kohei Okamoto, "Suburbanization of Tokyo and the Daily Lives of Suburban People," in P.P. Karan and Kristin Stapleton, ed., *The Japanese City* (Lexington: The University Press of Kentucky, 1997), 79.
86. Sanuki Toshio, *Seichō suru toshi, suitai suru toshi* (Tokyo: Jiji tsūshinsha, 1983), 79. The "Tokyo Metropolitan Region" consists of the twenty-three wards of Tokyo proper and the city's three adjacent prefectures: Chiba, Kanagawa, and Saitama.
87. Oda Mitsuo, *Kōgai no tanjō to shi* (Tokyo: Seikyūsha, 1997), 39.
88. Okamoto, 79.
89. The JHC shared the costs of infrastructural development—roads, schools,

One of the products of high-speed economic growth, then, was the "suburbanization of Japan." I borrow this wording from Kenneth Jackson, who has argued that the years after World War II witnessed the all-out "suburbanization of the United States."[90] In the United States, too, between 1950 and 1970, suburbs were the fastest growing regions of the nation. While center cities suffered a significant out-migration in these twenty years, the suburban population doubled from thirty-six to seventy-four million.[91] Yet the substance of this suburban growth differed significantly from Japan's. American suburbs grew at the expense of inner cities, draining them of residents, jobs, and revenue. They tended to be less dependent on their urban cores, often providing jobs as well as housing for their inhabitants. In Japan, postwar suburbs remained dependent on the city, especially for employment. They tended to grow not at the expense of but in tandem with major cities. Between 1955 and 1970, the twenty-three-ward area of Tokyo proper added 2.6 million workers to its labor force yet only one out of four of these people actually lived within the city limits. The other three lived in the suburbs and commuted to their jobs in the city. Gary Allinson, in *Suburban Tokyo*, noted: "rather than decay of the metropolitan center, *growth* in the center and periphery—of job opportunities, commercial districts, office buildings and government agencies—sped Tokyo's suburbanization."[92]

People and housing were pushed from urban centers because of rising land prices, but this did not mean that land ceased to be a problem for suburban

municipal offices—with local and prefectural governments. Train lines sometimes coordinated their expansion with *danchi* development, or the JHC built in the general vicinity of existing lines and coordinated bus service from the *danchi* to the train station. For an interesting account of how one private railway company coordinated its expansion with JHC development in Chiba Prefecture, see Shinkeisei dentetsu kabushiki kaisha shashi hensan jimukyoku, *Shinkeisei dentetsu gojū nenshi* (Tokyo: Shinkeisei dentetsu kabushiki kaisha, 1997).

90. Kenneth T. Jackson, *Crabgrass Frontier: The Suburbanization of the United States* (New York: Oxford University Press, 1985).

91. Ibid., 283.

92. Gary D. Allinson, *Suburban Tokyo: A Comparative Study in Politics and Social Change* (Berkeley: University of California Press, 1979), 150. This pattern of suburbanization has created a tremendous "donut effect" as populations empty out of cities at night. In 1960, the daytime population of central Tokyo was 2.38 times the nighttime population; in 1980, it was 6.38 times higher. This gap was greatest in the business and government wards of Chiyoda (1960: day to night population 5.51 times; 1980: 17.10 times) and Chūō (1960: 3.45 times; 1980: 7.94 times). Sanuki, 83.

developers. This was equally true for the JHC, which sought to acquire large tracts of land for its projects.[93] Japan's already fragmented landholding system was aggravated by postwar land reforms that greatly increased the number of small-scale landholders. Land reform reduced tenancy rates from over forty percent to less than ten, transforming former tenants to owner-cultivators and changing the property rights of over six million people.[94] The JHC was required to obtain forty percent of the land before beginning a project and was given the power of "pre-emption" which gave it "first option of purchase" when new land came on the market.[95] Even so, acquiring enough land for a *danchi* project sometimes required convincing hundreds of landholders to sell their land.[96] In the early years of the JHC's existence, this was quite difficult at times. The construction of Tokiwadaira *danchi* in Matsudo City in Chiba Prefecture starting in 1956 met with fierce opposition from sixty-nine of the over two hundred farmers who owned the land the JHC sought to build upon. It is well remembered in the annals of JHC history for the "*daikon* offensive" waged by opposing landowners who dumped truckloads of the long white radishes in front of JHC headquarters in Tokyo in protest.[97]

But it was the logic of development and the promise of profit that eventually eased JHC efforts to acquire land. The JHC developed most of its projects using methods of "land readjustment" (*kukaku seiri*) that relocated original landowners to plots of land (or within *danchi* complexes) approximately two-thirds the size of their original landholdings. The logic was that the one-third they "donated" would be more than recovered as the value of their land rose due to proximity to the newly developed *danchi*.[98] This, in fact, became the case. The *danchi* fueled development, accelerated suburbanization, and promoted peripheral

---

93. However, many of the early JHC complexes such as Hibarigaoka and Akabanedai were build on the location of former munitions and military installations. Hara and Shigematsu, 104.

94. See R. P. Dore, *Land Reform in Japan* (London: Oxford University Press, 1959).

95. André Sorensen, *The Making of Urban Japan: Cities and planning from Edo to the twenty-first century* (New York: Routledge, 2004), 187.

96. Ishida Yorifusa, "Nihon ni okeru tochi kukaku seiri seido shi gaisetsu 1870–1980," *Sōgō toshi kenkyū* 28, (September 1986): 57-59.

97. Miura Shigekazu and Takabayashi Naoki, et al. ed., *Chiba-ken no hyakunen* (Tokyo: Yamakawa shuppansha, 1990), 316.

98. See Ishida Yorifusa for a history of land readjustment in Japan. Also Luciano Minerbi and Peter Nakamura, et al., ed., *Land Readjustment: The Japanese System*, (Boston: Oelgeschlager, Gunn & Hain, Publishers, Inc., 1986).

development of businesses, transportation networks, and new residences.[99] A JHC study of peripheral development that accompanied the construction of seventy-six new *danchi* communities around Japan conducted in the 1960s indicated that sixty-two percent had brought new shopping centers, fifty-seven percent new private housing, thirty-three percent other locally or privately administered apartment housing, five percent new train stations, twenty-eight percent increased train service, forty-three percent new bus lines, seventy-eight percent increased installment of public phones, and thirty-four percent new post offices. In the 1960s, the joke in the halls of the JHC was that a JHC vehicle had only to drive through an area for land prices to rise.[100]

David Harvey calls the city that emerged in the United States after World War II the "Keynesian city." The very way in which urban space was restructured, he suggests, helped to address the problem of under-consumption that plagued the 1930s and 1940s.[101] Large-scale, debt-financed investment in urban infrastructure was one characteristic of the "Keynesian city," but so, too, were mass-produced suburbs. His point of reference is the American auto culture that enabled the expansion of suburbs but thereafter became virtually indispensable to their survival. The consumption of houses but also cars, gasoline, oil and all of the other things necessary to the suburban car culture meant that suburbanization itself became a "spatial fix" to the problem of under-consumption.[102]

In Japan, it was not the automobile but the train that promoted suburbanization and development. In the first decade of the twentieth century, private train lines such as Hankyū in Osaka or later, Tokyū in Tokyo, began developing small plots of land along their rail lines in order to increase numbers of regular customers. Later they began placing department stores at strategic hubs along their lines to allow their customers to shop and enjoy other leisure and cultural activities as they moved between work in the city and home in the suburb.[103] After the

99. *Nihon jūtaku kōdan jūnen-shi*, 177.

100. Nihon jūtaku kōdan, "Apaato danchi kyojūsha no shakai shinrigakuteki kenkyū, sono III: danchi to chiiki shakai," *Kenchikubu chōsa kenkyūka I* (May 1963): 35.

101. David Harvey, *The Urban Experience* (Baltimore: The Johns Hopkins University Press, 1989), 34-43.

102. Ibid., 39.

103. For the history of the relationship between private train lines and the development of suburbs and department stores see Wakuda Yasuo, *Nihon no shitetsu* (Tokyo: Iwanami shoten, 1981). In English: Katō Hidetoshi, "Service-Industry Business Complexes: The Growth and Development of 'Terminal Culture,'" in *Japan Interpreter: Journal of Social and Political Ideas* 7 (1972): 376-382. Also Louise

war, this linkage of train–department store–residence, became a primary logic of spatial and commercial development of land, homeownership, and a consuming middle-class. Suburbanization was not simply a product of high-speed economic growth but one of its engines.[104]

In retrospect, the speed and scale of Japan's postwar suburbanization makes it seem almost inevitable. Yet when the JHC began building its projects in the mid-1950s, the decision to locate housing for the urban workforce a fifty- or sixty-minute commute from city centers was a daring move. Just as it created the DK and stainless steel sink to appeal to its "middle-class" constituency, the JHC attempted to lure people to its distant communities by appealing to long-held associations of the suburban hinterlands with middle-classness. A pamphlet advertising Tokiwadaira Danchi in Matsudo, Chiba described it as "A residential satellite city in the garden" (den'en ni umareta eisei jūtaku toshi), evoking the "garden city" ideal inspired by Ebenezer Howard that was long associated with exclusive suburban communities such as Denenchōfu, built on the western periphery of Tokyo in the 1920s.[105]

Young "Marketing the Modern: Department Stores, Consumer Culture, and the New Middle Class in Interwar Japan," in International Labor and Working-Class History 55 (Spring 1999): 52-70, and Jordan Sand, House and Home in Modern Japan: Architecture, Domestic Space, and Bourgeois Culture, 1880-1930 (Cambridge, MA: Harvard University Asia Center, 2003).

104. For a discussion of the linked development of danchi complexes and train lines, see Hara and Shigematsu, Danchi no jidai.

105. Hasegawa Tokunosuke has characterized the expansion of Tokyo's residential areas as a movement from yama (mountain) to en (garden) to daira (plain) and oka (heights). By this, he refers to the popularity of each of these terms in the naming of residential enclaves on the periphery of the city in successive eras. The "yama" period was during late Meiji, when urban aristocrats and government bureaucrats took over abandoned samurai estates on the western periphery of Tokyo with names such as Shimazu-yama, Ikeda-yama, Goten-yama, and Daikan-yama. The second "en" period of the interwar and Taisho period was characterized by the creation of residential areas for both the wealthy and the growing "new middle class" of salaried workers outside the Yamanote periphery of Tokyo. Many of these areas appealed to the "garden city" ideal of Ebenezer Howard, reflected in names such as Shōtō-en, Taizan-en, and Denenchōfu. It was at this time that suburbanization began in earnest as private developers—particularly private train lines—began developing and selling individual plots of land for housing. It was hastened by the housing shortage that accompanied the economic boom of WWI and further accelerated by the devastating earthquake of 1923 that forced

As in the United States and England, the spatio-social coupling of the suburb and the middle class was a historical product of industrialization that sent urban middle-class families out into the proximate countryside to escape what they perceived to be the social and physical perils of increasingly overcrowded and slum-ridden cities. Like the home, the suburb became a spatial articulation of middle-classness. It developed hand-in-hand with new visions of family life; indeed, one helped define the other. Suburbs spatially promoted and reinforced many of the separations that defined middle-class life: the complete division between home and work, a gendered division of labor that placed women in the home and men in the workplace, and the formation of the insular nuclear family.[106] Suburban *danchi* communities promoted nuclear family life and reinforced these separations to an unprecedented degree. The location of communities meant that the average *danchi* husband commuted between one and two hours to work in the city.[107] Women typically were professional housewives or did piecework at home. Kon Wajirō likened *danchi* communities during the day to fishing villages where all the men were out to sea. They were "distant islands" that were "countries of only women" (*onna bakari no kuni*). Any "man that was a man was in the center city, earning a living."[108]

JHC policies and apartment sizes created a population that was extremely self-selecting. In essence, it consisted of families small enough to fit into tiny JHC housing, affluent enough to meet the JHC's stiff income qualifications,

many people to seek housing outside the city. The third "*daira*" and "*oka*" phase occurred after WWII with the massive expansion of suburbs into surrounding prefectures and the construction of *danchi* with names such as Hibarigaoka, Hikarigaoka and Tokiwadaira. Each successive phase pushed city limits outward and westward (until the final "*daira*" phase, when suburbs also began to develop east of the city). Hasegawa Tokunosuke, *Nihon no takuchi keisei-shi* (Tokyo: Sumai no toshokan shuppankai, 1988), 5-9. For the history of Denenchōfu see Ken Tadashi Oshima, "Denenchōfu: Building the Garden City in Japan," in *Journal of the Society of Architectural Historians* (June 1996): 140-51.

106. For a compelling argument about how suburbanization and the process of creating a model and ideology of middle class life have developed in tandem in the United States, see Richard A. Walker, "A Theory of Suburbanization: Capitalism and the construction of urban space in the United States," in Michael Dear and Allen J. Scott, ed., *Urbanization and Urban Planning in Capitalist Society* (New York: Methuen, 1981), 383-429.

107. *Nihon jūtaku kōdan nijū nenshi*, 68.

108. Kon Wajirō "Danchi no okusan-tachi: chiguhaku no fūkei," *Seikatsu-gaku: Kon Wajirō shū*, volume 5 (Tokyo: Domesu Shuppan, 1971), 275-77.

but still lacking the means to buy their own homes. JHC surveys conducted periodically over the 1960s indicated that the average *danchi* family had 3.4 family members—a husband, wife and one or two small children—the "typical nuclear family." The average age of the *danchi* husband was 36.2 years and seventy percent of *danchi* husbands were "typical mid-level salarymen."[109] JHC policies and priorities, then, created communities of young nuclear families, commuting husbands and stay-home wives. They also created communities that were socially homogeneous, spatially standardized, and physically separated from local populations. Unevenness with surrounding communities that often still lacked basic services such as electricity, indoor plumbing, and telephone service set apart the modern, high-rise concrete housing projects and gave them an air of exclusivity. They were semi-self-contained islands, surrounded by fences, and widely criticized for their insularity.[110] In their uniformity and social homogeneity, *danchi* communities had more in common with Levittown than Denenchōfu and were treated as such by many social scientists who considered the *danchi* Japan's version of the American suburbs.

One major difference between *danchi* communities and older suburban communities such as Denenchōfu (or newer ones such as Levittown, for that matter), was that most JHC housing consisted not of privately owned housing on individual plots of land but of blocks of rental apartments. In keeping with the government's priority of promoting homeownership, the JHC built some housing on lots or in apartment buildings to sell each year, but the apartments of "*danchi*" and "2DK" fame were the ones for rent. Just as public housing of all sorts was meant to be a temporary measure as national policy, to individual families, too, *danchi* life was meant to be a temporary, intermediary step between rental housing in the city and homeownership. As housing for the "mid-level salaryman," the *danchi* occupied an intermediate position along a career path,

---

109. *Nihon jūtaku kōdan nijū nenshi*, 68. These demographics remained remarkably steady over time. In 1979, the average age of the head of household renting a JHC apartment was 34.2 years old. The average size of household was 2.54 people. However, whereas in the late 1950s and early 1960s *danchi* residents were typically of the upper-middle income range, by 1979, they were slightly below the average income level for wage laborers. See "Tokushū: shin kōdan (sono 1): nihon jūtaku kōdan jūtaku kyōkyū no ayumi," *Jūtaku* (September 1981): 67.

110. A *danchi* fun fact: As of 1981, *danchi* communities were surrounded with a total of 3,000 kilometers of fencing, enough to circle the main Japanese island of Honshū. Honjō Masahiko, "Nihon jūtaku kōdan no ashiato o furikaette," in *Jūtaku* (September 1981): 3.

just as it occupied an intermediate spatial position within the suburbs. A merging of idealized life and spatial trajectories suggested that steady progress up the corporate ladder happened in tandem with progress up the "housing ladder," which led one farther from the city and deeper into the suburbs. As Oda Mitsuo observed, "In order for the tremendous number of people who turned to the city during the period of high-speed growth to live, they [successively] had to change their living situations, following this path: from a rented room or dormitory, to a wooden rented apartment, to the *danchi*, to 'my home.' Each change inevitably required diffusion to the outer reaches of the city."[111] Intermediacy was thus one of the defining attributes of the *danchi*. Spatially, they bridged city and countryside. To individual families, they were meant to bridge rental life and homeownership. Christie Kiefer suggested that *danchi* life also represented "a kind of status limbo—a symbol of half-way success that serves to whet the appetite for the payoff of the middle-class dream."[112]

The JHC's concerns about attracting residents were misplaced. After an initial slow year, apartments quickly filled up and by the late 1950s, the intense competition for JHC housing was itself newsworthy. (see figure 8) Applicants who met the income qualifications participated in a housing lottery with a placement rate of, at its most competitive in 1966, one in 145.[113] By its tenth anniversary, the JHC boasted it had built 300,000 housing units for rent and for sale throughout Japan, developed 10,000 hectares of land, initiated over 300 billion yen of construction, and "become a prototype of Japanese housing."[114] In the media, the JHC was often referred to as the "world's largest landlord."[115] The popularity of distant JHC housing reflected the severity of the ongoing urban housing shortage, but it also resulted from associations of the *danchi* with a new, middle-class lifestyle. As Construction Ministry official Hayakawa Kazuo observed, "At the start, there were few applicants to JHC housing . . . But gradually the number of *danchi* increased and as the white-collar class settled in as the *danchi*'s inhabitants, the apartments attracted attention as a new living configuration for Japan, and the term "*danchi* tribe" even gained currency."[116]

---

111. Oda, 33.

112. Kiefer, 292.

113. This was for the Tokyo area. For competition rates by year and region see *Nihon jūtaku kōdan nijū nenshi*, 420.

114. *Nihon jūtaku kōdan jū-nenshi*, 123 and 196.

115. Oya Sōichi, "Jūtaku kōdan: sekai ichi no dai yanushi," *Shūkan asahi* (October 19, 1958): 55.

116. In Seikatsu kagaku chōsakai, ed., *Danchi no subete* (Tokyo: Seikatsu kagaku chōsakai, 1963), 36.

As we will see in the next chapter, the *danchi* soon became as notorious for the "*danchi* tribe" that lived there as for its dining kitchens.

JHC attempts to middle-classify the *danchi* had been a success. It entailed creating a living space that appealed to the "consciousness of how to live" that helped to define the middle class. With policies, income requirements and apartment sizes the JHC created a *statistical* middle class that became known as the "*danchi* tribe." Although the "*danchi* tribe" represented an extremely limited cross-section of Japanese society that was noted more for its atypicality than its similarities with the rest of the nation, it eventually became synonymous with Japan's expanding "new middle class." The middle-classification of the *danchi* would be followed by the *danchi*-fication of the middle class.

Chapter Three

THE *DANCHI* VANGUARD

Enshrining a glittering blender in the center of their nearly bare dining table, people found it easier to dream about an affluent and tranquil family home in the future. The blender was both a symbol of the future and the first concrete step toward realization of the dream. In short, hope, desire, anticipation, and prophecy coalesced as people stared at the shining machine before them.

Tada Michitarō, 1971[1]

The New "New Middle Class"

Danchi housing projects loomed large in the social imaginary of the 1950s and 1960s. They appeared on the urban landscape and in the national imagination at the very moment that ideas about middle-class life were being rearticulated after World War II. At first they were notable for their very exclusivity and difference, a distant dream, an object of longing. But as they emerged as one of the first and most visible examples of postwar prosperity, they helped to redefine the material, social, and familial aspirations that, in turn, would become synonymous with postwar "middle-class life."

One quandary that faced social scientists of postwar Japan was the overwhelming tendency of people to identify themselves as members of the "middle class." Starting in the mid-1960s and continuing through the economic downturn of the 1990s, when asked in public opinion polls, up to ninety percent of Japanese identified their position in society as "mid-level" (*chūkan*) or "mainstream" (*chūryū*). Social scientists of every decade thus sought to identify the fault lines dividing society that were smoothed over by people's self-identification with the middle. Some claimed society remained fundamentally

---

1. In Tada Michitarō, "The Glory and Misery of 'My Home,' " in J. Victor Koschmann, ed., *Authority and the Individual in Japan: Citizen Protest in Historical Perspective* (Tokyo: University of Tokyo Press, 1978), 212.

divided between capital and labor. Others found the primary division to be between those working for large corporations and small. Still others claimed that class difference had essentially disappeared as people's lifestyles had gradually come to resemble one another—making Japan a "middle mass society."[2] Yet as William Kelly and others pointed out, the discourse on the middle class in postwar Japan often functioned to "declass" class and neutralize it as a marker of difference.[3] If "middle class" once stood for exclusivity and efforts by a self-identified middle class to differentiate themselves by a certain lifestyle and set of values, after the 1960s, it became a marker not of difference but of consensus and sameness. The notion that the Japanese people were "all equally middle class"[4] was one of the enduring myths of the postwar period.

Many trends contributed to this changed self-perception after World War II, including the leveling effects of the war, the development of a highly competitive yet egalitarian postwar educational system that created a standardized pathway to success, and a relative equalization of incomes during the years of high-speed economic growth.[5] Yet as studies over the decades indicated, there was a much greater diversity of family situations and socio-economic realities than the concept of "middle mass" suggested. Even into the 1980s, in the midst of the "economic miracle," only about half of high school graduates continued on to college, and only thirty to forty percent of men enjoyed the lifetime employment with large corporations that was the defining attribute of the middle-class "salary man."[6] "All equally middle class" was never a statement of objective reality but, as Kelly pointed out, a set of "mutually confirming aspirations" about work,

---

2.   Murakami Yasusuke, "The Age of New Middle Mass Politics: The Case of Japan," in *The Journal of Japanese* Studies 8.1 (Winter 1982): 29-72. For a summary of the various positions and debates about class and social stratification, see Ishida Hiroshi, "Class structure and status hierarchies in contemporary Japan," in *European Sociological Review* 5.1 (May 1989): 65-80.

3.   William Kelly, "Finding a Place in Metropolitan Japan: Ideologies, Institutions and Everyday Life," in Gordon, ed., *Postwar Japan as History* (Berkeley: University of California Press, 1993), 192.

4.   Koji Taira, "Dialectics of Economic Growth, National Power and Distributive Struggles," in ibid., 169.

5.   Andrew Gordon, "The Short Happy Life of the Japanese Middle Class," in Oliver Zunz, Leonard Schoppa, and Nobuhiro Hiwatari, ed., *Social Contracts Under Stress: The Middle Classes of America, Europe, and Japan at the Turn of the Century* (New York: Russell Sage Foundation, 2002), 116-125.

6.   William Kelly, "Rationalization and Nostalgia: Cultural Dynamics of New Middle-Class Japan," in *American Ethnologist* 13.4 (November 1986): 605.

home, and school that helped shape people's life goals and define the meanings of "mainstream" in postwar Japan.[7]

Thus aspiration, more than income, has been the defining attribute of the modern middle class, particularly for urban wage earners and their families who would come to be called the "new middle class." Differentiated from the "old" middle class of small business owners and landholders, the "new" middle class did not own property or the means of production but instead acquired status through the white-collar nature of their work. In his study of the formation of Japan's "new middle class" at the turn of the twentieth century, David Ambaras argued that this diverse group, whose numbers included government bureaucrats, school teachers, journalists, and company employees, in fact constructed itself as a category as members defined themselves in contradistinction to the unsophisticated peasants and physical laborers "below" them, as well as to the conservative and old-fashioned propertied classes "above."[8] Individuals associated with the new middle class, although never a unified or organized group, often positioned themselves as Japan's modernizers and "the principle promoters of national progress."[9]

With the dismantling of the hereditary status system of the early modern era and the introduction of the concept that individuals could and should endeavor to achieve their own positions in society, middle-class ambitions for the nation were matched only by those for themselves and their families. The accumulation of "cultural capital" through educational achievements, the white-collar nature of work, aspirations for children, and the enactment of a certain lifestyle through privileged consumption became key components defining membership in the "new" middle class.[10] After World War II, the nuclear family of the ambitious "salary man" husband, the professional housewife, and the hard-studying children would remain the core of the putative "new" middle-

---

7. Ibid., 604.
8. David Ambaras, "Social Knowledge, Cultural Capital, and the New Middle Class in Japan, 1895-1912," in *The Journal of Japanese Studies*, Vol. 24, No. 1 (Winter 1998), 30-31.
9. Ibid., 2.
10. See Jordan Sand, *House and Home in Modern Japan: Architecture, Domestic Space, and Bourgeois Culture, 1880-1930*, (Cambridge: Harvard University Asia Center, 2005) and Mark Jones, *Children as Treasures: Childhood and the Middle Class in Early Twentieth Century Japan*, (Cambridge: Harvard University Asia Center, 2010) on how middle –class aspirations formed and were performed through ideas about home and raising children.

class family. However, middle-class aspirations would also evolve in many ways and be rearticulated in the language of democratization and progress. Ambitions pertaining to school would become more strongly oriented toward entrance into competitive universities and career goals toward employment with large corporations that offered the security of life-time employment. Homeownership would become the ultimate middle-class dream, with more governmental and corporate inducements to support this goal. In the midst of high-speed economic growth, as physical reminders of the war disappeared, more and more people would begin to envision their lives in terms of these goals.

Both physically and ideologically, the vision of *danchi* life would help to mediate the transition of middle-classness from an exclusive and divisive category to an inclusive and homogenizing one. The physical space of the nDK (number of rooms plus dining kitchen), and eventually the nLDK (number of rooms plus living room and dining kitchen), became a prototype of postwar living space, suburban living became a reality for a large portion of the urban workforce, and the commodity-filled lifestyle exemplified by *danchi* inhabitants a reality for the majority of Japanese people. The *danchi* family also became the prototype of the idealized postwar family. Although by no means the single reality or even the statistical norm, this model family, labeled by one critic the "1955 system family" (*55-nen taisei kazoku*) of "corporate warrior and professional housewife," took on hegemonic status in postwar Japan.[11] In the words of Minami Hiroshi, the predominant perception of middle-class membership from the late-1960s on was at least partially due to the impression that people had "achieved for themselves in large part or small, the lifestyle of the *danchi* inhabitants."[12] As a vision of a life people longed for, *danchi* life would help to redefine the "middle-class dream."

The Show Window of Modern Life

The first *danchi* communities were considered vast social experiments, requiring the relocation of thousands of residents of similar age and socio-economic backgrounds to distant islands of urbanity on city peripheries. The homogeneity of residents and the thoroughly engineered qualities of their standardized apartments in identical concrete buildings fascinated the media and social scientists that used them as a kind of control group for studying the consequences of rapid social change and "modernization" on individuals and communities. More than a "housing phenomenon," one observer noted, the

---

11. Kanai Yoshiko, "Posuto 'kindai kazoku' no haujingu e," *Kenchiku zasshi: tokushū— yuragi no naka no kazoku to nLDK* 1371.110 (April 1995): 34.

12. Minami Hiroshi, *Zoku: Shōwa bunka, 1945-1989* (Tokyo: Keisō shobō, 1990), 28.

danchi were a "social phenomenon."[13]

In July of 1958, an article in the weekly magazine, *Shūkan Asahi*, gave birth to the *danchi* as a media spectacle by proclaiming the nation's approximately one million *danchi* residents the "backbone of the new city" and dubbing them the "*danchi zoku*" or "*danchi* tribe."[14] The nickname stuck and the *danchi zoku* became a media fixation and a household word.[15] Articles such as "Joys and Sorrows of the *Danchi* Housewife" (*Shufu no tomo*, 9/60), "*Danchi* Life: A Desert for Human Relationships" (*Fujin kōron* 2/61), "Will the *Danchi* Change Family Life?" (*FK* 9/63), "The Refined Life of the *Danchi* Madam" (*Yomiuri Shimbun*, 10/1/65), and "The Desires and Discontents of the *Danchi* Housewife" (*FK* 5/64) sensationalized *danchi* life by expressing a strange mixture of envy for its modern lifestyle and skepticism about family and community life in the "high rise villages."

Shioda Maruo, long-time *danchi* resident and prolific commentator on life there, noted that filling in questionnaires and surveys was "a monthly activity for residents of the *danchi*." He offered as proof of the "survey offensive" (*anketto kōsai*) the contents of the third drawer of his bureau containing "four thermometers, two wash cloths . . . an ashtray, three butane lighters, three soap sets, etc."—all gifts for participating in surveys.[16] Shioda recalled a time he and his wife sat together answering separate surveys, she on the "tofu preferences of *danchi* housewives" and he on Okinawan reversion. "Why do *danchi-zoku* want cars when they don't have garages? What kind of sex lives do the *danchi zoku* lead? How many mystery novels do the *danchi zoku* read per month? What is the average monthly income of the *danchi zoku*? . . . Every kind of question is hurled at the *danchi-zoku*," Shioda observed. "It is like newspaper reporters interviewing Martians visiting earth for the first time."[17]

Surveys and questionnaires had various objectives. Many were sponsored by marketing researchers investigating how to sell to this new group of urban consumers. Others were authored by home economics departments of women's colleges or sociologists interested in extrapolating from *danchi* data broader

---

13. Shioda Maruo, *Sumai no sengo-shi* (Saimaru shuppankai, 1975), 82.

14. The word "backbone" (*haikotsu*) was the same word used to describe the "new middle class" of the Meiji era. The word has long associations with the middle class. Ambaras, p. 5.

15. "Atarashiki shomin 'danchi-zoku' apāto sumai no kurashi no techō," *Shūkan Asahi* (July 20, 1958), 4.

16. Shioda Maruo, *Sumeba danchi* (Tokyo: Kōbundō, 1963), 53.

17. Ibid., 57.

conclusions about Japanese society. The Survey Research Section of the JHC itself conducted hundreds of surveys and studies in the interest of self-promotion and improvement. A three-part study sponsored by the JHC and conducted by scholars from Tokyo University on the social psychology of *danchi* apartment dwellers noted in its introduction, ". . . the various phenomena related to the so-called *danchi zoku* are intensifications of the most characteristic aspects of contemporary mass society. A social psychological study of the *danchi zoku* amounts to a study of the central aspects of contemporary society."[18] American scholars were drawn to the *danchi* for similar reasons. In the words of Christie Kiefer in his study of "Personality and Social Change in a Japanese *Danchi*," the *danchi* was a kind of "laboratory" in which "certain elements of the social structure had been artificially altered while most of the culture of its residents remained basically 'Japanese white collar.'"[19] In a later article, he continued to argue that the *danchi* could be seen as a "barometer of psychological change" in postwar Japan.[20] As social sciences flourished after World War II and methodologies of American social science were adopted by Japanese scholars, the *danchi*—isolated and self-contained—seemed to offer an ideal controlled setting and social petri dish for monitoring the impact of social and cultural change in Japan.

What made the *danchi zoku* so modern, according to the Parsonian assumptions of many of the sociologists analyzing them, was that they were perceived to be entirely cut off from the ascriptive privileges and responsibilities of the extended family and village community. They were believed to occupy an advanced position on a presumed trajectory from the interconnected and obligation-filled relationships of the traditional village toward the impersonal, "rational" interactions of the modern city. As white-collar families and members of the "new middle class," their positions in the world had resulted from their own achievements. Men's relationships with their workplaces were contractual. Marriages, it was believed, resulted from the partners' choice rather than family expectations. Relationships with neighbors were friendly but businesslike. The *danchi* served as the ideological "other" to the village of the spatial and temporal past.

---

18. Nihon jūtaku kōdan, "Apaato danchi kyojūsha no shakai shinrigakuteki kenkyū: ningen kankei to shakai ishiki o chūshin toshite," *Kenchiku chōsa kenkyūka* (September 1960): 1.

19. Christie Kiefer, "Personality and Social Change in a Japanese Danchi," (Ph.D. diss., University of California, Berkeley, 1968), 2.

20. Kiefer, "The Danchi Zoku and Metropolitan Mind," in Lewis Austin, ed., *Japan: The Paradox of Progress* (New Haven: Yale University Press, 1976), 280.

The government, too, took keen interest in *danchi* life. The 1960 White Paper on National Life announced that Japan was experiencing a qualitative and quantitative transformation of consumption habits that was transforming everyday life. The average consumption per capita was thirty to forty percent above what it had been before the war, it reported, and more fundamentally, the content and "quality" of that consumption had been transformed by increased availability of electrical goods, and Western foodstuffs and clothing. "This is often referred to as a revolution in consumption (*shōhi kakumei*)," the White Paper noted, "but the tremendous change in our daily lives is such that this can be considered a fundamental revolution in everyday life (*seikatsu kakumei*)." [21] But there was still unevenness in the progress of the revolution, the White Paper reported. Urban areas had progressed further than rural, and leading the urban transformation were the residents of the *danchi*, the vanguard of the "lifestyle revolution."

Charts and graphs compared *danchi* incomes, family sizes, hours spent in housework and leisure, ownership of electrical goods and even bread consumption (as a barometer of the extent of the "Westernization" of diets) to that of other Tokyo-ites.[22] Statistically, the "*danchi* tribe" was exceptional. *Danchi* families were smaller than the average Japanese family. Incomes, educational levels, and percentages of men working for large corporations were higher than average. *Danchi zoku* ownership of televisions, washing machines, and other appliances—the ultimate barometer of modernization in the late 1950s—was significantly higher than the national norm. *Danchi* women spent less time cleaning and more time pursuing "cultural activities" than other Japanese women (Charts 1–7, Appendix). *Danchi* children spent more time studying, less time playing, and had higher average test scores. *Danchi* men spent more time commuting and less time at home. In almost every way, the *danchi* family was a statistical anomaly.

Yet in all of the studies of *danchi* life in the 1950s and early 1960s, the anomalous and extraordinary "*danchi zoku*" functioned discursively to suggest national trends. The *danchi zoku* represented the urban trend, and the urban trend suggested a seemingly inevitable course that the rest of the nation would eventually follow. The small family structure, work, leisure, and consumption habits of the *danchi zoku*, the charts, statistics, and studies suggested, were the

21. Keizai kikaku chō, *Kokumin seikatsu hakusho*, Shōwa sanjūgo nen (Tokyo: Okurashō insatsu kyoku, 1961), ii.

22. Ibid., 137-45.

future of the Japanese nation. The White Paper concluded: "Although the lives of the *danchi zoku* differ greatly from those of average people, as the numbers of *danchi* grow and their influence widens, the new consciousness of how to live and consequently, the revolution in everyday life, will spread to and permeate (*shintō shite iku*) the general [public]."[23]

Treatments of the *danchi* and *danchi zoku* overlapped with a sizeable discourse on the "salary man" and the "new middle class" in the late 1950s and early 1960s. Often drawing upon prominent American publications on the white-collar, "new" middle class of the 1950s and 1960s, the "salary man" appeared as Japan's very own "organization man." As in the United States, the concern was that Japan was undergoing a massive middle-classification, with millions moving to cities, the agricultural sector shrinking, and the number of wage earners growing. In a forty-one part series titled "We Salary Men" which appeared in the *Yomiuri Shimbun* in the early months of 1961, authors noted that the "new" middle class was growing as small landowners "fell from above" and began working for wages and as the proletariat "rose from above" as their jobs became more managerial in nature. "Even the emperor, who never used to be seen without his military uniform, now has the salary man style" (*sarariiman sutairu*), it claimed.[24] The series, based on surveys and information gathered from forty-one *danchi* projects in Tokyo and Osaka, suggested that the vanguard of this massive middle-classification was the *danchi* salary man. Each installment included a photo titled "This is you" (*Kore wa anata desu*), featuring a *danchi* salary man on the train, in the city, at his desk, or his wife back at home shopping for groceries or participating in club activities, thus closing the gap between the reader and *danchi* life with one bold assertion.[25]

The fact that everyone was *not*, in fact, a *danchi* salary man was not lost on critical observers. The "middle class" targeted by the JHC was in the upper levels of the income range designated "middle" and in that way not typical at all.[26]

---

23. Ibid., 145.
24. Yomiuri shimbun shakai-bu, ed., *Warera sarariiman* (Toyko-yomiuri shimbun-sha, 1961), 12.
25. Ibid. The series was later published as a book.
26. Incomes for white-collar salaried employees in the late 1950s and early 1960s ranged from approximately 8,000 to 50,000 yen per month. This span was sometimes broken into a lower range of 8,000 to 20,000 / month and an upper range of 20,000 to 50,000 / month. Blue-collar incomes often overlapped with the lower range of white-collar incomes making many question the meaning of the divisions between the two. The income qualification of 30,000 to 35,000 yen

Thus "envy" and "longing" were the most common reactions to *danchi* life in the 1950s. Scholar Ishikawa Hiroyuki's recollection of his first 1958 visit to two JHC *danchi* complexes was typical: "I remember clearly even now that what I felt . . . was envy. Wide lawns, verandahs, dining kitchens filled with the 'three sacred treasures' . . . [I thought,] once I get married, I am going to do what I have to do to have a life like this."[27] Years later, Ishikawa managed to fulfill his dream and secure a JHC apartment. More generally, however, high income qualifications left the majority of Japanese people ineligible even to apply for JHC housing and for those who could, the lottery selection system with a placement rate of, at times, over one in a hundred, meant that *danchi* life was as distant as life in America to most Japanese people in the 1950s.

Critic Tada Michitarō noted this disparity, writing in 1961, "the qualification for entering [the *danchi*] is an income of thirty to thirty-five thousand yen per month *or over* . . . Why is the government putting so much effort into promoting '*or over*?'" The answer, he suggested, was that the *danchi* functioned as "Japan's display window." He concluded: "The government is spreading the image of the huge *danchi* to give all of the Japanese people a focus for their dreams . . . The *danchi zoku* is the 'vanguard' for the dream of the middle-classification of the entire country."[28]

"Dreams of middle-classification" sought to create consensus around issues of consumption and standard of living at a time of extreme social and political polarization in Japan. In the words of Andrew Gordon, the late 1950s were the time of the "knock-down-drag-out strike" with more work days lost to blue-collar labor stoppages between 1957 and 1961 than since the days just following the end of World War II.[29] Much more was at stake than basic issues of wages and working hours. The battle against labor at the end of the 1950s represented companies' efforts to retake power from combative unions that had formed after the war. At stake, argues Gordon, was the very "shape and pace of economic

/ month for JHC renters placed them well into the upper middle range. For a discussion of income statistics and their interpretations see Rōdō tōkei kenkyūkai, "Sengo nihon no 'chūkansō' ni tsuite: sono tōkei in yoru bunseki," in *Keizai hyōron* (November 1957): 64-83.

27. Quoted in Shioda, *Sumai no sengo-shi*, 82-83. The "three sacred treasures," a play on the concept of the "three imperial regalia," were the television, electric washing machine, and refrigerator.

28. Tada Michitarō, "Tsukiai no arachi, danchi seikatsu," *Fujin kōron* (February 1961): 71.

29. Andrew Gordon, *The Wages of Affluence: Labor and Management in Postwar Japan* (Cambridge, MA: Harvard University Press, 1998), 104.

growth."[30] Companies withstood long strikes in order to break the backs of their powerful opponents and endeavored to replace militant unions with the cooperative company-sanctioned organizations that became the hallmark of Japan's famous "cooperative unionism."

In the midst of labor conflict, the question of "new middle class" allegiance had real stakes. Observers noted that the Marxist prediction that society would bifurcate into two opposing forces of capital and labor as small business owners and land-owning farmers identified their interests with the wage-earning proletariat was complicated by the growth of the new stratum of white-collar wage earners who stood between capital and labor and mediated conflict between them. Their "middle-ness" had nothing to do with income, critics noted, rather it was their middle *mental* positioning that defined the middle-class salary man. In the words of the "We Salary Men" series, the salary man was "born as an assistant to management," and his "consciousness" was "neither that of capitalist nor labor."[31] In a 1957 article, Tsurumi Shunsuke argued that this "middle-class consciousness" (*chūkan-sō ishiki*) was spreading far beyond the confines of the "actually existing middle class" (*sonzai toshite no chūkan-sō*) to "society at large," and forestalling the possibility of creating a united front among the working class.[32] In the labor offensives of the late 1950s, although in some cases white-collar workers joined their blue-collar colleagues in labor stoppages, more often white-collar workers stood on the front line against militant labor on behalf of their companies.[33]

A key turning point in the postwar labor struggle was the 1960 defeat of

---

30. Ibid., 105.
31. Yomiuri shimbun shakai-bu, ed., *Warera sarariiman*, 13.
32. Kuno Osamu, Tsurumi Shunsuke, Miyamoto Kenji, "Nihon kyōsantō wa nani o kangaeteru ka," *Chūō kōron* 72.4 (1957): 262-266.
33. Konda Masaharu, who worked in the personnel section of the steel company Nippon Kōkan (NKK), recalled sleeping on a cot at work for two weeks at the height of a 1959 strike and facing a delegation of 120 union members alone one morning before his colleagues arrived at work. Konda, described by his wife as "the last soldier of the Imperial Japanese Army," later recalled of that morning: "I stood and faced them, resigned to a beating. Besides August 1945, when I was stationed at Atsugi Base awaiting the American arrival, these were the tensest days of my life." His boss, personnel manager Orii Hyūga, in 1973 wrote a memoir of the labor conflicts of the late 1950s in hopes, he noted, of conveying to contemporary readers how "negotiations back then were menacing to an extent impossible to imagine today." These and other recollections in Gordon, *The Wages of Affluence*, 18-19.

the year-long strike at Mitsui's Miike Mine, the "greatest in a series of defeats for a union-dominated workplace culture."[34] At precisely the time the state was celebrating a "lifestyle revolution," vowing to "cultivate the middle class" (*chūsan kaikyū no ikusei*) and promising that Japanese people would "double their income" within ten years, industrial laborers were being lured back to work and into "enterprise unions" with promises that in exchange for full cooperation with corporate rationalization efforts, they, too, would have access to middle-class lives. In the words of Gordon, the "labor-management cooperation" that resulted from these years of conflict was "part of a system that delivered unprecedented access to a middle-class life of clothing off the rack, home appliances, high school or college education for children, color television, travel, and the chance to own a car or home."[35] The salary man was not only the vanguard of the "middle class dream" but also of a postwar labor culture in which *both* white- and blue- collar labor eventually came to align their interests with the corporation.

Housing eventually became a central component of the "settlement" between management and labor. Larger companies began offering low-cost rental housing for their employees—much of it built by the JHC—and, increasingly, providing financial assistance to employees seeking to buy homes.[36] In 1953, the Housing Loan Corporation began providing low-interest loans and tax breaks to companies building employee housing, in essence encouraging private-sector corporations to help solve the housing crisis."[37] This "corporate housing welfare" had the effect of binding employees to the company and turning housing into a negotiable item for enterprise unions. As Iwao Sato noted, "Because labour unions in Japan were organized separately on an individual company basis, union demands regarding housing . . . were aimed at improving housing welfare provided by the company . . . [and] when in the 1960s corporations began actively helping employees to become homeowners, labour unions eagerly embraced that trend as well."[38] This was a win-win for corporations, too, as noted by Ann Waswo: "With the massive labor unrest of the 1950s still fresh

34. Andrew Gordon, "Contests for the Workplace," in Gordon, ed., *Postwar Japan as History*, 383.
35. Gordon, *The Wages of Affluence*, 148.
36. Nihon jūtaku kōdan nijū nenshi kankō iinkai, ed., *Nihon jūtaku kōdan nijū nenshi* (Tokyo: Nihon jūtaku kōdan, 1975), 109.
37. Iwao Sato, "Welfare regime theories and the Japanese housing system," in Yosuke Hirayama and Richard Ronald, ed., *Housing and Social Transition in Japan* (New York: Routledge, 2007), 73-93.
38. Ibid., 81.

in the minds of company directors, anything that might induce employees to associate their own interests with those of the enterprise for which they worked was extremely attractive—and if it cost the enterprise relatively little of its own money, as was the case with housing loans, so much the better."[39] Devotion to one's company became the price of achieving the middle-class dream.

Standard Lives

The consumption habits of *danchi* residents were of great interest at a time that the relationship between production and consumption was being redefined. In industrialized nations around the world, economic crises and mobilization for war in the 1930s and 1940s taught economists and governments that mass production required mass consumption and, more fundamentally, that the promotion of the latter was a way to create and maintain economic growth. The birth of the mass consumer thus requires historicization. Pent-up desire following the war and the conversion of wartime production to production for the domestic market are only part of the story. Consumers had to be cultivated, educated, and encouraged and the meanings associated with consumption redefined in societies where savings and frugality had been valorized and acquisitiveness viewed as "self-indulgence." In the case of the United States, Lizbeth Cohen argued, people from across the political spectrum actively worked to redefine consumption as "civic virtue" and inculcate the belief that "an economy and society built around mass consumption would deliver not only great prosperity but also more democracy and equality."[40]

The importance of domestic consumption to Japan's postwar economy has been a subject of debate for scholars. The "culture of thrift," carefully cultivated since the Meiji era to promote savings that could be mobilized for nation- and empire-building, was not easily changed and the government continued to encourage

---

39 Ann Waswo, *Housing in Postwar Japan: A Social History* (New York: RoutledgeCurzon, 2002), 94. Waswo also notes that providing housing had the added benefit of enabling corporations to offer lower wages, "provision of one scarce item essential for survival—housing—moderated demand for another—income." 92.

40. Lizabeth Cohen, "The Consumers' Republic: An American Model for the World?" in Sheldon Garon and Patricia L. Maclachlan ed., *The Ambivalent Consumer: Questioning Consumption in East Asia and the West* (Ithaca: Cornell University Press, 2006), 45-46. For a fuller analysis of the emergence of mass consumption in the U.S. after World War II, see Lizabeth Cohen, *A Consumers' Republic: The Politics of Mass Consumption in Postwar America* (New York, Vintage Books, 2013).

high savings rates in the years after World War II.[41] Into the 1990s, the average Japanese person saved more and consumed less than people of the other G7 nations, especially Americans.[42] At the same time, however, a growing recognition of the potential of domestic consumption to promote economic expansion, the increasing availability of installment buying, and a burgeoning advertisement industry combined to promote consumption. Simon Partner has discussed the new methods manufacturers of electrical appliances used to cultivate desire and along with it, a large market for their new products even during the 1950s when Japanese incomes were still relatively low and savings rates substantial. Did Japan's economic success have roots in popular savings that provided the capital for growth or in the development of acquisitive consumers determined to purchase the latest appliance? Partner suggested that the answer is both; growing incomes over the era of high-speed growth coupled with new methods of paying for purchases over time made spending *and* saving possible. Thus both saving and consumption played important roles in the story of Japan's postwar prosperity.[43]

To people living through the high-speed economic growth of the mid-1950s through the 1970s, changing attitudes toward consumption were noticeable and noteworthy. The basic rules of economics were being redefined, argued economist Ōkōchi Kazuo in his 1960 book, *The Japanese Middle Class*: "It is written in any economics textbook that you have the commodity on the one hand and income on the other and consumption occurs when the two come together. Actually, the opposite is true. Excessive amounts of commodities are produced, and in order to sell all of them, a latent, sleeping power to consume is whipped up and called into being."[44] New advertising strategies had "whipped up" this desire to consume, and new methods of spreading payments over time had enabled even the salary man of modest means to acquire the high-priced items—the washing machines, refrigerators, and televisions—that were reshaping the materiality of middle-class life.

---

41. Sheldon Garon, "The Transnational Promotion of Saving in Asia: 'Asian Values' or the 'Japanese Model'?" in Garon and Maclachlan ed., *The Ambivalent Consumer*, 166-170.

42. Charles Yuji Horioka, "Are the Japanese Unique? An Analysis of Consumption and Saving Behavior in Japan," in Garon and Maclachlan ed., *The Ambivalent Consumer*, 113-136.

43. Simon Partner, *Assembled in Japan: Electrical Goods and the Making of the Japanese Consumer* (Berkeley: University of California Press, 1999).

44. Ōkōchi Kazuō, *Nihon-teki chūsan kaikyū* (Tokyo: Bungei shunjū shinsha, 1960), 168-69.

In fact, it was his "new way of thinking about *things*" (*atarashii* mono *no kangaekata*) that most distinguished the postwar salary man from his prewar counterpart, according to Ōkōchi. [45] Rather than save for old age, as people had done before the war, "people think that while they are young, they should enjoy this life that only comes around once, find a good marriage partner, marry as young as possible, and if their wages are low, both husband and wife work hard and live in the *danchi*. In order above all to enjoy life, [they] bring a television, washing machine, and, if possible, a refrigerator into the home and worry about payments later."[46] It was this new way of thinking about consumption, argued the 1960 White Paper on National Life, that most set the *danchi* inhabitants apart from other Japanese people. They had "a new consciousness of living" (*atarashii seikatsu ishiki*) that sanctioned and encouraged acquisition and discarded the thrifty habits of old. "From the olden times of the Tokugawa period to the Second World War," the White Paper noted, "the fundamental attitude of the Japanese people in their daily lives emphasized frugality, saving, and economy. Frugality was considered a virtue in everyday life. But since the end of the war, as our exchanges overseas and contacts with Americans have increased, our country's ideas about how to live have changed tremendously. Our frugality has given way to a philosophy of enjoying life."[47] In the way they fostered this mentality, the White Paper suggested, the *danchi* vanguard was, first and foremost, a consumption vanguard.

If people had developed a new way of thinking about things since the war, as Ōkochi suggested, the postwar was also marked by the arrival of new things to think about. Most of the electric appliances that entered the Japanese home starting in the 1950s were simply not available before the war, or if they were, only to the very wealthy. Their significance to postwar history lay not simply in their increased affordability and accessibility but in the meanings attached to their consumption. Beyond their utilitarian purposes or even the association of objects such as washing machines and rice cookers with the "liberation" of the housewife, to many, the acquisition of these consumer goods signified the end of nearly two decades of hardship and deprivation caused by war and its aftermath. Author Amano Masako wrote of her grandmother's delight when the family installed a private bath for the first time around 1960 when Japan's "high-speed growth period" was just taking off. "To grandmother, 'those days' had nothing to do with ... 'high-speed growth.' To her, 'those days' was when she finally got a

---

45. Ōkōchi, 159. Emphasis in the original.
46. Ibid., 158.
47. Ibid., 14.

bath and could sit and enjoy a little time alone."[48] Another informant recalled the joy she felt the evening after she bought the washing machine for which she had saved for over one and a half years: "A washing machine! More than anything else, it was my dream . . . Whatever else I bought [in future years], I never again felt what I did that evening."[49] It was the acquisition of these new things, more than larger historical events, suggested Amano, which punctuated postwar life. For Japanese women, especially, it was the arrival of the washing machine that "raised the curtain on the postwar." [50]

As eventful and celebrated as their acquisition was, *things* as proof of the modernization and middle-classification of everyday life also fostered a sense of inevitable development over space and time. In the United States, Ōkōchi noted, "the age (*jidai*) when the salary man swooped down on televisions or automobiles is already past." The pursuit of boats and pools was now "the focus of the American-style 'consumption boom.'"[51] In 1960, Japan was still caught up in the pursuit of the television though, Ōkōchi predicted, it would eventually become as prevalent in the Japanese home as the radio.[52] "Ages" defined by consumption suggested that as people acquired these items one-by-one, their lives would start to look like that of the American middle-class or, at least Japan's version of such, that of the *danchi-zoku*.

In a sense, these predictions came true. A decade and a half of sustained economic growth and full employment, rising incomes, and a technological revolution in methods of mass production that made consumer goods affordable turned a lifestyle that was formerly enjoyed by a privileged few into a reality for many. By the early 1970s, over eighty percent of Japanese people owned the washing machines, electric fans, rice cookers, televisions, refrigerators, and other electrical appliances that were synonymous with modern middle-class life.[53] Living conditions popularized by the *danchi* had spread beyond

---

48. Amano Masako and Sakurai Atsushi, *"Mono to onna" no sengo-shi* (Tokyo: Yūshindō kōbunsha, 1992), 4.

49. Ibid., 142.

50. Ibid., 127-28.

51. Ōkōchi, 170.

52. Ibid., 144.

53. In 1955 less than ten percent of Japanese people owned washing machines, electric fans, rice cookers, televisions, refrigerators, and other electrical appliances while in 1973, over eighty percent of the people owned them. Kōdo seichō o kangaeru kai., ed., *Kōdo seichō to nihonjin: part II katei-hen: kazoku no seikatsu no monogatari* (Tokyo: Nihon edeitā sukūru shuppanbu, 1985), 66.

their complexes in other ways, as well. By the 1970s many of the floor plans, construction techniques, and fixtures developed for the *danchi* had diffused to private sector housing. Even if people did not live in *danchi* apartments, many had dining kitchens, stainless steel sinks, and pre-cast concrete walls inspired by them. The "revolution in everyday life" resulted in living conditions that were increasingly similar across space and social class, and this outward similarity ultimately contributed to the formation of the "middle-class myth." In the words of Louise Young, "middle-class identity has long been rooted in consumption and the association of the very idea of consumption with the middle class." The "universalization" of this identity occurred when "class consumption became mass consumption [and] the masses bought the class identity along with the consumer products."[54]

The facile conflation of lifestyle and social class was quickly noted by critics such as Kashiwagi Hiroshi, who argued that the standardized living space produced by high-speed growth functioned to create the great "alibi of postwar democracy": the perception that people shared "equal lives." He called the standardized space wrought by the mass consumption of mass produced items such as televisions, washing machines, and refrigerators a "metaphorical scene that substantiated the abstract phrase 'equal lives,'" referring at once to its materiality and the meanings attached to it.[55] "Throughout Japan," he noted, "whatever home you go to, there is the same refrigerator, the same vacuum cleaner, the same television . . . fundamental social and economic hierarchies are hidden by the sameness of the overcrowded rooms . . ."[56] Although Kashiwagi did not refer to the *danchi* specifically, they exemplified the "substantiated metaphorical scene" he described. *Danchi* apartments were mass produced, standardized living spaces filled with mass produced, standardized consumer goods. As Nishikawa Yūko noted, one could move from a *danchi* complex to another "far away in a different land" and "one's furniture would fit exactly in the same rooms and the same places."[57] As a metaphor, they stood for prosperity and the promise of a better life. Like Tada Michitaro's "shining blender" at the center

---

54. Louise Young,"Marketing the Modern: Department Stores, Consumer Culture, and the New Middle Class in Interwar Japan," in *International Labor and Working-Class History* 55 (1999): 68.

55. Kashiwagi Hiroshi, "Kōdo seichō ga motarashita mono: mikuro yūtopia toshite no kakukazoku," in *Sekai* 482 (December 1985): 79.

56. Ibid., 79-80.

57. Nishikawa Yūko, *Kariya to mochiya no bungakushi: 'watashi' no utsuwa no monogatari* (Tokyo: Sanseido, 1999), 181.

of the table, "hope, desire, anticipation, and prophecy coalesced" around them. Although difference and inequality remained, standardization helped hide their physical markers and contributed to perceptions of "equal lives."

The nLDK Family

Fascination with *danchi* dwellers went beyond interest in their consumption habits and lifestyles. The *danchi* were inhabited predominantly by small, nuclear families of husband, wife, and one or two small children. Some have argued that the compact *danchi* living space "created" the small nuclear family. "It wasn't housing for all of the diverse types of families," noted Nishikawa Yūko, "but the upside-down phenomenon where the size of *danchi* housing determined the size of the family . . ."[58] However, one could also argue that the JHC was simply catering to the type of family moving into cities in pursuit of employment. Between 1955 and 1960, thirty-one percent of the population growth in Tokyo resulted from the creation of "new households," contributing to the dire housing shortage which it was the JHC's mandate to address. But as large concentrations of families spatially removed from the ties of the extended family, *danchi* dwellers were once again believed to stand "at the extreme end of the social change continuum," and offer insights about Japan's changing family structure.[59]

The gradual decline of multi-generation families accompanied industrialization and urbanization starting in the nineteenth century, but after World War II, this decline took on new meaning as the nuclear family organized around the conjugal couple displaced the extended family, as the dominant ideal of family life. The prewar "family system" was stripped of its legal and ideological authority and criticized as a force of conservatism and a pillar supporting the emperor-centered "family state." The revised civil code abolished primogeniture rules of succession and inheritance and deprived the household head of decision-making power over marriage and other family matters. The nuclear family, long associated with the "new" middle class and coded the modern, urban "other" to the conservative, rural extended family thus gained new authority as the basis of postwar family life.[60]

---

58. Quoted in Hara Takeshi, *Takiyama komyūn 1974* (Tokyo: Kodansha, 2010), 36.

59. Christie Kiefer, "Personality and Social Change in a Japanese Danchi," 95.

60. Although after the war the *ie* was abolished as a legal entity, the extended, three-generation family persisted alongside the nuclear family as a model for organizing family life. In recent years, with the rapid aging of society, the three-generation family (as well as the three-generation family home) as a system for caring for the aged has been making a marked comeback. On the formation of the

As we saw in Chapter One, damning critiques of the prewar family and traditional home drove the agendas of many postwar architects. The very configuration of the traditional home was believed to reinforce the power of the household head. Democratization of the nation required democratization of the home, and this required young couples to break away from the expectations and surveillance of the household patriarch and mother-in-law (for new wives) and, in the words of Nishiyama, create "their own units of livelihood."[61] Many of these ideals became inscribed in the space of the "nDK" and eventually the "nLDK." Just as the "LDK' is the center of the acronym, so it, not the guest-focused, formal *zashiki* of the traditional house, was to be the site of a family-centered life. The "n" denoted bedrooms for the *number* of family members minus one, since a central assumption of the space was that each person would have his/her own bedroom except the husband and wife who would share.[62] Children required their own rooms to study for exams, and the fact that neither husband nor wife had a "private" room assumed that each spent most of the time in their respective workplaces, be it kitchen or corporation. Indeed, the "nLDK" expressed a spatial and familial division of labor that became the ideological basis of postwar society. According to architect Yamamoto Riken, it was the "nLDK" family model that people sought to buy when they purchased a home. He concluded: "we try to achieve the ideal family through the house."[63]

Studies of the 1950s and 1960s suggested that the small *danchi* family structure resulted from much more mundane causes. Men's jobs had required them to move to cities, and in-laws did not wish to uproot their lives to accompany their children and grandchildren to the *danchi* where there was little space for them in the typical 2DK apartment. A 1958 survey indicated that only twenty percent of families claimed they had moved to the *danchi* for the express purpose of "separating" themselves from the influence of the extended family.[64] Yet the type of separation that interested social scientists of the 1950s and 1960s concerned not simply the physical distance of *danchi* dwellers from their extended families but their changing attitudes and allegiances. One common survey topic concerned the religious practices of *danchi* dwellers, including

postwar "Japanese family system" see Ochiai Emiko, *The Japanese Family System in Transition: A Sociological Analysis of Family Change in Postwar Japan*, (Tokyo: Simul Press, Inc.), 1994.

61. Nishiyama Uzō, *Kore kara no sumai* (Tokyo: Sagami shobō, 1947), 125.

62. "Tokushū: yuragi no naka no kazoku to nLDK," 28.

63. Ibid., 25.

64. Kiefer, 96.

whether or not they placed Buddhist altars (*butsudan*) in their apartments to make offerings to deceased family members. Not surprisingly, very few families kept family altars—only ten percent in Kiefer's study of Hanshin Danchi in Osaka. Limited space was once again the culprit, but the impression that "the rationalized style of *danchi* life and the style symbolized by the *butsudan* do not go together" was also strong.[65]

Studies concluded that the loyalties of *danchi* families were not first to their extended families but to impersonal institutions such as the workplace and school. The *danchi* husband's first loyalty was to his corporation and the *danchi* wife's to her own nuclear family unit. Wives and mothers no longer relied on the expertise of older generations of women in keeping house and raising children but on the impersonal, "rational" advice of experts found in the pages of women's magazines. Parents aspired to "independence" in old age so as not to enmesh their own children in a web of family obligations.[66] It was such attitudes that seemed to hold the profoundest implications for the future of the extended family.

Many of the stereotypes of the *danchi* family would become the stereotypes of the postwar family. *Danchi* fathers were considered the original "lodger papas" and "Sunday guests" whose long commutes gave them little time at home. *Danchi* mothers were viewed as the original "education mamas" embroiled in intense relationships with their children who they over indulged even as they pressured them to study hard. *Danchi* children were caught up in the pressures of studying for the "examination hell" which was the gateway to the corporate life of their fathers and mothers. These understandings of the *danchi* family would participate in the creation of the normative ideal of postwar "nLDK" family life.

In reality, many other patterns of family life, including multi-generation families, single parent families, families with working mothers, and others coexisted alongside this model. As Mari Osawa points out, the model nuclear family of "salary man" husband and stay-at-home wife (plus children) peaked, statistically, at thirty-eight percent of married couples in the late 1970s but otherwise has averaged a mere thirty percent of the Japanese married population. Yet postwar corporate and social policy, including higher taxes on second incomes, rewarded this "stereotyped gendered division of labor" in which "one-third of society defined the norm." The value of this model, according to Osawa, was that it enabled men to devote countless hours to the

---

65. Ibid., 126.
66. Ibid., 96.

workplace while women oversaw the home and the education of children, and ironically in more recent years, performed social welfare tasks such as the care of the elderly.[67] The "hegemonic ideology" of the middle-class corporate family became a goal in itself as well as a system for reproducing itself and corporate-centered society.[68]

The nuclear family also became a driver of economic growth as each new household required a home and the things to fill it. It was in this sense, argued Kashiwagi, that the true role of the nuclear family, isolated in its standardized living space, manifested itself. The home had become a "micro-utopia": In the name of "liberating [itself] of messy relationships with the extended family and community," the small, nuclear family in fact had simply become the "best, smallest unit for consumption and production according to the logic of capitalism." Capitalism had produced the best and most effective "modern family."[69] To Kashiwagi and other critics, the postwar family model that had been invested with hopes for reforming the nation had instead become the basis of a new conservative *status quo* and a mechanism for economic growth.

---

67. Osawa, Mari, "Twelve Million Full-Time Housewives," in Oliver Zunz, Leonard
    Schoppa, and Nobuhiro Hiwatari, ed., *Social Contracts Under Stress: The Middle
    Classes of America, Europe, and Japan at the Turn of the Century* (New York:
    Russell Sage Foundation, 2002), 266. Osawa and Ochiai point out that here have
    been tensions between demands for women to care for the home and family,
    and persistent labor shortages between the 1960s and 1990s. Aggregate female
    participation in the postwar workforce has followed an "M"-shaped trajectory.
    Women have tended to work until marriage (forming the first peak of the "M,"),
    quit to bear and raise children (forming the trough), then return to the workforce
    in a part-time capacity after children begin school (forming the second peak).
    After the war, the trough was deepest for women born between 1926 and 1950,
    as more and more women began staying home. The trough is shallower for
    women born in subsequent years but there is still a marked tendency for women
    to quit work to raise children. This pattern has served the postwar economy in
    several ways: it freed up men to devote endless hours to work and company, made
    part-time female workers into a buffer labor force that could be hired and laid
    off according to need and, subsequently, in large companies, helped to protect
    "lifetime employment" for privileged male employees. For an analysis of female
    participation rates in the labor force, see Ochiai, 13-17.
68. Kelly, 215.
69. Kashiwagi, 85.

Shrinking Expectations

Already in 1961, Tada Michitarō noted that there was danger in designating the *danchi* the "advance guard" of the "dream of the middle-classification of the entire country." For with time, he predicted, the *danchi* would no longer be able to contain the dreams that had been invested in them. The problem was a simple and practical one: size. Already, he wrote, the *danchi* had turned into a "half-storage center" with the "dream goods" lined up, waiting in the *danchi* "until they can find a real home."[70] Infamous for their smaller-than-standard *tatami* mats designed to accommodate their thicker-than-standard concrete walls, the *danchi* simply could not accommodate all of the things people were acquiring. In the early years, manufacturers even designed special "*danchi*-sized" products to suit the *danchi* space. Shioda Maruo described his surprise during a visit to a department store to find "*danchi*-sized" chests of drawers, stereos, wall-clocks, refrigerators, and electric fans. "You can get anything '*danchi*-size.' There was even a '*danchi*-doll' (*danchi-bina*) . . . The only things in the *danchi* that are not *danchi*-sized are the people."[71]

Middle-class life defined by appliance ownership was outpacing middle-class life defined by housing. In the 1960s, this problem was labeled "imbalance" (*anbaransu*) within "modern living." Nishiyama Uzō, in a 1960 article on apartment life and "modern living" (*modan ribingu*), noted: "The imbalance is sharply evident in the electrification of the household (*katei denka*). It is a good thing that, since the war, there has been a tendency for [everyone] to enjoy life, from the top class to the lowest. And with the so-called consumption revolution, life within the home has changed greatly. However, this modernization has focused exclusively on equipping the inside [of the home] rather than on the home itself . . . What does it mean to chase after 'electrical life' in a small, shabby house?"[72]

The answer to this question, some ventured, was cramped living conditions in which the people were gradually being squeezed out by proliferating appliances and furniture. In response to a 1967 pronouncement by Prime Minister Satō that Japan's housing conditions were small but suitable for a young couple in love, the journal *Kurashi no techō* described the experiences of several families living in both JHC and privately rented housing. One man described his kitchen, packed with appliances, with the kitchen table and chair backed up to

---

70. Tada, 72.

71. Shioda, *Sumeba danchi*, 200. *Danchi*-sized products failed to catch on since most inhabitants hoped to move on to larger housing in the future.

72. Nishiyama Uzō, "Modan libingu," *Shūkan Asahi* (February 28, 1960): 43.

the toilet door. When his young daughter required use of the facilities during dinner, he was required to get up and move his chair to allow her access. "In our house, you can eat and eliminate within a space of two square meters. What a convenient and 'rational' life!"[73] Another noted with similar sarcasm: "What a convenient kitchen! You can reach everything without taking a step!"[74] Things were proliferating but the amount of space in the typical Japanese apartment was not. "At present," the article concluded, "our already-small homes are just getting smaller."[75] In the July 2, 1967, issue of the *Asahi Shimbun*, Hanamori Yasuji, editor of *Kurashi no techo* and a relentless critic of the government and the JHC, responded to this pronouncement: "There are people who live in a 4.5 *tatami* room with a piano, but have to eat ramen and have nowhere to sleep. Those people think that because they can buy a piano, their lifestyle is 'middle.' They look only for a piano that signifies 'middle.'"[76] Following upon the 1966 *White Paper on National Life* that announced that ninety-percent of Japanese people felt they lived a middle-level lifestyle (*chūryū no kurashi*) that was "neither low nor high," critiques such as this were meant to draw attention to the contradictions of the Japanese lifestyle.

In 1967, the JHC undertook a major redesign of the *danchi* space, adding an official "living room" to the DK configuration and giving birth to the "nLDK." The *Shūkan Asahi* that nine years prior had announced the arrival of the "*danchi-zoku*," proclaimed that the numbers of the "L-zoku" were still small but growing.[77] The 2DK, the article announced, had simply been too small. A typical family stuffed a piano, sofa, chest of drawers, stereo, television, not to mention the now-indispensable washing machine and refrigerator into a two-room apartment of six and 4.5 *tatami* mats (plus "DK"). Unlike the "DK" that had been designed to fulfill the principle of separating eating and sleeping and had required people to acquire dining tables and chairs at a time that these still rare, the "L" was designed at the height of "high-speed growth" to help accommodate the copious furniture that people already owned.[78] The "furniture jungle" in Japanese apartments, in the words of Hanamori, made it so that one had to "walk like

73. Ueda Tome, "Aishiatte itara, semakutemo, kurushikutemo, shiawase da to sōri daijin wa iu ga . . ." *Kurashi no techō* 100 (April 1969): 126.

74. Ibid., 132.

75. Ibid., 143.

76. Quoted in Sawada Tomoko, *Yuka-za, isu-za* (Tokyo: Sumai no toshokan shuppan kyoku, 1995), 146.

77. "Kore kara no mai hōmu wa L! Ribingu rūmu no yume to genjitsu," *Shūkan Asahi* (July 28, 1967): 30.

78. Sawada, 167.

a crab" around all of the furniture just to get to the toilet. Children from the *danchi*, he claimed, had even developed a "2DK-walk" of small steps.[79] The "L," predicted Hamamori, would not solve the problem. "Until now, we had children and lived our lives in coordination with the 2DK 'space.' In the same way, we will get used to the half-assed 'L' (*chūto hanpa 'L'*) and repeat human life the same as we did during the 2DK period."[80] For the problem, as Hanamori and others noted, was that even after adding a few meters to the *danchi* space, "'L' did not mean L-sized."[81]

To critics, a much more basic problem was that the endless pursuit of the newest appliance or piece of furniture had created a life that was perpetually "unsettled" (*fuantei*).[82] Though, in the early 1960s, examples of Japan's daily-improving-everyday-life such as the *danchi* were meant to signify the stabilization of the everyday and the acquisition of a certain level of comfort after long years of deprivation. The everyday life of Japan's "new middle-class," suggested Ōkochi, introduced new tensions, namely, the desire to "chase" (*oikakeru*) and the feeling of "being chased" (*oikakerareru*) by the latest commodity on the market. Keeping life unsettled was the only way to perpetuate the consumption necessary to mass production and was an essential component of postwar capitalism. "Surely," Ōkochi concluded, "this isn't what it means to 'enjoy life?'"[83]

This was certainly not the "revolution of everyday life" envisioned by early postwar reformers. A "deluge of things" had entered people's homes, complained Nishiyama Uzō. "With *danchi* life as the prototype . . . one after another, the waves of the 'revolution of everyday life' are surging upon the people."[84] The real revolution of home and family had been derailed by a consumption revolution led by corporations. "The craze for modern living is a result of changes in family life after the war: the fall of the absolute power of the family head, the elevation of the housewife, the demand for more efficient housework and the

---

79. "Kore kara no mai hōmu wa L!," 29.

80. Ibid., 34.

81. Ibid. The number of *tatami* mats / person—one standard by which improvements in living space was measured—increased steadily over the years in question. In 1953, the number was 3.3 per person. By 1963, the number had increased to 4.9 and by 1973, 6.6. Critics noted, however, that these increases could not keep up with the pace of furniture acquisition. Numbers taken from Sawada, pp. 146 and 168.

82. Tada, 72.

83. Ōkochi, 171.

84. Nishiyama Uzō, "Seikatsu kakushin no buizion," in *Jūkyo ron: Nishiyama Uzō chosaku shū* 2, (Tokyo: Keisō shobō, 1968), 622-629.

move toward a happy family life. That this is [now] being led by big monopoly enterprises is introducing distortions (*hizumi*)."[85] For Nishiyama, these "distortions" translated into "imbalance" between the home and the things that were taking over its interior, creating the illusion of "modern living" but, in fact, slowly eroding it. Harking back to the hopes he had expressed just after the war, Nishiyama insisted again that people had to create their own "revolution" in everyday life and "take back the power to make their own lives, by themselves."[86] This meant resisting the "deluge of things" that had washed into their homes and threatened to push the people out onto the streets again.

"Dreams of middle-classification" resonated powerfully in Japan of the 1950s and 1960s but so, too, did critiques that pointed out the many disappointments with middle-class life in the midst of high-speed economic growth. Once the life people "longed for," by the 1970s, the *danchi* would come to emblematize the life they *got*. As Carol Gluck noted, one of the paradoxes of postwar Japan has been the perception that the middle class is "both living better and not living well at one and the same time."[87] The *danchi* lent understanding to this paradox because they symbolized both. They were the shining symbol of "living better" in comparison with the lives of parents or grandparents in prewar or wartime Japan. But they eventually became an example of "not living well"—ironically in comparison with the very expectations they themselves had helped to create. As we shall see in the following chapters, the "*danchi* vanguard" that had served as such a powerful vision of an attainable middle-class life would also become a conduit for the expression of anxieties and disappointments that, in themselves, helped to define the middle-class experience. In the end, the myth of the universal middle class functioned to raise expectations, even as it lowered and eventually disappointed them.

---

85. Nishiyama, "Modan libingu," 43.
86. Ibid.
87. Carol Gluck, "Introduction," *Showa: The Japan of Hirohito*, Carol Gluck and Stephen R. Graubard, ed. (New York: W.W. Norton, 1992), xli.

Figures for
"The Life We Longed For"

Images are all courtesy of the Urban Renaissance Agency (*Toshi saisei kikō*), successor to the Japan Housing Corporation. Established in 2004, the URA is a semi-public agency that focuses primarily on urban renewal and the renovation and rental of over 750,000 housing units in Japan.

Figure 1 – Front view of a five-story *danchi* apartment building.

Figure 2 – "Star House" *danchi* apartment building.

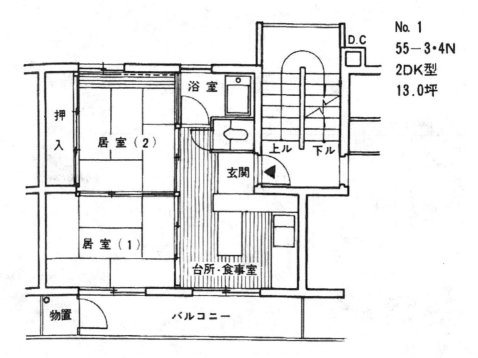

Figure 3 – Floor plan for 1955 2DK apartment.

Figure 4 – Original Dining Kitchen.

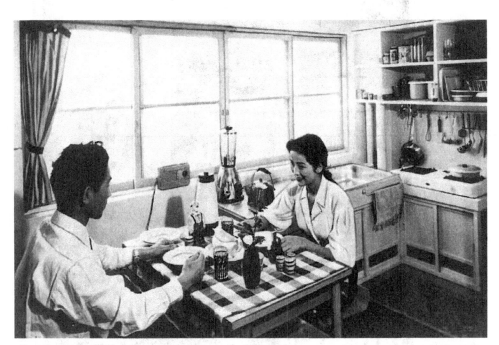

Figure 5 – Promotional photo of couple dining in the DK, 1956.

Figure 6 – *Danchi* playground.

Figure 7 – Aerial view of Matsubara *Danchi*, Saitama Prefecture.

Figure 8 – People queuing at JHC Tokyo Headquarters to apply for housing, 1962.

Figure 9 – Photo of Crown Prince Akihito and Princess Michiko inspecting Hibarigaoka *Danchi* in Chiba Prefecture, 1960.

Chapter Four

DANCHI DYSTOPIAS AND THE CRITIQUE
OF POSTWAR EVERYDAY LIFE

Modern living, though appearing to be glamorous, is the constant cause of
complications among human beings, producing thousands and thousands
of neurotic adults.

—Yoko McClain[1]

Behind steel doors

Modern housing often attempts to solve problems, to fix the dilemmas of society through the reorganization of living space. This was particularly the case of
twentieth century mass housing projects where "diverse forms of state paternalism" equated the reformation of living space with the modernization of society.[2]
As we have seen, the role of the *danchi* was largely corrective. They were built
to help solve Japan's housing crisis and raise living standards, and their interior
design was also the product of debates seeking to reform the prewar family and
community. They represented the possibility of a richer and transformed social
life; a new mode of relating to family and community away from the constraints
of the old "family system" and village. But once built, they engendered new debates—this time about what the *danchi* family and community predicted for
postwar society, for better and for worse. More than a concrete space for living,
the *danchi* also became a prominent discursive site through which architects,
journalists, social scientists, and even novelists and filmmakers explored the
tensions and anxieties that accompanied the reconfiguration of everyday life in

---

1. In "Ariyoshi Sawako: Creative Social Critic," in *The Journal of the Association of
   Teachers of Japanese* 12.2/3, (May & September 1977): 222.
2. Florian Urban, *Tower and Slab: Histories of Global Mass Housing* (New York:
   Routledge, 2012), 3.

the era of high-speed economic growth. While celebrating Japan's ever-improving-everyday life, much of this discourse also betrayed a profound ambivalence toward *danchi* life. The *danchi*, many suggested, had led to the destruction of meaningful community life, the isolation of housewives, and the total evacuation of husbands from the home as they spent all of their time at work or in transit. Rather than creating a new family and community, the *danchi* seemed to offer no family or community life at all. To many, the standardized, impersonal, concrete communities became synonymous with the alienation and anomie of modern life.

Ironically, many of the alienating features of *danchi* life were also among their most celebrated. Concrete walls and steel doors with locks and keys became markers of a modern lifestyle in which privacy was at a premium. Unlike the sliding outer doors of homes in the countryside that allowed neighbors and other callers to enter at will, making the entryway a kind of ambiguous semi-public space, the new door very clearly defined the boundary between inside and outside, private and public. The item that allowed one to pass easily between the two was the key. The phrase "with one key" (*kagi hitotsu de*) became a metaphor for the ease and freedom of *danchi* life, especially for the housewife. "The metal door connects and divides the family and society," claimed one magazine feature on *danchi* life, "and the key is the talisman that allows the housewife to go out freely."[3] It also allowed the housewife to define her degree of involvement in the *danchi* community. In the words of resident Yamaguchi Yoshiko, "with one key, we can go out or isolate ourselves from the neighbors and enjoy our own private lives. *Danchi* life lies in the successful mix of individual and collective life."[4] Yet to many, these markers also signified the loneliness of modern life. Recalling his first night living in Takanedai Danchi, Takenaka Tsutomu noted that the only sign of life "beyond the concrete walls" was a lonely toilet flushing in the night. "Privacy of the concrete box, isolated behind the steel door," he concluded, "is in conflict with [people's] humanity."[5]

"Privacy"—pronounced as the English word *puraibashii*—thus became one of the defining attributes of *danchi* life. It suggested a broader set of meanings within the theories of modernization that permeated studies of *danchi* and

3.   "Fujin o kaihō suru danchi 'kagi' zoku no shutsugen," *Fujin kōron* (October 1958): 245.

4.   In Nihon jūtaku kōdan, *Apāto danchi kyojūsha no shakai shinrigaku-teki kenkyū: ningen kankei to shakai ishiki o chūshin toshite* (Tokyo: Nihon jūtaku kōdan, 1960), 59-60.

5.   Takenaka Tsutomu, *Danchi nanatsu no daizai* (Tokyo: Kōbundō, 1964), 22.

salary man life in the 1950s and early 1960s. "Privacy" suggested a shift from "pre-modern" community-based relationships governed by tradition and group expectations to "modern" and rational relationships based on democratic association. One survey of human relationships in the *danchi* compared the number of "privacy types," defined as those who sought to "limit relationships with neighbors to functional matters," with "sociability types," who were more neighborly and possessed "feelings prior to modern individualism." Predictably and in keeping with the study's hypothesis, the survey found more "privacy" than "sociability" types in the *danchi*, especially the further one moved out into the suburbs.[6] *Puraibashii* thus situated the *danchi* in space and time. The very English-inspired pronunciation of the word rendered the entire concept modern and foreign and suggested an advanced stage of development on a spatial and temporal trajectory away from the old-fashioned village or plebian urban neighborhood. As one *danchi* resident observed, "there is the belief that having meddlesome relationships with neighbors is 'pre-modern' and that we have been freed of such things; that the reason we mustn't get involved with our neighbors is that it is pre-modern."[7]

The postwar "privatization" of the family and everyday were not unique to Japan. Elaine Tyler May, writing on the American family during the Cold War, interpreted the turn inward as a form of "domestic containment" aimed at keeping newly re-domesticated women in the home and the threat of civil discord and nuclear war out of it.[8] Kristin Ross has linked the privatization of the everyday in postwar France, "the withdrawal of the new middle classes to their newly comfortable domestic interiors," with a corresponding withdrawal from empire and the reorientation of colonizing energies from overseas to the domain of everyday life.[9] In Japan, attempts to separate, isolate, and enclose the family were not new to the postwar. From late Meiji on, the discourse on hygiene and kitchen reform often centered on eliminating maids and other "outsiders" who might bring disease or other social contaminants into the home through

---

6. Nihon jūtaku kōdan, *Apāto danchi kyojūsha no shakai shinri gakuteki kenkyū*, 63-64. See too Hoshino Ikumi, "Apartment Life in Japan," for a survey of studies about "privacy" versus "sociability" types in English. *Journal of Marriage and Family* 26, No. 3 (August 1964): 312-317.

7. "Gōsuto taun ni hana wa saku," *Chūō kōron* (March 1960): 291.

8. Elaine Tyler May, *Homeward Bound: American Families in the Cold War Era*, New York: Basic Books, 1988.

9. Kristin Ross, *Fast Cars, Clean Bodies: Decolonization and the Reordering of French Culture* (Cambridge MA: The MIT Press, 1996), 11.

the portal of the kitchen.[10] The postwar, however, brought a whole new set of possible contaminants, not the least of which was history itself. The *danchi* were imagined to be impervious to external threats and dangers. Popular myth had it that a fire could be raging next door and the *danchi*'s concrete construction would prevent it from spreading to one's own apartment, a myth not borne out in experience. The supposed inflammability of concrete walls thus promised not only to protect residents from fires next door but to quarantine them from such devastating conflagrations as those of the recent wartime past. Housing innovations based on the principle of separation and the promotion of individual and family "privacy" served not only to divide generations—to separate the generation that fought the war from the one that would rebuild the nation— but they separated past from present and sealed the latter in an "emerging clean, bright space" from which, in the words of Igarashi Yoshikuni, "traces of loss and the past seemed to be fast disappearing."[11]

In Japan and elsewhere, it is no coincidence that the focus on privacy and containment coincided with the "consumer revolution" after World War II. "Privacy" was enabled by the privatization of various functions that had previously been communal. In many parts of Japan, exposure to the modern appliances of the postwar was initially a communal experience with women from one neighborhood sharing the same washing machine or entire neighborhoods gathering around televisions situated on street corners to watch popular sports events and other programs.[12] Privatization required the replication of the consumption of these items on a household basis. In the 1950s, the *danchi* became a dramatic example of this replication. At a time when most Japanese people still utilized public bathing facilities, the inclusion of private baths in the *danchi* was a revolutionary departure, especially for collective housing. Indeed, the *danchi zoku* were best known for what they owned and even criticized for their conspicuous consumption and the need for everyone to keep up with

---

10. See Jordan Sand, *House and Home in Modern Japan: Reforming Everyday Life, 1880-1930* (Cambridge, MA: Harvard University Asia Center, 2003), 68-69.

11. Yoshikuni Igarashi, *Bodies of Memory: Narratives of War in Postwar Japanese Culture, 1945-1970* (Princeton: Princeton University Press, 2000), 132.

12. A farming woman in Chiba prefecture recalled: "Each house would use the washing machine we bought collectively for three days then after finishing, we would carry it on our backs to the next member's house. It was just when people were starting to use washing machines (1954)." In Amano Masako and Sakurai Atsushi, ed., *Mono to anna no sengo-shi* (Toyko: Yūshidō Kōbunsha, 1992), 142. For accounts of group viewings of corner television sets, see Partner and Igarashi.

the Suzuki's. One of Christie Kiefer's informants told of women in his *danchi* community who would "buy small things in department stores and have them delivered instead of merely carrying them home, so that the neighbors will see the impressive delivery take place."[13] Popular accounts of *danchi* life described stories—many certainly apocryphal—of "chain reaction purchasing" as door-to-door salesmen moved from one apartment to the next.[14] Privatization was thus a motor of mass consumption. It required the individualization of consumption that, as we saw in Chapter Three, also functioned to standardize and homogenize everyday life.

Ironically, achieving "private life" also required dedication to work and company. Workers relied on corporations for the jobs and promotions that would allow them to purchase the amenities of modern life but also, increasingly, for the home loans that allowed the dream of acquiring "my home" to become a reality. Large companies had long provided housing for employees in small apartments or dormitories but starting in the late 1960s, many also began encouraging their employees to purchase homes by providing loans. Expectations that both blue- and white-collar employees would spend their entire careers with the same company made "the person's employment rather than the property he purchased . . . collateral for the loan . . ."[15] Tomiko Yoda noted: "The spirit of my-homeism . . . encouraged the ethos of masculine workaholism and loyalty to the employer—'working bee' (*hataraki bachi*) fathers and 'gung-ho employee' (*mōretsu shain*) fathers."[16] Tada Michitarō called this "the paradox and the strategy of my-homeism . . . The company, on behalf of the whole society . . . intrudes into my-home, supposedly the fortress of the private sphere."[17]

---

13. Christie Kiefer, "Personality and Social Change in a Japanese Danchi," (PhD diss. University of California, Berkeley, 1968), 35.

14. Takenaka Tsutomu, *Danchi nanatsu no daizai* (Tokyo: Kōbundō, 1964), 13-14. This particular account was of a door-to-door salesman who reportedly sold over one thousand double bed mattresses in one *danchi* complex.

15. Ann Waswo, *Housing in Postwar Japan: A Social History* (New York: RoutledgeCurzon, 2002), 93-94.

16. Tomiko Yoda, "The Rise and Fall of Maternal Society: Gender, Labor, and Capital in Contemporary Japan," in Tomiko Yoda and Harry Harootunian, ed., *Japan After Japan: Social and Cultural Life from the Recessionary 1990s to the Present* (Durham: Duke University Press, 2006), 247-248.

17. Tada Michitarō, "The Glory and Misery of 'My Home,'" in *Authority and the Individual in Japan: Citizen Protest in Historical Perspective*, J. Victor Koschmann, ed. (Tokyo: University of Tokyo Press, 1978), 210.

One common criticism of the *danchi* was that they provided no "natural" place to gather. Informal gathering places such as the public bath had been replaced with the "community meeting room," the site of organized club activities. The back door (*katteguchi*) where housewives popped in for a quick visit or to borrow a cup of *misō* had been eliminated and replaced with a single metal door at the front of the apartment that required a more formal visit. The engineered quality of the *danchi*, where every space had a specific function, made it difficult to engage directly and spontaneously with neighbors. Writer Tada likened *danchi* life to riding in an air-conditioned express train. Unlike the slow-moving local that picked up passengers of all social classes who mingled and chatted amiably along the way, the express train was filled with salary men speeding to the city, sitting shoulder to shoulder, unspeaking and feeling "ill at ease." Thick glass windows and air conditioning separated passengers from nature and the modern, engineered quality of the space separated one passenger from another. "If you have a problem," Tada noted, "you don't look to the person next to you but ask for the mediation of an official."[18] The problem, Tada concluded, was that the modern salary man and his family had no real need for the community. They turned to the company, labor union, or government with their problems—not to neighbors who were now simply a nuisance. The *danchi*, Tada concluded, was a "desert for human relationships."[19] It was a "ghost town," concluded another writer. The *danchi* might be "a machine for living," he noted, "but it gives no feeling of life."[20]

Ambiguous spaces and natural "communal territorial space" had been eliminated. Community relations were safely housed in the planned and "rationalized" space of the community room and the *danchi* playground and mediated by JHC planners. JHC-appointed "home helpers," often the wives of JHC employees, coached new inhabitants in the ways of community living, such as how to properly dispose of garbage, and tread quietly in hallways.[21] Indeed, this

---

18. Tada Michitarō, "Tsukiai no arachi, danchi seikatsu," *Fujin kōron* (February 1961): 69.

19. Ibid.

20. "Gōsuto taun ni hana wa saku," 290.

21. The helpers were eventually replaced with a short initiation film titled "Introduction to the *Danchi*" that featured a happy *danchi* couple giving married friends a tour of the public and private spaces of the Hibarigaoka complex. In the film, the housewife-narrator-tour guide demonstrates how to wrap and dispose of garbage, walk softly in hallways, beat the dust from the futon quietly, and stoke up the bathtub in such a way as not to set fire to the entire apartment. At the end of the film, while the men shake up cocktails in the living room with the television

was a mediated space *par excellence*. Between steel door and vestibule, kitchen and bedroom, were numerous interventions: a plan that sought to separate space by function and people by generation, and of the state that sought to re-insinuate itself in postwar life.

These mediations created a space that was fraught with tensions and contradictions. Observers such as Ōya Sōichi noted the tension between JHC goals of "collectivization" and "individualization" of everyday life.[22] Less noted was that *danchi* life, famous for being isolated and closed, was in fact open and exposed to public scrutiny. This most "private" of living spaces was also, ironically, highly visible. Neighbors viewed each other through lace curtains, comparing belongings and keeping track of others' movements. The verandah was where *danchi* housewives, quite literally, aired their laundry. A sensationalist 1960 article on "the joys and sorrows of the *danchi* housewife" in *Shufu no tomo* described the "*nozokare noiroze*" (neurosis of being watched) of "Mrs. E." who was unable to get out of her bath without having her husband check that no neighbors were watching. More serious, however, was the case of "Mrs. O" who feared neighbors thought *she* was watching *them* and "wore out her nerves trying and trying not to look, ending up with a serious case of neurosis."[23] *Danchi* life, many concluded, infected people with an entire array of nervous conditions. Concrete walls induced feelings of claustrophobia. Metal doors eliminated the communal interchange around household entrances and, in the opinion of Isoda Kōichi, imbued vestibules with "feelings of anxiety" and "fear of an unexpected visitor."[24] Through the peephole, concurred Takenaka, every visitor became "an enemy, intruder, or pushy salesman."[25]

The problem was not just being *seen* but also being *heard*. The fortress-like concrete walls, it seems, conducted sound. Anne Imamura's ethnography of a *danchi* community outside Tokyo described the experience of one couple who retreated to the bathroom out of hearing range of the children to discuss family finances only to learn later that their conversation had carried through the

---

flickering in the background, the visiting wife takes over the kitchen and cooks dinner. She proclaims that she had quickly learned how to "use these facilities— surrounded by community life—to make a wonderful life for him and me." *Danchi e no shōtai*, Nikkei Films, November 1960.

22. Ōya Sōichi, "Jūtaku kōdan: seikai ichi no ōya-shū," *Shūkan asahi* (October 19, 1958): 56.

23. "Danchi fujin no yuutsu to tanoshimi," *Shufu no tomo* (September 1960), 195.

24. Isoda Kōichi, "The Dilemma of Domestic Sensibilities," translated by Alan Tansman in *The Journal of Japanese Studies* (Winter 1995)21.1: 56.

25. Takenaka, "Tsukiai no arachi," 7.

walls and become the latest topic of gossip in the *danchi* community.[26] Christie Kiefer's study described *danchi* couples occasionally going to a hotel "for bouts of sexual self-expression" out of the earshot of neighbors.[27] The metal door and concrete walls might discourage spontaneous visits from neighbors, but the very anonymity of the *danchi* community seemed to encourage eavesdropping and voyeurism. "Privacy" described a specific mode of relating—or not relating—to the community, not the reality of everyday life.

The *danchi* were exposed not only to the eyes and ears of neighbors but to the national and international gaze as well. *Danchi* apartment complexes were among the most scrutinized spaces in Japan of the 1950s and 1960s. Beyond the countless social science surveys and exposés in newspapers and women's magazines which analyzed all aspects of *danchi* life, they also became a "must-show" attraction to foreign diplomats and visiting dignitaries. In the late 1950s and early 1960s, ambassadors from Belgium, Australia, Italy, Canada, and the United States, engineers and housing authorities from Colombia, Bangkok, Bolivia, Guatemala, Chile, and officials from the World Bank and the United Nations were just some of the visitors who were taken to the outer reaches of Japan's developing suburbs to see the *danchi*.[28]

In the context of the Cold War, the *danchi* were offered as proof of Japan's recovery from war, commitment to improving living standards, and status as an "advanced" country. American Ambassador Douglas MacArthur II, nephew of General Douglas MacArthur, in three highly publicized visits to Tokyo-area *danchi* projects in December of 1957, commended the JHC for "stabilizing housing conditions" and thereby "stabilizing the country and warding off communism."[29] David Riesman, during a two-month lecture tour in Japan in 1961, took special interest in the *danchi* as the ultimate manifestation of "modern Japan," and his guides were equally eager to display them as evidence of Japan's very own "lonely crowd."[30] To observers from "developing" nations in Asia or

26. Anne Imamura, *Urban Japanese Housewives: At Home and in the Community* (Honolulu: University of Hawaii Press, 1987), 58-59.

27. Kiefer, 41-42. A famous comical representation of the utter *lack* of privacy in latter day apartment buildings appeared in the 1983 film *Family Game*—where husband and wife have to retreat to the family car—the newest "private" space—to talk or engage in a little bit of necking.

28. Visits were proudly chronicled in the JHC's inhouse magazine, *Ienami*, in the late 1950s and early 1960s.

29. *Ienami* (January 1958): 28.

30. Riesman observed: "In reflecting on the interest in *The Lonely Crowd* shown here, I have the feeling that the Japanese want to have all of the 'neuroses' of the West and

South America, the trips to the *danchi* were educational tours aimed at training third-world engineers in housing technology. Thus the *danchi* functioned to "place" Japan firmly in the first and developed world.

One of the most memorable *danchi* tours was by Japan's own Crown Prince Akihito and his new bride, Princess Michiko, to the Hibarigaoka complex located on the western outskirts of Tokyo in September of 1960. Hibarigaoka had opened to great fanfare the previous year. Built on the site of a former military aircraft manufacturer, it was the JHC's largest project to date with 2,714 apartments, as well as a park, a baseball field, tennis courts, an elementary school, a supermarket, a branch of city hall, a post office, and other amenities within its grounds. The JHC's first "mammoth" *danchi* and a "one set community,"[31] it became a prototype of the "new towns" it would build in growing numbers during the 1960s and 1970s.

It was no coincidence that it was the young crown prince and princess, not the patriarch Emperor Hirohito, who toured Hibarigaoka since room for the extended family had been designed out of this space. Residents were instructed to show the crown prince and princess "life as it really was" in the *danchi*, and so the couple was greeted by drying laundry and airing *futon* bedding hanging from apartment balconies. They were taken to see the 2DK apartment of advertising executive Mr. Hiroi and his wife, chosen as "typical" JHC housing residents and members of the "new middle class." Princess Michiko was immediately escorted to the kitchen that she proclaimed was "conveniently designed, healthy, and bright." The trip to Hibarigaoka, the JHC magazine noted, allowed the royal couple "to take a peek at the lives of citizens, from the kitchen to the bedroom."[32] If imperial viewership had previously focused on troops, weapons and national pageantry, in the postwar, the dining kitchen and refrigerator as symbols of a peaceful, everyday life were the objects commanding the imperial gaze.

At the end of their visit, the crown prince and princess had their photo taken standing on the apartment verandah, with t-shirts, diapers, and other laundry clearly visible drying on the balcony below. The caption under the photo, featured in the JHC's in-house magazine, noted: "in the contrast between the royal couple and the laundry below, you can feel the wave of a new age." (See Figure 9)[33] In

not be deprived of a single one." David Riesman and Evelyn Thompson Riesman, *Conversations in Japan: Modernization, Politics, and Culture* (New York: Basic Books, 1967), 8-9.

31. *Nihon jūtaku kōdan 20-nenshi*, 11.

32. Ibid.

33. *Ienami* (October 1960), 27. The laundry was subsequently cropped out of the photo for inclusion in the JHC's official ten-year history published in 1965.

a country where images and photographs of the emperor and imperial family were carefully controlled, the vision of the royal couple surrounded by diapers indeed suggested a departure from the past. This was a time when efforts were being made to rework the image of the imperial family, tarnished through years of war waged in the divine emperor's name, into something more suitable to the nation's post-WW II democratic image.[34] The widely publicized courtship and wedding of the crown prince and his popular and fashionable commoner bride the previous year had gone a long way toward updating the royal image and reviving interest in imperial affairs. After the wedding, details of their domestic life were daily fare in newspapers and women's magazines. The once inaccessible imperial family was recast as the image of the family next door—or, in this case, upstairs.

Visibility, Henri Lefebvre observed, is an attribute of modernist spatial practice. In the case of the modern apartment building, fragmented into "stack after stack of 'boxes for living,'" the result is that the "spectator-cum-tenant" is able to envision his or her apartment as part of the larger project; and envision themselves as metaphors, "images, signs, and signals . . . doubles of themselves in prettified, smiling, and happy poses."[35] In the case of the danchi projects, this logic must be expanded. As Japan's "show window of modern life,"[36] another larger group of spectators, of "spectators-cum-aspiring-tenants," looking in from the outside, could envision themselves as danchi dwellers. Alongside its modern dining kitchen and appliance-filled interior, "puraibashii," and even the various neuroses believed to infect danchi life were among the objects on display. For better or worse, they defined danchi life as "modern," Japan as modernizing, and made "private life" within the danchi an object of scrutiny, desire, and ultimately, concern.

Making Time

The danchi were often referred to as places dedicated to the "reproduction of the salary man." This phrase is apt because it captures the primary objective of the danchi space: labor and its reproduction. The danchi were all about work. They were built for the urban workforce, those who would "rebuild Japan." Their locations were defined in terms of commuting distances. As sites of "reproduction," studies showed the danchi to be places where children studied diligently

---

34. See Kenneth J. Ruoff, The People's Emperor: Democracy and the Japanese Monarchy, 1945–1995 (Cambridge, MA: Harvard University Asia Center, 2003).

35. Henri Lefebvre, The Production of Space (Malden, MA: Blackwell, 1991), 98.

36. Nihon jūtaku kōdan jū nenshi, 142.

to follow in their parents' footsteps as white-collar employees working for large corporations.[37] "Reproduction" also referred to the role of the home as a place for regenerating the salary man's energy on a daily basis so that he could return to his company ready to work again the following day.

The *danchi* interior was also designed to promote the efficient use of female labor, and space was carefully calibrated in terms of its function. In the words of Ann Waswo: "The ergonomics of daily life within the home—everything from slicing onions to undressing for a bath—had been studied and what was considered just the right amount of space for the activity provided."[38] So while the *danchi* represented efforts to create a space suitable to the age and Japan's place in the world, they also sought to coordinate time and space in an efficient, work-centered everydayness. These two projects were not unrelated: "rationalizing" the space of the home was believed key to its modernization. But just as the "therapeutic" space of the *danchi* created its own neuroses, the rational space of the *danchi* created its own irrationalities. Contemporary critiques suggest that the *danchi* were spatially and temporally dysfunctional—places where women had too much time on their hands, and where men had too little time and even less space. These dysfunctionalities produced cultural representations of the bored wife trapped in the home and the harried husband longing to escape from it.

Women's labor was a major concern of postwar reformers. Many of the debates over reforming and democratizing the home after the war centered on the issue of how best to rationalize women's labor and thereby create time for its reproduction.[39] The project of lightening housework was tied to goals of democratizing the home and "liberating" women from endless chores so as to give them more time for "self-cultivation." The quest for private space was thus closely linked with the quest for private time.

Lightening housework was also tied to the marketing of the various electrical appliances that were then just entering the Japanese marketplace. Simon Partner has written of how manufacturers of electrical appliances hawked their wares in the name of lofty postwar goals. One advertisement for Matsushita electrical goods indicated that Japan lagged far behind in the international leisure race, claiming that the average American housewife devoted four hours to housework and nine to leisure compared with the typical Japanese housewife who worked ten hours and had only two hours of free time. A Matsushita electric rice cooker,

---

37. Hashizume Sadao, *Kawariyuku katei to kyōiku: danchi bunka ga yotei suru mono* (Tokyo: Reimei shobō, 1962).

38. Waswo, *Housing in Postwar Japan*, 81.

39. These debates are discussed extensively in Chapter One.

the ad suggested, would help Japan close the leisure gap.[40] Once again, statistics suggested that the *danchi* housewife was closest to the American standard. The 1960 economic White Paper on National Life reported that *danchi* housewives had a third more "cultural, social time" compared with the average salary man housewife in the Tokyo area and fifty percent more leisure time than the housewives of "ordinary workers" nationwide.[41] The ever-shrinking number of hours women devoted to housework thus became another barometer of Japan's "lifestyle revolution." And the goal of reducing housework was finally accomplished by privatizing it on a household basis through the acquisition of the "labor-saving" devices produced by Matsushita and other companies. Many of the new things entering the home after the war—from washing machines and refrigerators to new instant foods and ready-made clothes—were sold in the name of reducing housework and "liberating" women for other activities. In this way, advertisers suggested, the new consumption was made productive—it "made time."[42]

In the opinion of some critics, however, new labor saving devices made *too* much time. "Rationalization" was a worthy goal in industry where profit was the objective, claimed writer Uramatsu Samitarō, but in the home, the problem

---

40. Described in Simon Partner, *Assembled in Japan: Electrical Goods and the Making of the Japanese Consumer* (Berkeley: University of California Press, 1999), 154.

41. The average salary man housewife in the Tokyo area spent nine hours and two minutes per day doing housework and had four hours and thirty-one minutes of "cultural, social time" (*bunka-teki, shakai-teki jikan*), while the average *danchi* housewife spent six hours and fifty-two minutes working and had almost the same amount of time, six hours and forty-one minutes, to do as she pleased. *Kokumin seikatsu hakusho, Shōwa 35-nen*, 144-45.

42. Many have noted that the new appliances created new standards of cleanliness as well as the possibility of "*nagara*" chores—doing more than one chore at once— thus adding to women's workload. Even so, appliances such as washing machines, rice cookers, and vacuum cleaners have been widely credited with reducing hours devoted to housework. Hours full-time housewives devote to housework have decreased steadily since the 1950s. A study conducted by the Labor Ministry in 1949 found that the average housewife devoted ten hours and sixteen minutes to housework. By 1959, for salary man housewives, the amount of time had dropped to nine hours and two minutes. A study conducted by the prime minister's office in 1973 found that housewives spent six hours and forty-three minutes in housework. Figures cited in Kōdo seichō o kangaeru kai, ed., *Kōdo seichō to nihonjin part II katei-hen: kazoku no seikatsu no monogatari* (Tokyo: Nihon edeitā sukūru shuppanbun, 1985), 204-205.

was "what to *do* with the labor and time saved by the washing machine." If one didn't use these effectively, he noted, "you might save [labor and time] on one hand but waste them on the other."[43] Critics in the 1950s believed that this was precisely what was happening: housewives were squandering the time "saved" by their new appliances. This question was taken up in a long-ranging debate on the role of the housewife in the mid- and late-1950s. In a series of articles published in the women's journal, *Shufu kōron* between 1955 and 1959 and subsequently labeled the "housewife debate" (*shufu ronsō*), intellectuals and readers discussed the role of the housewife in the transformed postwar home. The debate was sparked by an article by Ishigaki Ayako titled "On the Housewife as a Second Profession" (*Shufu to iu dai-ni shokugyō ron*) published in the February 1955 issue of the journal. Ishigaki started by criticizing young women who chose professions according to where they could meet the most promising future husband and who left the workforce after marriage to begin their "second professions" as housewives. Although this was the professed goal of many young women in the workforce, Ishigaki noted a profound "discontent" among housewives with their daily lives at home. This discontent was the product of a historic shift in the function of the housewife due to the changing role of the home in capitalist society. Whereas the housewife of pre-industrial society was a productive and equal member of the family—weaving, sewing, or making soy sauce—these tasks had all been commodified and taken over by machines and factories. Now even housework was being taken over by machines: "Modern civilization," she noted, "has been mobilized to omit the labor of the housewife." The housewife had become fundamentally a consumer and "parasite" of men. While they complained they were "busy, busy," Ishigaki claimed they were in fact idle and wasted their time gossiping with other bored housewives. Wasting this "precious time of human life," housewives stagnated while their husbands who interacted with the world everyday continued to grow. Ishigaki's conclusion was that women should remain in the workforce or, at the very least, find meaningful ways to spend their time in service to "society."[44]

The debate that resulted from Ishigaki's provocative article covered a full range of opinions about the value and function of the housewife in postwar Japan.[45] Ethnographer Umesao Tadao agreed with Ishigaki's analysis, noting that

---

43. Uramatsu Samitarō, "Gōrika, ryūkō, kakumei," in *Kurashi no techō* 40 (1957): 166.

44. Ishigaki Ayako, "Shufu to iu dai-ni shokugyō ron," in Ueno Chizuko, ed., *Shufu ronsō o yomu I* (Tokyo: Keisō shobō, 1989), 6-11.

45. This rich debate has been published in its entirety in a volume edited by Ueno Chizuko cited above. Also see Mizuda Tamae, "Kaji rōdō ronsō," in *Onna no sengo*

the housewife had "lost the meaning of her existence" and become "superfluous" as machines had replaced her labor.[46] Many more writers disagreed with Ishigaki, however, arguing that the housewife she described was still a minor exception in Japan. "Hasn't Ishigaki mistaken Japan for America?" asked Ōkuma Nobuyuki. "[Her description] applies to only a very small number of people in Japan above the middle class."[47] Another participant agreed: ". . . the fruits of capitalism have not reached the vast majority of households that need them. And the ordinary Japanese housewife continues doing her sundry household chores in a house that is beyond all attempts to organize it."[48]

   Although the *danchi* housewife was not mentioned by name in the "housewife debate," in the popular discourse on *danchi* life, she was the hyper-representation of the housewife of Ishigaki's critique. Although many *danchi* housewives actually had jobs outside the home, took in piecework, or were involved in various volunteer and community activities,[49] the typical portrayal of the "*danchi-zuma*" was of someone with way too much time on her hands. Despite her lighter-than-average housework burden and her higher-than-average proportion of "free time," critics suggested that she did nothing useful with all this highly desired time, squandering it in idle gossip or excessive shopping. Indeed, the housewife's boredom was considered one major source of her various psychoses and the overall dysfunctionality of the *danchi* community. "Just what does the *danchi* housewife do?" asked Takenaka Tsutomu. "She sends off her husband at seven and finishes straightening and cleaning by ten. Then, for women with no children, the time until three is the time of the white devil . . . She waits for her husband. All day, she waits."[50] Some *danchi* housewives reportedly stayed "closed

shi II: Shōwa 30-nendai, Asahi jyānaru, ed. (Tokyo: Asahi shimbunsha, 1985), 205-212; and Kōdo seichō o kangaeru kai, ed., *Kōdo seichō to nihonjin,* 198-200.

46. Umesao Tadao, "Tsuma muyō ron," in Ueno, ed., 201.

47. Ōkuma Nobuyuki, "Shufu no shisō," in ibid., 139.

48. "Kaji rōdō wa shufu no tenshoku de wa nai," in ibid., 40.

49. Anne Imamura's ethnography of women living in the danchi provides a much more nuanced understanding of their involvements than these stereotypes. See *Urban Japanese Housewives: At Home and in the Community* (Honolulu: University of Hawai'i Press, 1987).

50. Takenaka, 20-21. This question is what motivated Anne Imamura to conduct a study of Japanese housewives in the mid-1970s. Watching the daily routines of *danchi* women in a Tokyo suburb and noting that their husbands were seldom home, Imamura wrote: "I knew that keeping such a small apartment clean could not occupy a woman's entire day and that, especially after the children were in school, the housewives must have many hours to fill. What, I wondered, did they

up" inside their apartments, staring at their "televisions, living rooms, and lace curtains," victims of *danchi* neurosis.[51] Others had "stairwell meetings" (*kaidan kaigi*) with neighbors—modern day gossip sessions that, critics were fond of observing, had replaced the traditional gossip sessions around the well (*itabata kaigi*). Others poured all of their time and energy into their children. The *danchi* housewife, Christie Kiefer noted, was "Education Mama with a vengence."[52]

Ariyoshi Sawako, in her novel *Yūhigaoka Apartment Complex Number 3* (*Yūhigaoka sango-kan*), provided a scathing critique of *danchi* housewives with too much time on their hands. Ariyoshi is better known for novels such as *The River Ki* (*Kinokawa*) and *The Twilight Years* (*Kōkotsu no hito*), which feature strong and intelligent female protagonists. The females that inhabit "Complex Number 3" are far from strong and intelligent, however. Most are petty, backbiting and neurotic, including the protagonist, Tokieda Otoko. After quickly becoming the target of *danchi* gossip, Otoko spends most of her days inside, cleaning her already spotless apartment and managing the education of her teenage son. In her boredom, she looks through her husband's and son's belongings and makes startling discoveries: pornographic magazines in her son's room; and a matchbook from a hostess bar in her husband's pocket. As she confronts her son and husband, they rail at the violation of their "privacy" and conspire against her—buying a desk that locks to keep their personal items from her prying eyes. Shut in her apartment by gossipy neighbors and shut out of the lives of her son and husband, Otoko's life in the *danchi* is portrayed as alienating and lonely.[53]

Journalist and self-described "*danchi* critic" (*danchi hyōronka*) Shioda Maruo, suggested that once all of the material desires of the *danchi* housewives had been met, they would be left with "only one: unfulfilled sexual desire." It was only a matter of time, he predicted, before *danchi* housewives, like bored suburban housewives in America, would begin to fill the "long, long hours" until their husbands came home with illicit sexual liaisons.[54] The real sexual habits of *danchi* (and American!) housewives notwithstanding, the image of

---

do all day?" Imamura, 2.

51. Ibid.

52. Kiefer, 39. On *danchi* women and children's education, see Hashizume.

53. The novel was originally serialized in the *Mainichi Shimbun* between April and December of 1970. Ariyoshi Sawako, *Yūhigaoka sango-kan* (Tokyo: Shinchō-sha, 1971).

54. Shioda Maruo, "Kōgai danchi fujin no kokkyū to fuman," *Fujin kōron* (May 1964): 303-306.

the lonely and isolated *danchi* housewife soon became the material of sexual fantasy. In the early 1970s, Roman Porn developed an entire genre of "*danchi*-housewife pornography" featuring scenes of "what she is thinking about in her tiny apartment within the mammoth *danchi*, as she waits for her tired husband to return."[55] Depictions of *danchi* housewives in other novels and films also often showed them as lonely, bored, and sexually promiscuous. The male protagonist of Abe Kobo's 1967 detective novel, *The Ruined Map*, is dangerously drawn to the mysterious *danchi* housewife sitting behind the yellow curtains of her apartment, smoking cigarettes and drinking beer day and night. Although he is unable to remember her face after leaving her apartment or even when she leaves the room to refill her beer, he is drawn to the sexually charged space behind the yellow curtains like a moth to a flame. A more recent novel by Tatematsu Wahei, *Distant Thunder*, features a *danchi* housewife who has a series of wild affairs with local farmers. In both novels, the protagonists, men from outside the *danchi*, are destroyed by their affairs. The detective in *The Ruined Map* is drawn into the anonymous vortex of the *danchi* and loses his identity; the farmer in *Distant Thunder* murders the *danchi* temptress and ends up in jail.[56] In the cultural imagination, *danchi* housewives (indeed, women in general), with too much time on their hands spelled trouble.[57]

The 1963 film *She and He* focused directly on the problem of the *danchi* housewife. Directed by documentary filmmaker Hani Susumu, the film's gritty, disjointed, black and white camera work gives a feeling of reportage to the drama. Like Hani's other films of the early 1960s which focused on juvenile delinquency and other social issues, *She and He* had a definite social agenda. In an article published just after the film was released, Hani warned against the isolationism of the new family of "only two" represented by the *danchi*. Isolationism was spreading beyond the walls of the *danchi*, Hani warned, and

55. Imamura Shōhei, et al., ed., *Nihon eiga no genzai*, Vol. 7 (Tokyo: Iwanami shoten, 1988), 303.

56. Abe Kobo, *The Ruined Map*, translated by E. Dale Saunders (New York: Kodansha International, 1993); also Tatematsu Wahei, *Distant Thunder: A Novel of Contemporary Japan*, translated by Lawrence J. Howell and Hikaru Morimoto (Rutland, VT: Charles E. Tuttle Company, 1999). *Distant Thunder* (Japanese title *Enrai*) was originally published in 1980. It is set in rural Japan at the height of the "bubble economy" and describes what happens to members of a farming community after they sell their land for the construction of a *danchi* community.

57. This was not a new cultural trope. Too much time was one of the problems of Tanizaki's Naomi as well.

"psychological metal doors are being built at the entrances of our homes."[58] The message of Hani's film was that it was up to women, with their greatly increased opportunities to become involved with the outside world, to "renew" links with society. "A new consciousness of human relationships," he insisted, "will take root not in the husband but in the wife."[59]

As the order of pronouns in the title of the film suggests, the protagonist of *She and He* is the wife, not the husband. "She," a woman named Ishikawa Naoko, is in many ways a typical *danchi* housewife. She lives in a modern apartment replete with an appliance-filled dining kitchen, private bath, television, washing machine, and big double bed. She wears crisp, Western-style dresses, cheerfully sees her husband off in the morning and patiently awaits his return in the evening. But in other ways, she is the complete antithesis of the stereotypical *danchi* housewife. Far from isolating herself "behind metal doors," Naoko interjects herself into the lives of the people around her—knocking on strangers' doors to return lost toys, innocently inviting the laundry man into her apartment for a shower and change of clothes after he falls in the mud, and intervening in children's games to teach them the proper rules. The story revolves around Naoko's relationship with a ragpicker named Ikono and his blind, adopted daughter, Hanako, who are from the slum community just down the hill from the *danchi*. Unlike other residents who chase off the ragpickers who pick scrap metal from their garbage and push to have authorities build a fence around the slum, Naoko refuses to recognize any separation between the *danchi* and the slum. She goes there day after day to visit Ikono and Hanako and eventually invites them into her home.

Despite Hani's insistence that it was up to women to "renew" links with society, the message of the film is that these attempts were absolutely futile. Naoko's neighbors do not return her friendly gestures; in fact they gossip behind her back. Her attempts to referee the children's games are ignored and result in her being dragged into the dirt and having her blouse torn. Her new friend, the ragpicker Ikono, betrays her trust and confidence when he steals a trophy from her entryway after a visit to her home. And her efforts to nurse an ailing Hanako back to health end disastrously when the child is removed from her adopted father and taken to a charity hospital. More than a parable of the cold, impersonal life in the *danchi*, *She and He* is the story of a woman desperately resisting the closed life of "only two." Toward the end of the film, Naoko discloses to her husband that through her relationship with the ragpickers, she had been trying

---

58. Hani Susumu, "Danchi wa katei seikatsu o kaeru ka," *Fujin kōron*, September 1963, 59.

59. Ibid., 63.

to "find the confidence" to have his child. Rejecting her husband's insistence that what happens in the slum has nothing to do with them, she responds: "They are important to us." The film contains a dire message for women with the kind of "social consciousness" Hani and others called for. When the ragpickers' slum is razed to make way for a new golf course at the end of the film, Naoko finally has nothing to do but stay home. In the final scene, Naoko lies in bed beside her husband, staring at the ceiling. "She" has finally been contained within the concrete walls of the *danchi*.

"Geography matters to gender," Doreen Massey has argued.[60] The suburban community is a perfect example of how space functions as a form of social control. The "liberated" *danchi* housewife with her key and labor-saving devices was at the same time confined to distant suburban communities that made it difficult for her to engage in anything but part-time work or piece work at home. Distance reinforced and justified a gendered division of labor. The distance of *danchi* communities from city centers added hours to men's workdays and meant that they were seldom home. Busy husbands who devoted endless hours to company and commuting, required someone else to perform labor in the home and see to the "reproduction" of their labor. In the words of Esashi Akiko: "As populations began to concentrate in cities in the early 1960s, the salary man had no choice but to commute long distances. Added to long work hours in the company and factory, they returned home seeking a little rest and to store up energy for the following day. It was the role of the housewife on the home front to send those corporate warriors back to the battle field the next day."[61] It is ironic but telling that gendered differences were being reinforced at the very moment that class differences were being denied through the "middle-class myth."[62] Both supported and made possible high- speed economic growth.

Lost in Space

The division between home and workplace, women's roles and men's roles, was reinforced by what Nishikawa Yūko called the "genderization" of inside and outside, private and public spaces.[63] One result of the project of redesigning

---

60. Doreen Massey, *Space, Place and Gender* (Minneapolis: University of Minneapolis Press, 1994), 177.

61. Quoted in Kōdo seichō o kangaeru kai, ed., *Kōdo seichō to nihonjin*, 210.

62. Elaine Tyler May makes this observation of the postwar suburban home in America. It holds equally true for Japan. May, 162.

63. Nishikawa Yūko, "Otoko no ie, onna no ie, seibetsu no nai heya," in Wakita Haruko and S.B. Hanley, ed., *Jendā no nihon-shi, volume II* (Tokyo: Tokyo daigaku shuppankai, 1995), 621. Tomiko Yoda argues that the "middle-class matricentric

the "feudalistic" Japanese home, she noted, was the elimination of what had formerly been "privileged spaces of the husband" (*otto no tokken-teki kūkan*). The former formal *tatami* room was where the head of the household received guests and the study the place he retreated to be alone. The postwar nLDK space eliminated both of these, replacing them with the dining room and living room, both widely considered "women's domains."[64] So as women were being "shut out" of society, or, in the words of Imamura, separated "from anything resembling a community,"[65] men were being shut out of the home. A common criticism of postwar living space was that it provided no space for men.[66] The JHC *danchi,* the suburban "island of only women and children" and originator of the DK and LDK, was the prototype of this "feminized" space.

So if *time* and what to *do* with it was a particular problem of the *danchi* housewife; *space* and where to *be* was a particular problem of the *danchi* husband. According to Shioda Maruo, this was why men and women reacted entirely differently to *danchi* life. "To women, he noted, "[the *danchi*] is a 'new town.' To men, it is a 'bed town.'"[67] Corresponding to the stereotype of the *danchi* housewife as bored and sexually promiscuous, was the stereotype of the *danchi* husband as an outsider, "Sunday visitor" or someone who was lost or loathed coming home. There were comical tales of husbands returning late at night to identical but wrong apartments or panicking after arriving home drunk, having forgotten the number of their apartment. Takenaka described his reaction after forgetting his apartment number: "I looked around but all I saw were identical buildings with the same standard staircases and windows . . . Fifteen thousand people living in almost identical 'boxes' . . . I suddenly envisioned a beehive.

domesticity" that emerged in Japan in the 1960s was "far from unique." She continues, "Rather, many of its features are typical of those found in a society in the process of industrial capitalism, the construction of home as 'personal space' (of affect and psyche) existing outside the relation of economic production, and the identification of home/family with women." What was peculiar to Japan, she notes, was the degree to which this ideal became generalized to Japanese of all social classes. Tomiko Yoda, "The Rise and Fall of Maternal Society: Gender, Labor and Capital in Contemporary Japan," in Tomiko Yoda and Harry Harootunian, ed., *Japan After Japan: Social and Cultural Life From the Recessionary 1990s to the Present* (Durham: Duke University Press, 2006), 250.

64. Ibid.

65. Imamura, 3.

66. See Waswo, 129-130. Also Miyawaki Mayumi, *Otoko to onna no ie* (Tokyo: Shinchōsha, 1998).

67. Shioda Maruo, "Danchi seikatsu no kiken na kankei," *Fujin kōron,* (April 1966), 152.

Bees have a homing instinct but people in the *danchi* have, first and foremost, a 'number' to identify where they live. If they should forget that number, they become vagabonds, just like me."[68]

In Yamakawa Masao's 1960 short story, "The Talisman" (*Omamori*) the standardized space of the *danchi* was not only a place where salarymen got physically lost but where they lost their identities, as well. His salary man protagonist Sekiguchi returns home one night to find another man in his apartment. The man looks so much like Sekiguchi that his own wife does not notice and indeed, our protagonist, peering in at the man sitting in his kitchen, begins to doubt his own identity: "'I' was paging through the newspaper . . . Another 'I' was in there. But if that's the case, this man standing here with the blank look on his face . . . who was this 'I'? Which one was the real 'I'? And where should this 'I' go home to?"[69]

Sekiguchi and his wife had won the lottery to live in the *danchi* and "it was just like we'd gone to heaven . . . finally liberated from others' eyes and noises, all we wanted was a room with a key."[70] Yet after this incident, Sekiguchi begins to feel uncomfortable in his new home. "I know that people in the *danchi* live in standardized spaces. But what I realized is that without knowing it, even our lives had become the same . . . not just the exterior aspects but down to the core."[71] He becomes paralyzed imagining total temporal and spatial synchronicity within the *danchi* and his every move being replicated above and below him. "You go to the toilet. And at that moment, in the room above and below you, you can hear the toilet flushing." Whenever his wife called his name, he heard "all the wives in the *danchi* calling out in a great chorus."[72]

Sekiguchi begins to search for a way to differentiate himself from the mass of other salary men inhabiting the *danchi*, insisting, "I am not him. I am not one of the salaried men who look like me. I am not one of endless numbers of 'me'! I am ME!"[73] He begins carrying a "talisman"—a stick of dynamite—to make himself unique from the others. The story ends as Sekiguchi hears news of an explosion on a bus near the *danchi* the previous evening that had killed three people. A man from the *danchi* had been carrying dynamite in his shoe.Sekiguchi's quest

---

68. Takenaka, 3-4.
69. Yamakawa Masao, "Omamori," in *Yamakawa Masao zenshū 3* (Tokyo: Chikuma shobō, 2000), 266. This story has been translated into English: Yamakawa Masao, "The Talisman," in *Life* (September 11, 1964).
70. Ibid., 264.
71. Ibid., 268.
72. Ibid., 269.
73. Ibid., 271.

for a unique self-identity within the homogenized space of the *danchi* had failed.

The tropes of getting lost and losing one's identity were critiques of the standardization of living space. But they were equally a critique of salary man life, in general. The fantasy of getting lost or becoming a vagabond—not by accident but on purpose—has been a major counter-theme to dominant images of responsible, hardworking salary man life.[74] Popular author Ishikawa Tatsuzō wrote several "salary man novels" in the 1950s, each depicting downtrodden salary men trapped between the tyranny of boss and wife. The protagonist of one novel longs for some difference in his unchanging daily routine moving between home and office: "Working in the office was disagreeable; working for a whole month and getting paid on pay day was no less stupid. Boarding the same train every day to return to the same house where he found a wife looking no different from the day before in bed with that same sulky look on her face, what stupidity all this was! He wanted to go home to a different house and find a different woman waiting for him once in a while."[75] The salary man protagonist of another novel ponders finding freedom by getting lost: "For human beings, I think, it is necessary for them to be missing now and then; otherwise they will always be chained to the world around them . . . In such a rigid way of life, there is one way, only one way, to enjoy freedom . . . and that is to run away somewhere by yourself. Yes, to get lost completely!"[76] The only way to escape the "rigid" salary man life was to enter a liminal space that could not be located on the spatio-temporal grid of labor-driven everyday life. It was the bar, pachinko parlor, or Turkish bath where, the detective in *The Ruined Map* noted, men went to "play the game of missing persons."[77]

Getting lost is the central theme of Abe Kobo's novel *The Ruined Map*. It is a detective novel about a young private investigator hired to locate an apartment resident who has vanished into a small manhole on the *danchi* compound. The novel is filled with men who have walked away from their conventional lives.

---

74. One example is the long-running series *Otoko wa tsurai yo* (It Is Tough to Be a Man) about the travels and adventures of the itinerant *teki-ya*, Tora. Novelist Inoue Hisashi, discussing reasons for the popularity of the series, noted: "[Tora] was free, he could go where he wanted, when he wanted. These days, seventy percent of adult males are salaried employees, limiting their own freedom in exchange for salaries. They envy the carefree Tora and go to the movie theater to see him." In Inoue Hisashi, *Tora-san taizen* (Tokyo: Chikuma shobō, 1993), 1.

75. Ishikawa Tatsuzō, *Evil for Pleasure*, translated by Paul T. Konya (Tokyo: Yohan Publications, Inc., 1972), 65.

76. Ishikawa Tatsuzō, *Resistance at Forty-Eight*, translated by Kazuma Nakayama (Tokyo: The Hokuseido Press, 1960), 30-31.

77. Abe Kobo, 225.

The investigator himself has left his wife and former life to work for a two-bit detective agency. During his investigation, he discovers a taxi company that operates as a front for men who have "disappeared" and now spend their days "driving other people around for their purposes." One of the disappeared drivers comments: "I can't understand how you can assume, as if it were a matter of course, that there is some right that lets you seize a man who has gone off of his own free will."[78] At the end of the novel, the detective suffers what we suspect to be the lost man's fate. After spending the night with the missing man's wife in the *danchi*, he leaves the apartment only to discover that he knows neither *where* nor *who* he is. Now a detective on his own case, he searches his pockets and wallet for clues to his own identity. In his disoriented state, he gets in a taxi to search for something familiar but is terrified at the sight of the immense housing development of four-story apartment buildings. In a panic, he screams at the driver: "'Turn back, quick! Get out of this development as quick as you can!' I had to get to a place where freedom of space was secure. If I had anything to do with a place like this, I would lose even space, to say nothing of time."[79] In the end, the detective decides to remain lost, to "forget looking for a way to the past." As he evades the woman from the *danchi*, who is now looking for him in the same way she had searched for her lost husband, the detective concludes: "Nothing would be served by being found. What I needed now was a world I myself had chosen by my own free will. She searched; I hid."[80]

The Ruined Map is an unconventional mystery novel. If the mystery novel is the quintessential modernist genre in which the detective puts clues together like puzzle pieces to create a complete and coherent picture of a crime to restore "order" to a temporarily broken society, Abe's novel represents the modernist project gone awry. Scenes are not arranged sequentially, clues lead nowhere, the mystery is never solved, and the detective ends up losing himself. It is as if Abe has "ruined" our "map" for reading and interpreting a mystery novel.[81] This is at least partially a reflection of Abe's distinctive style, but the larger issue is the novel's setting in the *danchi*. Abe depicts the *danchi* as a temporal vacuum—a place where only the now exists. It is a place of utter spatial standardization and temporal synchronization in which "within a five-minute period hundreds of filing cabinets are unlocked at one click and swarms

---

78. Ibid., 115.
79. Ibid., 295.
80. Ibid., 298-99.
81. I am indebted to James Hyre for this insight. *Tokyo: City as History* seminar, New York University, Spring 2001. Also, the comments of Naveen Koshy and other members of the seminar greatly enhanced my reading of the novel.

of different but indistinguishable workers, like a wall of water released from the floodgates of a dam, suddenly throng the streets."[82] The temporal vacuum of the *danchi* makes it an impossible setting for a mystery novel because it is a place where it is virtually impossible to reconstruct the past. *The Ruined Map* suggested the ultimate danger of life in the *danchi* was not getting lost but losing one's identity—none other than one's past—in the routinized life in the labyrinth of identical buildings.

Representations of the *danchi* tapped into fundamental anxieties about the routine of work-driven everyday life. But it also suggested that there was slippage between time and space that offered the possibility of "getting lost" if even temporarily (or through the fantasy of fiction). Separate from the "leisure time" that was integral to the cycle of labor and its reproduction, these small gaps revealed if not the possibility, at least the desire, to find a place truly outside the twenty-four hour, one-day unit of work-centered everyday life.

Searching for "Home"

The home is often idealized as a refuge against change, in the words of David Harvey, "a private museum to guard against the ravages of time-space compression" caused by capitalism.[83] One of the most famous idealizations of the Japanese home was Watsuji Tetsurō's 1935 book on climate and culture which argued that the industrial development and division of labor that were reshaping the rest of Japanese society had left the home a "tiny centre of unity in the middle of the wide world." [84] Though challenged by reformers such as Nishiyama Uzō and Hamaguchi Miho, who recognized that capitalism had fully infiltrated the home and changed people's living habits, the conception of the home as "refuge" and locus of tradition had deep roots.[85]

Yet in postwar discourse, the *danchi* fulfilled an entirely different function: that of a cultural/social pressure chamber and laboratory for measuring the effects of modernization and change. According to critic Isoda Kōichi, the establishment of the JHC and the creation of the *danchi* totally changed "domestic sensibilities." On the one hand, Isoda claimed, the *danchi* had made it possible for "the merits of postwar civil law to penetrate to the mass level in the

---

82. Abe Kobo, 20.

83. David Harvey, *The Condition of Postmodernity* (Cambridge, MA: Blackwell Publishers, Inc., 1997), 292.

84. Watsuji Tetsurō, *Climate and Culture: A Philosophical Study*, translation of *Fūdō* by Geoffrey Bownas (Tokyo: The Hokuseido Press, 1961), 165.

85. See Chapter One for an analysis of these ideas.

form of housing."[86] But with the creation of this functional and "sanitary" living space, the home had been "emptied of its status as myth and assigned the status of dwelling."[87] Postwar Japan, Isoda suggested, was in need of new myths, best expressed through literature. "Might the new generation of authors write novels that make high-rise housing their 'home' [*kokyō*]? The question of whether the *danchi* can obtain the status of 'home' [*kokyō*] will decide not merely the course of literature, but of culture itself."[88] Isoda's use of the word "*kokyō*" is telling for it refers not to a physical structure or house but to the more mythical ideal of "homeland" or "native place," traditionally situated in the time and space of the Japanese countryside. The *danchi* were none other than a radical rejection of the "*kokyō*" of old, the "native place" represented by the countryside. In fact, it was "'shame' toward agricultural life," claimed Isoda, that led postwar Japanese to embrace the Westernized *danchi* space in the first place.[89] Having physically and ideologically displaced the former "*kokyō*," could the *danchi* possibly become a place where meaning and myth would be restored to postwar life?

A new generation of authors and filmmakers did choose the *danchi* as the setting for their stories but they certainly did not find their "home" there. In fact, the *danchi* generally represented the antithesis of home in films and novels. They were depicted as places devoid of history, devoid of culture, indeed, devoid of life. More than anything else, they tended to function as a device for expressing loss and waxing nostalgic about steadily disappearing tradition and culture. This loss occurs not only within the *danchi*. The *danchi* play the role of modernization itself: consuming the landscape, taking over the countryside, and displacing and destroying older and culturally richer ways of life. In this way, literary depictions of the *danchi* were often what Marilyn Ivy has called "discourses of the vanishing," that articulate what culture *is* at the moment and site of its "disappearance."[90] In the film *She and He*, the slum community below the *danchi* is displaced to build a golf course. In the novel *Distant Thunder*, an agricultural village is dispersed and destroyed by housing projects that buy up and build on its land. In each, what has been displaced are entire ways of life—the meanings of which only become clear in contrast with the *danchi*. In the slum and among the former villagers there is still a semblance of community life. The ragpickers in *She and He* gather at night to cook, eat, drink, and dance around the fire while in the *danchi*, families

86. Isoda Kōichi, 52.

87. Ibid., 55.

88. Ibid., 63. I have used Alan Tansman's translation of Isoda.

89. Ibid., 52.

90. Marilyn Ivy, *Discourses of the Vanishing: Modernity, Phantasm, Japan* (Chicago: University of Chicago Press, 1995).

of "only two" sit in their individual apartments watching television or each other. The villagers in *Distant Thunder* hold an old-fashioned three-day wedding—a raucous, drunken affair—while the women from the *danchi* watch curiously from a distance. The village and slum appear anachronistic, disorderly, and far from "rational," but life and human relationships there, these two works suggest, are richer and more meaningful than modern life in the *danchi*.

Depictions of the *danchi* in film and literature complicate notions of modernization as an even process of spatial and temporal convergence. The advance of the *danchi* and accompanying infrastructure over the landscape is met not with desire and willingness to converge, but with antagonism and resistance. Hani's film has several disturbing scenes of war "games" between the children from the *danchi* and from the slum. It quickly becomes evident that these are no games. The children charge at each other with sticks and rocks—this is literally class warfare. Naoko tries to intervene and force "rules" on the children, but the differences between the two sides are irreconcilable. Similarly, her attempts to convert the ragpicker Ikono to a salary man lifestyle fail. He rejects the job Naoko's husband offers him, saying angrily, "Don't take this work from me." Not everyone envied and desired *danchi* life after all.

Neither were they able to emulate it. The former farmers in *Distant Thunder* have the outward trappings of modern life. They live in costly houses that opportunistic real estate agents coaxed them into building after they sold their land to the *danchi*. But they do not know how to inhabit a modern house. The protagonist's grandma crouches on chairs as if sitting on *tatami*; the family covers their leather sofa with a *futon*, and the house is covered with grime and dust. The family is oblivious to modern habits of hygiene, and its living habits are unchanged even in this new, modern space.

Distant Thunder suggests that the effects of the *danchi* on the lives of the people around them are much more insidious, transforming life not from the outside in but from the inside out. The arrival of the *danchi* destroys the old village as well as its families. Grandma, as the keeper of tradition and all of the old stories, plays the role of history. But she is reduced to irrelevance after the family sells its land. She spends her days in front of a blaring television, babbling like a crazy woman about the past or chanting incantations to the gods as she had done as a young midwife, but her stories and prayers go unheard. Protagonist Mitsuo's father loses his moral bearings. He runs off with a barmaid, and is last seen wearing a pink negligee, lipstick, and rouge. His best friend has an affair with a woman from the *danchi*, but eventually kills her, lands in jail, and destroys his family. All of this misfortune, Mitsuo believes, was brought on by the *danchi*:

"It's all the fault of those damned apartments," he claims when he hears of the murder. "The bastards came and brought us nothing but evil."[91]

Mitsuo assumes the mantle of tradition after his grandmother dies. He refuses to sell the family's tiny remaining plot of land and insists on making his livelihood on the soil—even if it is only contained within a hothouse for growing tomatoes. His traditional wedding at the end of the novel brings the old village back together like the old days. However, this reunion will not stem the tide of change. As Mitsuo observes repeatedly, there is no village left. It remains only as a memory and an ideal. At the end of the novel, Mitsuo stands listening to the rumble of thunder off in the distance and concludes: "Though still some distance off, there could be no doubt that a storm was on its way."[92] For even as Mitsuo continued farming and Ikono continued his life as a ragpicker, their lives and livelihoods had been irrevocably altered by the appearance of the *danchi,* and, ironically, dependent upon them. Mitsuo depends on the women from the *danchi* to buy his tomatoes and Ikono makes a living picking tin cans from the *danchi* garbage to sell for scrap metal. *The Ruined Map* also exposes a shadowy underworld of unruly labor gangs, prostitution, and makeshift drinking establishments dependent upon the construction of the *danchi.* Perhaps the most fundamental critique of postwar modernization is to be found in these works of fiction. All of them suggest that modernization had different effects on different people, perpetuating and producing new disparities rather than smoothing old ones away.[93]

In many fictional accounts of the *danchi,* Japan suffers the fate of the detective in Abe's novel. It loses its identity and past as traditions and rich communal life are displaced by anonymous apartment blocks. While these were the very traditions and communal relations that had been criticized and judged dispensable in early postwar critiques, works such as these suggested that nothing had taken their place; that the *danchi* had *not* become a new "home" after all. Nostalgia for *danchi* life that emerged in the early twenty-first century would reconsider this conclusion, but to novelists and other observers in the midst of rapid social, spatial, and economic change, the *danchi* became a device for describing and then mourning what "home" was at the very moment of its perceived vanishing.

---

91. Tatematsu Wahei, 202.

92. Ibid., 263.

93. Selling land also made many farmers rich. *Distant Thunder* was written in 1980 as Japan was entering the "bubble economy" years. The novel continually suggests that the farmers brought their woes upon themselves. They had exchanged their lives and traditions for a pot of gold.

Chapter Five

Futures Past

These ruins are our own, and the society they indict is ours as well.

John Patrick Leary[1]

The Housing Reverse Course

The early 1970s would bring an end to the era of high-speed economic growth as Japan, along with other industrialized nations, entered its first serious recession since the end of World War II. The nation's average ten percent annual growth rate of the 1960s had slowed to half that by the early 1970s, and in 1974 the economy did not grow but contracted. The oil embargo in 1973 led to a near tripling of fuel costs, triggering dramatic inflation and creating shortages of consumer goods. The United State's sudden normalization of relations with China and equally abrupt abrogation of fixed dollar-yen exchange rates, the so-called "Nixon shocks," threatened to redefine Japan's political and economic relationship with its closest ally and sponsor. A sense of economic and political crisis engendered deep feelings of anxiety as people recognized anew the extent of Japan's interdependence on the global economy, especially its reliance on foreign oil.[2] People's confidence in both the public and private sectors was shaken as large corporations and the government attempted to shirk responsibility for

1. John Patrick Leary, "Detroitism," in *Guernica: A Magazine of Art & Politics*, January 15, 2011, http://www.guernicamag.com/. Accessed August 1, 2014.
2. Laura E. Hein, "Growth Versus Success: Japan's Economic Policy in Historical Perspective," in Andrew Gordon, ed., *Postwar Japan as History*, (Berkeley: University of California Press, 1993), 116.

industrial pollution and its shocking human costs. But more than anything else, the crises of the 1970s raised questions about the promise of perpetual growth and forced people to take stock of the tremendous toll almost two decades of breakneck development had taken on the nation's environment and their everyday lives.

The end of high-speed growth was also the end of the "golden age" of *danchi* housing. By now, the JHC *danchi* no longer represented "modern" living. Once the vanguard of housing and the modern lifestyle, by the 1970s, in the estimation of Shioda Maruo, they had "stagnated" and been "left behind" (*torinokosareta*). The phrase, "We live in the *danchi*," noted Shioda, now elicited not envy but empathy.[3] He observed that in the 1969 edition of the *Kōjien* dictionary, the adjective "modern," used in earlier editions to modify "*danchi*," had now been deleted. The *danchi* were built with the mandate of aiding "people suffering from housing difficulties" (*jūtaku konnan-sha*), yet, a headline in the *Asahi Shimbun* in January of 1971 announced, "2DK inhabitants are the latest people suffering from housing difficulties."[4] The design and size of *danchi* apartments had transformed and grown over the years yet were crammed to bursting with home appliances and dining and living room sets, barely leaving people space to move within the "furniture jungle."[5] By the late 1960s, *danchi* complexes were located an average of ninety minutes from city centers, subjecting residents to exhausting commutes.[6] As the buildings continued to grow in height and developments to expand in scale, they stopped representing a new experiment in social relationships and "modern living" and began to signify an everyday life that had become standardized, homogenized, and dehumanized.

To people who lived not *in* but *near* the *danchi*, the large apartment blocks also came to be considered one of the many pollutants plaguing urban life.

---

3. Shioda Maruo, *Sumai no sengo-shi* (Tokyo: Saimaru shuppankai, 1975), 95.
4. Ibid.
5. The average size of a rental danchi unit in 1955 was 41.2 square meters. In 1960 it was 43.2; in 1966, 51.6; 1971, 54.3; and 1974, 62.8 square meters.
6. This was the time that the Tokyo train system gained international notoriety for its white-gloved "pushers" charged with packing people onto rush hour trains and catching them when the doors opened again. Statistics kept by the Tokyo Metropolitan Government on crowding levels on Tokyo trains and subways indicated approximately a 260 percent congestion rate in 1968. 250 percent was considered "Bodies affected by jolts of train and cannot move, even hands," and 300 percent described as "Physically almost impossible, dangerous." Noted in Roman Cybriwsky, *Tokyo* (New York: John Wiley & Sons, 1998), 45.

"*Kogai*," or pollution, was ubiquitous in the 1970s, both as a reality of everyday life in congested and smog-filled cities and in the news. Stories of industrial dumping resulting in deforming diseases and death made people aware of the extent to which *they*, not corporations investing in industrial safety standards, had been forced to absorb the adverse impacts of development. Yet conceptions of *kogai* were not limited to contaminated air and water, and referred also to the many problems threatening the quality of people's daily lives in the 1970s including noise, congestion, even high rise apartment buildings that blocked one's sunlight. In more fundamental ways, too, as André Sorensen has noted, "rapid and unplanned urban growth contributed to environmental degradation in Japan."[7] The lack of zoning which led to residential neighborhoods being constructed in close proximity to industrial sites, as well as the "scattered" nature of suburban development resulting from Japan's fragmented land holding patterns, gave birth to a particular form of sprawl. This made it difficult to evenly provide infrastructure such as roads and sewage and, as land prices rose, for developers to acquire tracts of land large enough for development.[8] Although the main culprits of sprawl were small housing developments of ten or a dozen houses, the JHC also contributed to the creation of a "half-rural, half-urban"[9] urban perimeter. The patchwork nature of development is also one of the factors that sent the JHC farther and farther out into the suburbs, in search of contiguous tracts of land large enough to develop.[10] In the 1970s, a growing concern with "sprawl" paralleled that with *kogai*; both were environmental costs of rapid, haphazard urbanization. Whether factories or housing blocks, development was visible and ugly, and contributed to a sense that the nation's natural beauty was among the many things being sacrificed to high-speed growth.[11]

---

7. André Sorensen, *The Making of Urban Japan: Cities and planning from Edo to the twenty-first century* (New York: Routledge, 2002), 207.
8. Ibid., 204-207.
9. Ibid. 207.
10. Nihon jūtaku kōdan ni-jū nenshi, 46.
11. Although housing developers and agencies such as the JHC have been blamed for urban sprawl, Sorensen has pointed out the role of small farmers who "release" their land gradually and in a piecemeal fashion in accordance with rising land prices in the creation of sprawl. This forces developers to look ever farther from city centers to find lower priced land, "jumping over large amounts of still undeveloped land." "In Japan, small-scale farmers . . . remain the dominant political and development actor in processes of urbanization . . ." Andre Sorensen, "Post-Suburban Tokyo? Urbanization, Suburbanization, Reurbanization," in Nicholas Phelps and Fulong Wu, *International Perspectives on Suburbanization*

In response to sprawl, many local governments and prefectures pushed for greater control over the development of their own communities. The City Planning Law of 1919, which was the foundation of urban development even after World War II, was finally revised in 1968 with the New City Planning Law. The new law attempted to control the pace and direction of development by designating areas for immediate versus eventual development. While the 1919 law mandated that the central government plan and implement development nationwide, the revised law gave a much larger role to municipalities and prefectures—at least in theory.[12] Localism was also at the heart of Prime Minister Tanaka Kakuei's 1972 plan to "rebuild the Japanese archipelago" (*Nihon rettō kaizō-ron*). This initiative was meant to revitalize local economies and direct flows of capital and population away from overcrowded cities (and major pork into the hands of Tanaka's rural supporters).[13] His initiative resulted in the construction of some major highways and train lines in far-off rural areas but failed to redirect capital and business away from cities, especially Tokyo. As Roman Cybriwsky wrote, ". . . Tokyo kept growing though all of this, and, despite considerable earnest investment that went elsewhere . . . strengthened its primacy over the rest of the country. Instead of de-concentration on a national scale, what took place was an unprecedented sprawl of the built-up area onto surrounding terrain, and incorporation of almost all of the nearby cities, small towns, and farmlands, as well as substantial portions of Tokyo Bay, into its urban-industrial orbit."[14] As the sprawl worsened, land prices rose. One of the unintended consequences of Tanaka's plan was a "frenzy of land speculation" as developers sought prime locations along new highways and train routes.[15] Dramatically rising land prices were thus another manifestation of the 1970s crisis.

While the JHC maintained its authority to develop across municipal and

---

(New York: Palgrave, 2011), 222.

12. Sorensen describes how the central government maintained the power to "legislate the rules and goals which local governments had to follow" as well as significant control over finances. Personnel transfers between the central and prefectural or local governments also helped to maintain central oversight and control over planning. See *The Making of Urban Japan*, 215.

13. Tanaka Kakuei, *Nihon rettō kaizō-ron* (Tokyo: Nikkan kōgyō shinbunsha 1972). Also in English: *Building a New Japan: Remodeling the Japanese Archipelago* (Tokyo: Simul Press, 1972).

14. Roman Cybriwsky, *Tokyo: The Shogun's City at the Twenty-first Century* (New York: John Wiley & Sons, 1998), 27.

15. Sorensen, *The Making of Urban Japan*, 229.

prefectural boundaries and was not bound by the development permission system resulting from the New City Planning Law, its work was severely hampered by this pervasive spirit of localism. Local and prefectural governments, once eager to have *danchi* developments come to their towns, began to oppose their construction, citing destruction of the environment and the high cost of sharing the expense of providing schools, roads and other supporting services. The *Twenty Year History of the Japan Housing Corporation*, published in 1975, reflected this changed context. Exhibiting little of the optimism and exuberance of the *Ten Year History*, its authors noted, "in recent years, the concerns of local people have grown stronger, on the one hand opposing the traffic issues, blockage of sunlight, and radio interference that come along with mass housing, and on the other demanding more parks and green space. Together [this means], not even local public groups are able to obtain land for public facilities such as sewage and garbage treatment, schools, etc. . . ."[16] Locals opposed the *danchi* for other reasons, too, as the *Twenty Year History* candidly admitted, "*Danchi* are isolated and closed from the community. This is because they are dominated by people who commute to the city, because they are composed predominantly of nuclear families, because they are a transient population with loose ties to the region, and because there is a gap between their living standards and those of the surrounding community. The so-called '*danchi* ego' and '*danchi* Monroe Doctrine' have become reasons to withdraw cooperation and refuse the advance of the *danchi* . . ."[17] In an attempt to stem the tide of criticism and become more conciliatory toward local governments, the JHC lightened the financial burden on them and began picking up a larger portion of infrastructural costs. It committed itself to building facilities such as parks, libraries, and nursery schools for local communities and changed its resident selection processes to give preference to local people in need of housing.[18]

Even with these adjustments, the 1970s would become a fundamental turning point in the history of the Japan Housing Corporation. As of 1973, the national goal of providing "one housing unit per household" had been fulfilled and with this, the JHC vowed to turn its priorities from "quantity" to "quality." Coupled with land prices which, by the early 1970s, were thirty-five times what they had been in 1955, the JHC could not continue its early pace of development.[19] The

16. *Nihon jūtaku kōdan ni-jū nenshi*, 46.
17. Ibid., 78.
18. "Tokushū: shin kōdan (sono 1): Nihon jūtaku kōdan jūtaku kyōkyū no ayumi," *Jūtaku*, Vol. 30, No. 9, 1981, 21. Also *Nihon jūtaku kōdan nijū nenshi*, 73.
19. *Nihon jūtaku kōdan ni-jū nenshi*, 45.

year 1971 marked the quantitative peak of JHC housing with the construction of a record 85,000 units—60,000 of them for rent. Construction numbers dropped precipitously the following year, never to return to former levels. Yet it was not easy to shift away from the objectives of that earlier age. Institutional interests were now entrenched, and despite the original objective that state-sponsored housing be a temporary, stopgap measure until the private market recovered, the JHC began to compete with private rental housing. The crisis also produced new opportunities. In Japan, as in other industrialized countries, economic restructuring resulting from the crises of the early 1970s reconfigured national space as some regions died, others flourished, and entire sectors of industrial labor became obsolete. The JHC entered this vacuum in the early 1970s, "redeveloping" old industrial sites in center cities.[20] As the importance of redevelopment grew and land acquisition became more difficult in an environment of competition with private developers, in 1981 the JHC was combined with the Residential Land Development Corporation (*Takuchi kaihatsu kōdan*) to form the Housing and Urban Development Corporation (H.U.D.—*Jūtaku toshi seibi kōdan*).[21]

In many parts of the world, the economic crises of the 1970s brought an end to the romance with mass-produced, state-sponsored housing projects. Global recession was only part of the problem. Around the world, the disillusionment with mass housing was accompanied by the recognition that the social experiment had largely failed. Vast concrete housing projects from Chicago to Venezuela, built to house the urban poor but now "second ghettoes" in their own right, were testament to the fact that attempts to reform behavior through architecture had been a miserable failure.[22] "Some of the very projects that had come with an unprecedented rhetoric of hope," noted Florian Urban, "subsequently became the incarnation of social dystopia."[23] The mass-produced, public housing project thus became a favorite object of critique in reevaluations of the modernist project of the early and mid-twentieth century. Although they served as an important solution to housing problems throughout the world, especially after World

20. "Tokushū: shin kōdan," 13.
21. The *Takuchi kaihatsu kōdan* was created in 1974. In 1991 the HUD would be reorganized into the Urban Development Corporation (*Toshi kiban seibi kōdan*), and in 2004 it would be reorganized into the present-day Urban Renaissance Agency (*Toshi saisei kikō*). With each reorganization, the housing mandate would become smaller and the urban redevelopment mandate would increase.
22. See Arnold Hirsch, *Making the Second Ghetto: Race and Housing in Chicago, 1940–1960* (Chicago: University of Chicago Press, 1983).
23. Florian Urban, *Tower and Slab: Histories of Global Mass Housing* (New York: Routledge, 2012), 17.

War II, the scale, social agendas, and functionalist homogeneity of large public housing projects came to stand for all that was wrong with massive planning.[24] It was in this vein that Charles Jencks, in an often-quoted pronouncement, claimed that the "symbolic end of modernism" occurred precisely at 3:32 p.m., July 15, 1972, when Pruitt-Igoe, a low-income housing project in St. Louis, was dynamited.[25] Although housing projects like Pruitt-Igoe continued to be built and remained important parts of urban infrastructures around the world, Jencks suggested that what had been torn down was the belief in large-scale planning, social engineering, and a state-sponsored lifestyle.

While the "golden age" of the JHC also ended in the 1970s, the critique of the *danchi* took place within a larger discourse on the shortcomings of housing policy since the end of the war. "Thirty years have passed since the end of the war," Shioda wrote in the introduction to his 1975 book, *The Postwar History of Housing.* "In thirty years, a person is born, grows up, goes to school, is married, has children, and becomes a member of society as an adult. Has Japan, reborn thirty years ago, become an adult in this time?" When it came to food and clothing, he wrote, Japan had matured appropriately but when it came to housing, "unfortunately, I cannot say [Japan] has grown to adulthood."[26] "Housing," Shioda concluded, "was omitted from the progress of high speed growth."[27] International assessments concurred with Shioda. An article in *The New York Times* in 1969 noted that the Japanese people were the "worst housed" among people living in "advanced industrial countries."[28] The phrase "rabbit hutch," in Japanese, "*usagi goya*," became entrenched as a popular referent to Japanese housing in the 1970s after an EU commissioner referred to Japan as a nation of "workaholics" living in "rabbit hutches." The suggestion that housing standards were out of synch with the nation's other economic accomplishments made the home, once again, the site of "imbalance" and temporal unevenness. The *danchi*, formerly imbued with such lofty expectations, became emblematic of the very stunted growth of housing it had been designed to overcome.

Critiques of housing and the *danchi* followed a story line specific to postwar Japan: that of the "reverse course." The paradigm of the "reverse course" has

---

24. This critique is neatly articulated by James Scott, *Seeing Like a State: How Certain Schemes to Improve the Human Condition Have Failed* (New Haven: Yale University Press, 1998).
25. Noted in Harvey, 39.
26. Shioda, *Sumai no sengoshi*, 1-2.
27. Ibid., 41.
28. "In Japanese Cities, 'Home' Translates into 'High-Rise,'" *The New York Times* (October 19, 1969).

played an important role in postwar intellectual history as a narrative of revolutionary possibility derailed. The phrase refers specifically to a "reverse" in the objectives of the Allied Occupation of Japan after the beginning of the Cold War. The Occupation which initially sought to democratize and demilitarize the country, purge the government and industry of militarists, and create new, democratic legal institutions, changed gears in 1947 with the onset of the Cold War in Europe and especially after 1950 with the start of the Korean War. Now the objective of the Occupation became to ensure Japan's economic recovery and partnership with the United States so that the country could stand as a bastion against the Soviet Union in Asia. The left was purged, radical unionism banned, remilitarization encouraged, and the old guard welcomed back to public life. To many intellectuals, this "reversal" was a betrayal of the promise of a new and democratic Japan.[29]

The housing story followed a similar trajectory of revolutionary potential betrayed. One of the earliest and most famous critiques, one that many architects later claimed had profoundly influenced their thinking, was a 1958 essay titled "Banzai to Small Home Design" written by Isozaki Arata, Itō Teiji, and Kawakami Hideyoshi. It was less a criticism of the JHC and other developers than of architects who they claimed had sold out to the project of "developing new owners" through the uncreative work of arranging tiny blocks of space labeled "B" (bedroom) and "L" (living room) in single family homes. They claimed the age of small housing design as the "vanguard" of social change was over and architects involved in such efforts were no longer fulfilling any revolutionary function. The "development" of new owners was necessitated by the development of land for housing construction by private and public developers, including the JHC. The old family system, based on landownership, had been replaced by a new one based on the same. Only now, urban and suburban land was so expensive and parcels of land so correspondingly small that the home that could accommodate only the nuclear family had become a self-fulfilling prophesy. Using the "ideology" of "having a living room, separating eating and sleeping, lightening housework, [and] respecting the independence of the individual," architects were simply perpetuating the new bourgeois goal

---

29. For a history of the Occupation and the reverse course, see John W. Dower, *Embracing Defeat: Japan in the Wake of World War II* (New York: W.W. Norton & Company, 1999). Also Bruce Cumings, "Japan's Position in the World System," in Andrew Gordon, ed., *Postwar Japan as History* (Berkeley: University of California Press), 34-63.

of small-home acquisition.[30] The social agenda, as well as the quality of housing, were forfeited to the project of creating the infrastructure for economic growth. Many shared the opinion of architectural historian Funo Shūji who claimed that architectural contributions to postwar housing peaked in the 1950s with the creation of the DK. Once the DK became a prototype, however, "postwar housing lost its direction."[31] In this sense, the DK came to represent both the very best and the very worst of postwar housing.[32]

But by the 1970s, the role of the *danchi* as "vanguard" had already been fulfilled. The "lifestyle revolution" had been accomplished. The years of high-speed growth had transformed the materiality of the Japanese home and filled the majority of houses with the refrigerators, television sets, and washing machines that once stood for *danchi* prosperity. Even through economic crisis, the vast majority of Japanese continued to identify themselves as members of the "middle mass." And by the 1970s, the dream of homeownership had become entrenched as "an essential element of middle-class life and identity."[33] "*Mai homu*" (my home) had become the primary object of people's *akogare* or "longing."

Yet while homeownership was easier to achieve in the countryside or small towns, in large cities, particularly Tokyo, rising land prices made fulfilling the dream increasingly difficult. The pursuit of middle-class life through university education and employment with a prestigious company—both endeavors that required moving to large cities where the best schools and jobs were located— was at odds with the other middle-class pursuit of "my home." Indeed, one middle-class dream robbed the other. Urban middle-class families determined to purchase their dwellings were left with basically two choices: purchasing privately built "*manshon*," condominiums which were "essentially JHC clones— that is 2DK apartments,"[34] that began appearing in redeveloped sections of cities in the late 1960s, or buying homes at least a ninety-minute commute from the city. Many urbanites, Tokyoites especially, continued to rent housing and spend their money instead on hobbies and consumer goods.[35] The latter, of course,

30. Itō Teiji, Isozaki Arata, Kawakami Hideyoshi, "Shōjūtaku keikaku banzai," *Kenchiku bunka* 13. 4 (April 1958,): 4-10.

31. Funo Shūji, 265.

32. For a retrospective of the significance of the "nLDK" to postwar architecture, see "Tokushū: yuragi no naka no kazoku to nLDK: sengo nihon no kazoku to jūtaku" *Kensetsu zasshi* 10.1371 (April, 1995): 15-67.

33. Ann Waswo, *Housing in Postwar Japan* (New York: RoutledgeCurzon, 2002), 92.

34. Ibid., 100.

35. Ibid., 123. In 1983, forty percent of people in the Tokyo metropolitan region owned their own homes, forty-four percent owned homes in Osaka and sixty-two

only contributed to overcrowded living conditions. The criticisms leveled at the JHC *danchi*—too expensive, too small, too far—were applicable to urban living conditions in general.

However a key transformation had occurred in the two decades of high-speed growth because what was being criticized in the 1970s and beyond was national life itself. Standard of living was not considered a problem of inequality or unevenness but one plaguing the nation as a whole, a problem of substandard living conditions believed to be shared equally. The *danchi*, no longer the vanguard of middle-class "modern living," was now the vanguard of the equally middle-class "rabbit hutch."

The spirit of the *danchi*

Historical assessments of the crucial decade of the 1970s have shifted in recent years. From the perspective of the "bubble-era" of the 1980s, the decade was seen as one of painful but necessary restructuring which, with the aid of Japan's famous "administrative guidance," would shift the locus of the economy from heavy to light industry, reduce the nation's dependence on foreign oil, deal effectively with industrial pollution, and position the economy for global prominence.[36] From the frenetic growth of the 1960s and the restructuring of the 1970s would emerge Japan, the economic superpower and "model" to both developing and developed nations.

From the perspective of the early twenty-first century, however, the 1970s appear differently. Continuously rising land and stock prices would contribute to the unsustainable "bubble" that would burst in devastating fashion in the early 1990s. The entrenchment of the conservative business practices and government-industry linkages, the hallmarks of "Japan, Inc.," would be viewed as the very forces hampering the flexible, innovative thinking required to be competitive in the digital age. The glorious 1980s would now be recognized as an era of excess and hubris—and Japan of the "economic miracle" not permanent but the product of a very specific historical moment, one now passing. Economic stagnation since the 1990s, during the so-called "lost decades," called into question the very institutions and cultural attitudes which once seemed to make the nation "unique" and worthy of emulation. What would define "Japan after

---

percent owned them nationwide. Waswo, 112.

36. Chalmers Johnson, *MITI and the Japanese Miracle: The Growth of Industrial Policy, 1925-1975* (Stanford: Stanford University Press, 1982).

Japan"?[37] This is a question which has yet to be answered.

Among the anxieties gripping "post-bubble" Japan was the fear that the age of the mass middle class was ending. Many feared that the social contract between labor and management forged in the late-1950s was being broken as the economic crisis loosened companies' commitment to lifetime employment and other components of the "Japanese employment system."[38] In the midst of layoffs and hiring freezes, diligence and sacrifice no longer promised the reward of a corporate job. Growing numbers of high school and college graduates found themselves unable to secure full-time employment of any variety, and were forced to settle for temporary, part-time work as "*furītā*"—a status which placed them firmly outside of the social mainstream.[39] As Martin Fackler noted in *The New York Times*, "Japan has already created a generation of young people who say they have given up on believing that they can ever enjoy the job stability or rising living standards that were once considered a birthright here."[40] The Labor Ministry's revelation in October of 2009 that it had been secretly compiling poverty statistics since 1998, and that a shocking 15.7 percent of Japanese people lived in poverty, rocked the nation and made it clear that the economic crisis was not suffered evenly by "all Japanese." Discussions of social class were no longer focused on over-identification with the middle but with the emergence of "*kakusa*"—inequality and difference—in a nation now known to be *above* average in income inequality among advanced nations.

In a switch, employers and the government encouraged workers to spend more time with their families—to go home at five and take Saturdays off. An emerging critique of the "middle-class matricentric domesticity" that had prevailed since the 1960s suggested that the loss of the presence and authority of the father in the home was one cause of the nation's woes. Calls for "paternalism"

---

37. I borrow this phrase from the title of the edited volume by Tomiko Yoda and Harry Harootunian, ed., *Japan After Japan: Social and Cultural Life from the Recessionary 1990s to the Present* (Durham: Duke University Press, 2006).

38. See Olivier Zunz, Leonard Schoppa, and Nobuhiro Hiwatari, ed., *Social Contracts Under Stress: The Middle Classes of America, Europe, and Japan at the Turn of the Century* (New York: Russell Sage Foundation, 2002).

39. Mary Brinton, *Lost in Transition: Youth, Work, and Instability in Postindustrial Japan* (New York: Cambridge University Press, 2011). The term "furītā, a combination of the English word "free" (freelance) and the German word "arbeit" (work) was coined in the late 1980s to describe underemployed people or those able to secure only part-time work.

40. Martin Fackler, "Japan Goes from Dynamic to Disheartened," *The New York Times* (October 16, 2010).

suggested that "fathers who [had] lost their jobs or who fear[ed] getting squeezed out of their 'corporate domicile' (to which they have hitched their fortune and self-identity) [were] desperate to find their way back 'home.'"[41] Yet tales of laid-off salary men pretending to go to work and spending their days in public parks or in internet cafes captured the public imagination and suggested that "going home" was not easily done.[42]

Housing was no longer emblematic of one's middle class status but of the degree of vulnerability in rough economic times. The most vulnerable—whether day laborers turned out of boarding houses or people who had stretched beyond their means to buy houses now foreclosed—were the first to lose "my home." Many urbanites who had managed to achieve the middle-class dream of homeownership in areas where land prices were so inflated during the bubble years, now found themselves in a "negative equity trap" with loans to repay that exceeded the post-bubble value of their property.[43] Iwao Sato noted, "Whereas in postwar Japan the government strove to nurture and stabilize the middle class by promoting homeownership, in the 1990s homeownership itself became a destabilizing factor in the lives of the middle class."[44] Twenty-four-hour internet cafés and blue plastic tarp shanties in public parks, the refuges of growing numbers of homeless people, became the housing emblems of post-bubble Japan. [45] "The downsizing of Japan's ambitions can be seen on the streets of Tokyo," noted Fackler, "where concrete 'micro houses' have become popular among younger Japanese who cannot afford even the famously cramped housing of their parents or lack the job security to take out a multi-decade loan."[46] Often measuring less than 300 square feet, micro houses made the *danchi* apartment appear palatial by comparison.

It has been against this backdrop of economic uncertainty that the most recent chapter of the *danchi* story has unfolded. The HUD and its successor

41. Tomiko Yoda, "The Rise and Fall of Maternal Society," 240.
42. The award-winning 2008 film, *Tokyo Sonata*, directed by Kurosawa Kiyoshi, captured the anxiety and disillusionment of post-bubble Japan. It centers on the attempts of a middle-class family man to maintain the illusion of employment after losing his job and the quiet disintegration of his family that results.
43. Waswo, *Housing in Postwar Japan*, 109.
44. Iwao Sato, "Welfare regimes and the Japanese housing system," in Hirayama and Ronald, ed., *Housing and Social Transition in Japan*, (New York: Routledge, 2007), 88.
45. Masami Iwata, "Homelessness in contemporary Japan," in Misa Izuhara, ed., *Comparing Social Policies: Exploring new perspectives in Britain and Japan* (Bristol, UK: The Policy Press, 2003).
46. Fackler, "Japan Goes from Dynamic to Disheartened."

institutions—the Urban Development Corporation (1991–2004) and the Urban Renaissance Agency (2004–present)—focused increasingly on urban redevelopment and less on housing provision. In recent years, the Urban Renaissance Agency has "withdrawn from tract housing projects, has stopped construction of new rental housing, is selling as much of its existing housing stock as possible to the private sector, and wherever possible is outsourcing the management of remaining buildings to private companies."[47] In 2007 the Agency announced that it would reduce its current stock of 770,000 rental units by thirty percent by 2048 and identified *danchi* complexes slated for reconstruction, consolidation, and demolition.[48]

These shifting priorities were part and parcel of a general privatization of the "three pillars" of postwar housing policy. In 2007, the Housing Corporation, the first "pillar" and the agency that played the greatest role in nurturing the dream of homeownership, was reorganized into the Housing Loan Support Agency (*Jūtaku kinyu shien kikō*). Suffering from growing numbers of loans in default and payments in arrears, its role has shifted from financing homes to assisting potential buyers to secure housing loans from the private sector. As for the second pillar, Public Housing, construction of new social housing dropped more than half between 1995 and 2004, and "income levels determining eligibility for public housing are gradually being lowered, resulting in a marked shrinking of the socio-economic class to which public housing is available."[49] After two decades of economic crisis, "housing marketisation appears to have become the sole purpose of housing policy."[50]

As the Urban Development Corporation and Urban Renaissance Agency began renovating the *danchi*, a new set of priorities emerged. Once known for the homogeneity of its residents, the *danchi* now had a diversity of inhabitants: blue-and white-collar workers, single people, even foreign laborers. With the aging of Japanese society, housing geared to the needs of young, nuclear families

---

47. Iwao, 87.
48. "Toshi saisei," UR toshi kikō, accessed July 1, 2014, http://www.ur-net.go.jp/ rebuild/.
49. There were 51,030 public housing construction projects in 1994 and only 21,278 in 2004. Iwao, 86-87.
50. Richard Ronald, "Home Ownership, Ideology and Diversity: Re-evaluating Concepts of Housing Ideology in the Case of Japan," in *Housing, Theory, and Society* (2004): 21, 62.

was remodeled to accommodate growing numbers of elderly inhabitants.[51] Interior designs once based on rigid functionalism were re-envisioned as the agency experimented with creating a "you-make house" (*yū meiku jūtaku*) with flexible floor plans utilizing moveable *tatami* mats and walls.[52] Harking back to the farmhouse of the countryside, the remodeled Kangetsuko Danchi in Kyoto even included an apartment design featuring a "*doma*"—not of earth as in the traditional farmhouse, but of concrete—where inhabitants could wear their shoes and utilize it as an interior workspace or atelier, reuniting work and living in one place.[53] In many ways, the approach to interior space was the inverse of the JHC's nearly a half-century earlier.

With many projects slated for reconstruction and demolition, a new generation of *danchi* enthusiasts emerged. The first decade of the twenty-first century witnessed a spate of new publications on the *danchi*, some of them on practical topics such as how to remodel and renovate apartment interiors, but many more of them retrospectives on their unique architecture and significance to postwar history. Self-labeled "*danchi* maniacs"(*danchi mania*) and "*danchi* lovers" (*danchi aikōka*) formed a new "*danchi* tribe," of sorts, through websites, blogs, and live gatherings such as tours and "*danchi* talk" events in cafes and performance spaces.[54] Many websites were dedicated to photographing *danchi* around the country, with some dedicated to specific aspects of the *danchi* such as their building numbers or water towers.[55] The *danchi*, it seems, had become a focus of "*otaku*" or "obsessive fan" culture, replete with "goods"—mugs and cups featuring the *danchi*, punch-out paper *danchi* models, and *danchi*-shaped cookies and cakes.[56]

51. The Urban Renaissance Agency reports that as of 2005, thirty-five percent of its inhabitants were sixty-five or older. By 2018, that percentage is estimated to increase to fifty-five percent. "Toshi saisei," UR toshi kikō, accessed July 1, 2014, http://www.ur-net.go.jp/rebuild/.

52. Pamphlet "Kenchiku gijutsu shikenjo," Jūtaku toshi seibi kōdan, 1998, 5.

53. "Kangetsukyo Danchi," UR Toshi kikō, accessed July 1, 2014, http://www.ur-net.go.jp/kangetsukyo/.

54. The "Project D" blog lists links to nineteen separate *danchi* websites including "Danchi mappu," "Danchi hyakkei," "Kōdan wōkā," "salon de 2DK," and "Danchi-ing.com." Purogekkuto D burogu, assessed July 15, 2014, http://codan.blog120.fc2.com/.

55. The blog, "Nangou towa?" (Which number?) at www.belle-danchi.blobspot.com features photographs of the numbers on the sides of *danchi* buildings; and the blog, "Nihon kyūsui tō" (Japanese water towers) at kyusuitou.blog87.fc2.com focuses on *danchi* water towers. Both were last accessed July 1, 2014.

56. Salon de 2DK, accessed July 1, 2014, http://salon2dk.blogspot.com/.

Although the majority of these enthusiasts were born well after the heyday of the *danchi* was past, as the trailer to the 2008 documentary, *A Good Day for Danchi*, asserted, "The *danchi* are always by your side"; the narrator adding, "even if you never lived in one, they are part of the landscape."[57] In a nation where homes stand for an average of twenty-five years, the *danchi*, especially those built in the late 1950s and 1960s, formed a constant backdrop to people's everyday lives and had come to represent part of the nation's architectural heritage. But in a switch, *danchi* complexes, once islands of urbanity in the midst of the countryside, were now notable for their wide-open green spaces with fully grown trees and diverse plant life which stand in stark comparison with the dense urban sprawl and taller buildings that have grown up around their edges. As Terui Keita, creator of the website, "Codan Walker" noted, "recently a movement is growing to recognize the nature within the *danchi* as irreplaceable; people are reevaluating the environment of the *danchi*."[58]

In many other ways, as well, the *danchi* has come to represent a lifestyle opposite that of their original inhabitants. Young single people were drawn to them not for the "privacy" they offered but because the clusters of four- and five-story buildings seemed to offer the possibility of a richer community life than was possible in anonymous urban condominiums.[59] No longer associated with a frenetic pace of life in the midst of high-speed growth, many of the older *danchi* were now associated with a "slow life"[60] As invoked by young people of the *"furītā"* generation, Mark Driscoll noted, the concept of "slow life," served as an "implicit critique of the ideology of sacrifice and deferred gratification" of earlier postwar generations.[61] That would no doubt include the original inhabitants of the *danchi*.

One popular motif of the new "mania" was the *danchi* tour where professional and amateur photographers traversed Japan cataloguing and photographing the *danchi*.[62] Hase Satoshi, the creator of the website, "100 Views of the *Danchi*,"

---

57. *Danchi biyori* (Tokyo: Albatros, 2008).

58. "Danchi no miryoku," Kodan wōkā, accessed June 18, 2014, http://codan.boy.jp/intro/index.html

59. Hara Takeshi and Shigematsu Kiyoshi, *Danchi no jidai* (Tokyo: Shinchosha, 2010), 229.

60. *Danchi biyori.*

61. Mark Driscoll, "Debt and Denunciation in Post-Bubble Japan: On the Two Freeters," in *Cultural Critique* 65 (Winter 2007): 172.

62. Many books and websites warn would-be *danchi* tourists not to disturb the residents. "The *danchi* are really wonderful so we understand that they may excite

claimed, "Our purpose is to chronicle and photograph the *danchi*, the object of people's longing in the Shōwa Thirties [referring to the decade between 1955 and 1964], before they disappear."[63] Some are drawn to decaying or dilapidated complexes, or those on the verge of demolition.[64] In his book *Danchi Pilgrimage*, photographer Ishimoto Kaoru focused on several *danchi* sites—including some that are still in commission or in the process of renovation. But, in the vein of his earlier photography collection of Japan's "war ruins,"[65] Ishimoto displayed a special fascination with what might be called "*danchi* ruins." Though he never lived in the *danchi* and at the beginning of his "pilgrimage" admitted to not knowing the difference between a *danchi* and a condo, Ishimoto set out to discover the "spirit of the *danchi*" (*danchi no kami*). His camera sought out rusting mailboxes, overgrown pathways, rusting bicycles, torn *shoji* screens, old magazines and yellowing calendars—the detritus of everyday life left behind by decades of inhabitants. As he explored a section of Saitama Prefecture's Higashi Miyashita Danchi that had been abandoned and was on the verge of demolition, Ishimoto discovered a photograph of a nude woman and speculated, "'Father' must have bought this then hidden it somewhere, away from the eyes of his wife. He certainly forgot he even bought it. Then transcending time and space, it has emerged. I felt close to that 'father' I had never met."[66] Through such feelings of connection, Ishimoto discovered the "spirit" of the *danchi*. "While *danchi* are inanimate buildings, they have become something more than that . . . They are the beauty and fascination you see with your eyes, but also the history and drama that you cannot see with your eyes but that resonate in your heart."[67] On the verge of their demise, it seems that the *danchi* had finally achieved the status of myth.

Demolition was the greatest threat to the *danchi*, but in the estimation of many enthusiasts, so was renovation. Renovation often entailed the consolidation of buildings and the addition of floors, elevators, and parking lots. Efforts updated and modernized complexes but also rewired communities, and changed their

you but, in the end, they are people's homes! Be careful not to cause them any disturbance!" Ōyama Ken, Satō Dai and Hayazumi Kenrō, *Danchi-dan* (Tokyo: Kinema Junposha, 2012).

63. Danchi hyakkei, accessed July 18, 2014, http://danchi100k.com/.
64. The documentary *Danchi biyori* toured several dilapidated complexes including Hibarigaoka Danchi and Asagaya Jutaku.
65. Ishimoto Kaoru, *Sensō kaikyo* (Tokyo: Mirion shuppan, 2006).
66. Ishimoto Kaoru, *Danchi junrei* (Tokyo: Futami shobō, 2008), 128.
67. Ibid., 172.

overall appearance. The "Codan Walker" lamented, "Once *danchi* are rebuilt, they become no different from private condominiums. With only a parking lot, a small park, and a building, [they become] very uninteresting *danchi*."[68] And "after they are rebuilt," political scientist and *danchi* commentator Hara Takeshi added, "they are no longer called '*danchi*.' Building placards are changed to foreign-inspired names such as 'Green Town' and 'Sun Rafre' . . . Once they are rebuilt, are no longer called '*danchi*' and are given condo-esque names, even the fact that there once was a *danchi* there will be forgotten."[69] Noting the same phenomenon, Ishimoto asked, "Will the *danchi* disappear along with their names?"[70]

Even as they were being demolished and renovated beyond recognition, *danchi* were also being preserved and memorialized in museums around the country. In local, prefectural, and national museums, the turn of the century witnessed a "Shōwa Thirties boom." Museums in the Tokyo wards of Katsushika, Arakawa, and Meguro, the art museum in Utsunomiya, the Tohoku Historical Museum in Sendai, and the National Museum of Science in Tokyo, among others, created exhibits displaying home appliances or replications of various living spaces, urban and rural, to show how the "lifestyle revolution" transformed daily life in the 1950s and 1960s.[71] The Edo-Tokyo Museum, which focuses on the history of Tokyo from the early modern period through the end of World War II, followed its exhibit of the firebombing and occupation of Tokyo with a display of household appliances and photographs of the *danchi*. Similarly, the controversial Shōwa-kan Museum in Tokyo, which takes as its main focus daily life in Japan during the war, also followed its war display with an exhibit of shiny televisions, washing machines, and other items emblematizing postwar recovery. In both museums, the placement of these displays within the larger exhibits reproduced what had become the formulaic narrative of the "lifestyle revolution" as the happily-ever-after ending to the story of the war. Appliance-filled daily life was the phoenix that rose from the ashes of the destroyed city and defeated nation.

One of the most elaborate exhibits focusing specifically on the *danchi* was created by the Matsudo Municipal Museum in Chiba Prefecture. "The Lifestyle

68. "Hibarigaoka," Kōdan wōkā.

69. Hara and Shigematsu, 190-91.

70. Ishimoto, *Danchi junrei*, 84.

71. Described in Aoki Toshiya, *Saigen shōwa 30-nendai: danchi 2DK no kurashi* (Tokyo: Kawade shobō shinsha, 2001), 118-123.

Revolution in Postwar Matsudo" opened as a permanent exhibit in the autumn of 2000 and included a full-scale replication of a JHC-built 2DK apartment, circa 1962, filled with appliances, furniture, and other household goods of the age. The city of Matsudo had a special place in the annals of JHC history. Forty-four years earlier, local farmers had opposed the construction of Tokiwadaira Danchi by sitting in front of bulldozers and dumping truckloads of *daikon* radishes in front of JHC headquarters in Tokyo. Yet the history of protest and opposition had a small place in the display that focused mainly on the material transformation of daily life in the 2DK. According to museum curator Aoki Toshiya, the exhibit sought to convey the specific local history of Matsudo and its postwar transformation from rural farmland to a Tokyo residential suburb, as well as the broader history of the "lifestyle revolution" experienced throughout Japan.[72]

Preserved in Matsudo and other museums were not the *danchi* and 2DK as they changed and developed but the *danchi* as they had appeared on the landscape and in the national imaginary in the mid- and late- 1950s. Exhibits were as much about the age as about the 2DK space, although the two could not be separated. In postwar histories, the transformation of daily life in the home was the "event" that had come to define the Shōwa Thirties no less than defeat and occupation defined the Shōwa Twenties (1945–1954) and war the Shōwa Teens (1935–1944). The Matsudo museum surveyed guests on their "images" of the Shōwa Thirties. Responses described the decade as a "time of changes in daily life," a time marked by feelings of "*maemuki*"—literally "forward-lookingness"—and a time when "people's longing for a new life was just beginning to be realized."[73] People expressed nostalgia for what they believed to be the prevailing optimism of the 1950s and 1960s.[74] "In the nostalgia we feel for the Shōwa Thirties," Aoki noted, "we take stock of what we have lost in the present."[75] It was now the *danchi* that were the object of nostalgia and the passing of 2DK life the symbol of loss. But from the vantage point of the anxiety-ridden turn of the twenty-first century, what had been "lost" was not the 2DK lifestyle, which was simply an

72. Ibid., 122.
73. Ibid., 118-119.
74. On the broader phenomenon of nostalgia for the "Showa Thirties," see Jordan Sand, "The Ambivalence of the New Breed: Nostalgic Consumerism in 1980s and 1990s Japan," Sheldon Garon and Patricia L. Maclachlan, ed., *The Ambivalent Consumer: Questioning Consumption in East Asia and the West* (Ithaca: Cornell University Press), 105-107.
75. Aoki, 119.

earlier version of contemporary daily life, but the promise of the "bright life" and perception that life was getting better by the day. Looking back, people felt nostalgia for the feeling of "looking forward."

"Nostalgia," wrote Svetlana Boym, "is not always for the *ancien regime* or fallen empire but also for the unrealized dreams of the past and visions of the future that became obsolete."[76] Japan's postwar middle-class dream, seeming to promise security and the comforts of middle-class life to those who worked diligently and loyally, was born of the era of high-speed growth. This was an unrealized dream for many, even at the height of postwar prosperity. Indeed, the true legacy of the *danchi* lies less in what they revealed of postwar society than what they sought to conceal: difference and economic disparity. This legacy continues today as the "2DK lifestyle" and "*danchi* mania" evoke uniting sentiments of nostalgia for the Showa Thirties past. But more fundamentally, current nostalgia for the *danchi* suggests that one of the most important manifestations of the era of high-speed economic growth was the feeling of longing itself. More than any single aspect of "middle-class life," it is this longing in anticipation of a better future that has become increasingly elusive. The aging *danchi*, relics of a better time, stand as reminders of that optimism for futures now past.

---

76. Svetlana Boym, *The Future of Nostalgia* (New York: Basic Books, 2001), xvi.

Appendix

Charts 1-7. Comparative statistical charts about the danchi from the 1960 White Paper on National Life. From Keizai kikaku chō, *Kokumin seikatsu hakusho, shōwa sanjū-go nen,* 138-145.

Chart 1
Occupations of Residents (%)

	Commerce/ Industry	Management	Office/ Engineer	Blue-collar	Self-employed	Primary	Other
A. Tokyo (males)	21	7	23		49		—
B. Tokyo (all households)	27	11	30	23	—	1	4
C. *Danchi*	4	11	75	4	—	0	4

Sources: A: 1955 National Census
B and C: Ad Search Circle (*Ado sāchi sākuru*) study February 1960

Chart 2
Income Levels (%)

	JHC residents (October 1958)	Tokyo labor force (1958 average)
0-24,000 yen	1.4	24.8
24,000-32,000 yen	14.3	24.4
32,000-40,000 yen	35.5	18.3
40,000 yen and over	48.8	32.5

Sources: JHC statistics from "Survey of finances and incomes of residents of rental housing"
Others from Prime Minister's Office Statistics Bureau "Survey of Family Finances"

Chart 3
Educational Levels / March 1960 (%)

	Elementary	Secondary	Higher	Totals
JHC residents				
Males	6.6	27.9	65.6	100.0
Females	5.0	86.7	8.3	100.0
Tokyo 23 Wards				
Males	39	34	27	100.0
Females	46	46	8	100.0

Source: JHC study: "Social Psychological Study of *Danchi* Apartment Dwellers"
(*Apāto danchi kyojūsha no shakai shinrigakuteki kenkyū*)

Chart 4
Bread Consumption (%)

	Danchi	Tokyo
Every day	44	34.7
Several times per week	36	
Once or twice per week	14	
Never	6	
Total	100	

Source: Ad Search Circle study, February 1960

Chart 5
Family Size

	Tokyo labor force 1958 average	JHC *danchi* October 1958
Average family size	4.4 people	3.5 people
2 member family	8.9 %	25.4 %
3 member family	17.8	27.4
4 member family	26.9	26.4
5 member family	25.1	13.4
6 member family	12.6	3.5
7 member family	8.7	1.5
Unclear	0	2.5

Sources: JHC statistics from "Survey of finances and incomes of residents of rental housing"
Others from Prime Minister's Office Statistics Bureau "Survey of Family Finances"

Chart 6
Comparisons of Time Housewives Devote to Housework, Free Time

	Danchi	Wives of Tokyo "Salarymen"
Housework	6 hours 52 minutes	9 hours 02 minutes
Comparison	(76.0)	(100)
Cultural, social time	6 hours 41 minutes	4 hours 31 minutes
Comparison	(148.1)	(100)
Newspaper	55 minutes	
Radio	1 hour 13 minutes	
Television	2 hours 07 minutes	
Magazine	46 minutes	
Total time devoted to mass media	5 hours 01 minutes	

Source: Ad Search Circle study (February 1960) and
Labor Ministry Survey "Opinion survey of housewives' free time" (February 1959)

Chart 7
Ownership of Consumer Durables (February 1960) (%)

	Danchi residents	Tokyo (23 wards)
Sewing machine	79.2	71.4
Radio	90.5	84.8
Transistor radio	22.5	22.0
Washing machine	76.0	49.2
Electric rice cooker	56.0	25.1
Refrigerator	20.5	13.7
Gas or electric stove	63.2	37.1
Electric fan	22.2	35.7
Television	61.1	60.6
Phonograph	21.7	28.5
Camera	69.6	59.2
Eight millimeter projector	3.6	3.8
Piano	1.6	3.1

Source: Ad Search Circle survey and Economic Planning Bureau survey
"Survey predicting consumer trends"

Bibliography

Journals and Periodicals

Asahi shinbun (1945–1957)
Chūō kōron (1959–1961)
Fujin kōron (1950–1964)
Ienami [inhouse magazine of the Japan Housing Corporation] (1956–1962)
Jūtaku (1952–1956)
Kurashi no techō (1955–1961)
Shin kenchiku (1946–1957)
Shufu no tomo (1950–1961)
Shūkan asahi (1950–1967)
Toshi mondai (1955–1956)

Films

Danchi e no shōtai. Nikkei Films, 1960.
Kanojo to kare. Hani Susumu, 1963.
Danchi biyori. Albatros, 2008.

Studies

Nihon jūtaku kōdan, ed. *Apāto danchi kyojūsha no shakai shinri gakuteki kenkyū sono II: chiikisa no bunseki o chūshin ni shite.* Tokyo: Nihon jūtaku kōdan, 1961.
———, ed. *Apāto danchi kyojūsha no shakai shinri gakuteki kenkyū sono III: danchi to chiiki shakai.* Tokyo: Nihon jūtaku kōdan, 1963.
———, ed. *Apāto danchi kyojūsha no shakai shinri gakuteki kenkyū: ningen kankei to shakai ishiki o chūshin toshite.* Tokyo: Nihon jūtaku kōdan, 1959.

Websites

Danchi hyakkei. Accessed July 18, 2014. http://danchi100k.com/
Kodan Wōkā. Accessed June 18, 2014. http://codan.boy.jp/intro/index.html
Purogekkuto D burogu. Assessed July 15, 2014. http://codan.blog120.fc2.com/
Salon de 2DK. Accessed July 1, 2014. http://salon2dk.blogspot.com/
UR toshi kikō. "Kangetsukyo Danchi." Accessed July 1, 2014. http://www.ur-net.go.jp/kangetsukyo/.
———. "Toshi saisei. Accessed July 1, 2014 http://www.ur-net.go.jp/rebuild/.

Dissertations and Unpublished Materials

Kiefer, Christie. "Personality and Change in a Japanese Danchi." Ph.D. diss. University of California, Berkeley, 1968.

Kuroishi, Izumi. "Kon Wajirō: A Quest for the Architecture as a Container of Everyday Life." Ph.D. diss. University of Pennsylvania, Philadelphia, 1998.

All other sources

Abe Kobo. *The Ruined Map: A Novel.* Translated by E. Dale Saunders. New York: Kodansha International, 1993.

Allinson, Gary D. *Suburban Tokyo: A Comparative Study in Politics and Social Change.* Berkeley: University of California Press, 1979.

Amano Masako and Sakurai Atsushi, eds. *"Mono to onna" no sengo-shi.* Tokyo: Yūshindō kōbun-sha, 1992.

Ambaras, David. R. "Social Knowledge, Cultural Capital, and the New Middle Class in Japan, 1895–1912." *Journal of Japanese Studies* 24, no. 1 (1998): 1-33.

Aoki Toshiya. *Saigen Shōwa 30-nendai: danchi 2DK no kurashi.* Tokyo: Kawade shobō shinsha, 2001.

Ariizumi Tōro. *Kyūyo, kōei jūtaku no kenkyū.* Tokyo: Tōkyō daigaku shuppankai, 1956.

Ariyoshi Sawako. *Yūhigaoka sanko-kan.* Tokyo: Shinchō-sha, 1971.

Atoriekochi [Atelier Kochi], ed. *Danchi rinobe kurashi.* Tokyo: Asupekuto, 2013.

Beer, Lawrence W. "Japan 1969: 'My Homeism' and Political Struggle." In *Asian Survey* 10, no. 1 (January 1970): 43-55.

Betts, Paul, and Greg Eghigian, eds. *Pain and Prosperity: Reconsidering Twentieth Century German History.* Stanford: Stanford University Press, 2003.

Boym, Svetlana. *Common Places: Mythologies of Everyday Life in Russia.* Cambridge, MA: Harvard University Press, 1994.

———. *The Future of Nostalgia.* New York: Basic Books, 2001.

Brinton, Mary C. *Lost in Transition: Youth, Work, and Instability in Postindustrial Japan.* New York: Cambridge University Press, 2011.

Building Center of Japan, ed. *A Quick Look at Housing In Japan.* Tokyo: The Building Center of Japan, 1998.

Coaldrake, William H. *Architecture and Authority in Japan.* New York: Routledge, 1996.

Cybriwsky, Roman. *Tokyo: The Shogun's City at the Twenty-First Century.* New York: John Wiley & Sons, 1998.

De Certeau, Michel. *The Practice of Everyday Life.* Berkeley: University of California Press, 1984.

Dower, John W. "Peace and Democracy in Two Systems: External Policy and Internal Conflict." In *Postwar Japan as History,* Andrew Gordon, 3-33. Berkeley: University of California Press, 1993.

Fackler, Martin. "Japan Goes from Dynamic to Disheartened." *The New York Times* (October 16, 2010).

Fishman, Robert. *Bourgeois Utopias: The Rise and Fall of Suburbia*. New York: Basic Books, 1987.

Fowler, Edward. *San'ya Blues: Laboring Life in Contemporary Tokyo*. Ithaca: Cornell University Press, 1996.

Fujimori Terunobu. "Dainingu ki'chin tanjōki: gakumon mo mare ni katsu." *Jūtaku tokushū* (April 1988).

———. *Shōwa jūtaku monogatari*. Tokyo: Shin kenchikusha, 1990.

Funo Shūji. *Suramu to usagi goya*. Tokyo: Seikyūsha, 1985.

Gluck, Carol. "Introduction." In *Showa: the Japan of Hirohito*. Edited by Carol Gluck and Stephen R. Graubard, xi-lxii. New York: W.W. Norton & Company, 1992.

———. "The Past in the Present." In *Postwar Japan as History*. Edited by Andrew Gordon, 64-95. Berkeley: University of California Press, 1993.

Gordon, Andrew. "Contests for the Workplace." In *Postwar Japan as History*. Edited by Andrew Gordon, 373-394. Berkeley: University of California Press, 1993.

———. "The Short Happy Life of the Japanese Middle Class." In *Social Contracts Under Stress: The Middle Classes of America, Europe and Japan at the Turn of the Century*. Edited by Olivier Zunz, Leonard Schoppa, Nobuhiro Hiwatari, 108-129. New York: Russell Sage Foundation, 2002.

———. *The Wages of Affluence: Labor and Management in Postwar Japan*. Cambridge, MA: Harvard University Press, 1998.

Hamaguchi Miho. *Nihon jūtaku no hōkensei*. Tokyo: Sagami shobō, 1953.

———. "Seikatsu jikan, seikatsu kūkan." In *Kenchikugaku taikei: jūkyo-ron I*, Kenchikugaku taikei henshū iin, ed., 285-371. Tokyo: Shōkokusha, 1954.

Hamaguchi Ryūichi. *Hyūmanizumu no kenchiku*. Tokyo: Kenchiku jyānaru, 1995.

———. *Hyūmanizumu no kenchiku—sairon*. Tokyo: Kenchiku-ka kaikan, 1994.

———. *Nihonjin no seikatsu kūkan*. Tokyo: Shinchōsha, 1959.

Hara Takeshi and Shigematsu Kiyoshi. *Danchi no jidai*. Tokyo: Shinchosha, 2010.

Hara Takeshi. *Danchi no kūkan seiji-gaku*. Tokyo: NHK shuppan, 2012.

———. *Takiyama komyūn 1974*. Tokyo: Kodansha, 2010.

Harada Sumitaka. "Sengo jūtaku hōsei no seiritsu katei." In *Fukushi kokka 6*, ed. Tokyo daigaku shakai kagaku kenkyūjo "fukushi kokka" kenkyūkai. Tokyo: Tokyo daigaku shakai kagaku kenkyūjo, 1985, 317-396.

Harloe, Michael. *The People's Home? Social Rented Housing in Europe and America*. Cambridge, MA: Blackwell, 1995.

Harootunian, Harry. *History's Disquiet: Modernity, Cultural Practice, and the Question of Everyday Life*. New York: Columbia University Press, 2000.

———. *Overcome by Modernity: History, Culture, and Community in Interwar Japan*. Princeton: Princeton University Press, 2000.

———. "Shadowing History: National narratives and the persistence of the everyday." *Cultural Studies* 18, no. 2/3 (March/May 2004): 181-200

Harrison, David. *The Sociology of Modernization and Development*, New York: Routledge, 1988.

Harvey, David. *The Condition of Postmodernity: An Enquiry into the Origins of Social Change*. Cambridge, MA: Blackwell, 1990.

———. *The Urban Experience*. Baltimore: The Johns Hopkins University Press, 1989.

Hasegawa Tokunosuke. *Tokyo no takuchi keisei-shi*. Tokyo: Sumai no toshokan shuppankyoku, 1988.

Hashizume Sadao. *Kawariyuku katei to kyōiku: danchi bunka ga yotei suru mono*. Tokyo: Reimei shobō, 1962.

Hein, Carola. "Rebuilding Japanese Cities after 1945." In *Rebuilding Urban Japan After 1945*. Edited by Carola Hein, Jeffry Diefendorf, and Ishida Yorifusa. New York: Palgrave Macmillan, 2003, 1-16.

Hinokidani, Mieko. "Housing, Family and Gender." In *Housing and Social Transition in Japan*, . Edited by Yosuke Hirahama and Richard Ronald, 114-139. New York: Routledge, 2007.

Hirayama Yosuke and Richard Ronald, eds. *Housing and Social Transition in Japan*. New York: Routledge, 2007.

Hirayama, Yosuke. "Housing policy and social inequality in Japan." In *Comparing Social Policies: Exploring new perspectives in Britain and Japan* Edited by Misa Izuhara. Bristol, UK: Policy Press, 2003, 151-171.

———. "Reshaping the Housing System: Home Ownership as a Catalyst for Social Transformation." In *Housing and Social Transition in Japan*. Edited by Yosuke Hirahama and Richard Ronald, 15-46. New York: Routledge, 2007.

Hirsh, Arnold A. *Making the Second Ghetto: Race and Housing in Chicago, 1940–1960*. Chicago: University of Chicago Press, 1998.

Honma Yoshihito. *Mai hōmu gēmu*. Tokyo: Ōtsuki shoten, 1980.

———. *Naimushō jūtaku seisaku no kyōjun: kōkyō jūtakuron josetsu*. Tokyo: Ochanomizu shobō, 1988.

Hoshino, Ikumi. "Apartment Life in Japan." In *Journal of Marriage and Family*, 26, n. 3 (August 1964): 312-317.

Housing & Urban Development Corporation. *'ING Report: Searching for a New Conversation with the Times: Changes and Related Technological Development in Housing Facilities Built by the Housing & Urban Development Corporation*. Tokyo: Building Technology Laboratory, HUDC, 1997.

Huyssen, Andreas. "Mapping the Postmodern." *New German Critique* 33 (Fall 1984): 5-52.

Igarashi, Yoshikuni. *Bodies of Memory: Narratives of War in Postwar Japanese Culture, 1945–1970*. Princeton: Princeton University Press, 2000.

Imamura, Anne E. *Urban Japanese Housewives: At Home in the Community*. Honolulu: University of Hawaii Press, 1987.

Ishida, Hiroshi. "Class Structure and Status Hierarchies in Contemporary Japan." *European Sociological Review* 5:1 (1989): 65-80.

Ishida Yorifusa. *Nihon kindai toshi keikaku no hyakunen*. Tokyo: Jijitai kenkyūsha, 1992.

———. "Nihon ni okeru tochi kukaku seiri seidoshi gaisetsu 1870–1980," *Sōgō toshi kenkyū* 28 (September 1986).

Ishikawa, Tatsuzō. *Evil for Pleasure*. Translated by Paul T. Konya. Tokyo: Yohan Publications, Inc., 1972.

———. *Resistance at Forty-Eight*. Translated by Kazuma Nakayama. Tokyo: The Hokuseido Press, 1960.

Ishimoto Kaoru. *Danchi junrei*. Tokyo: Futami shobō, 2008.

———. *Sensō kaikyo*. Tokyo: Mirion shuppan, 2006.

Ishikawa Hiroyoshi and Fujitake Akira, eds. *Amerikan karucha*. Tokyo: Sanseidō, 1981.

Ishizuka Hiromichi and Narita Ryūichi, eds. *Tōkyō-to no hyakunen*. Tokyo: Yamakawa shuppansha, 1986.

Itō Teiji, Isozaki Arata, Kawakami Hideyoshi. "Shōjūtaku keikaku banzai." *Kenchiku bunka* 13: 4 (April 1958), 4-10.

Ivy, Marilyn. *Discourses of the Vanishing: Modernity, Phantasm, Japan*. Chicago: University of Chicago Press, 1995.

———. "Formations of Mass Culture." In *Postwar Japan as History*, Edited by Andrew Gordon, 239-258. Berkeley: University of California Press, 1993.

Iwao Sato. "Welfare Regime Theories and the Japanese Housing System." In *Housing and Social Transition in Japan*. Edited by Yosuke Hirahama and Richard Ronald, 73-93. New York: Routledge, 2007.

Iwata, Masami. "Homelessness in Contemporary Japan." In *Comparing Social Policies: Exploring New Perspectives in Britain and Japan*. Edited by Misa Izuhara, 191-210.

Jackson, Kenneth T. *Crabgrass Frontier: The Suburbanization of the United States*. New York: Oxford University Press, 1985.

Jain, Purnendra. *Local Politics and Policymaking in Japan*, New Delhi, India: Commonwealth Publishers, 1989.

Jarausch, Konrad H., and Michael Geyer. *Shattered Past: Reconstructing German Histories*. Princeton: Princeton University Press, 2003.

Jones, Mark Alan. *Children as Treasures: Childhood and the Middle Class in Early Twentieth Century Japan*. Cambridge, MA: Harvard University Asia Center, 2010.

Judt, Tony. *Postwar: A History of Europe Since 1945*. New York: The Penguin Press, 2005.

Jūtaku ki'nyū kōko. *Jūtaku ki'nyū kōko sanjū nenshi*. Tokyo: Jūtaku ki'nyū fukyū kyōkai, 1980.

———. *Shiryō de miru nihon no jūtaku mondai*. Tokyo: Jūtaku ki'nyū fukyū kyōkai, 1980.

Jūtaku toshi seibi kōdan, jūtaku toshi shiken kenkyūjo, ed. *Kōdan chōsa kenkyū, gijutsu kaihatsu no ayumi*. Tokyo: Jūtaku toshi seibi kōdan, 1993.

Kagoyama Takashi. "Kokumin seikatsu no kōzō." Compiled by Ishikawa Hiroyuki, *Yoka goraku kenkyū kiso bunkenshū, dai nijūni maki*, Tokyo: Daikūsha, 1990.

Kashiwagi Hiroshi. "Kōdo seichō ga motarashita mono: mikuro yūtopia toshite no kaku-kazoku." *Sekai* 482 (December 1985), 77-85.

Kasza, Gregory J. "War and Welfare Policy in Japan." *The Journal of Japanese Studies*, 61:2 (2002): 417-435.

Katō, Hidetoshi. "Service-Industry Business Complexes—the Growth and Development of 'Terminal Culture.'" *Japan Interpreter: Journal of Social and Political Ideas* (July, 1972): 376-382.

Kawai, Takao, ed. *Kindai nihon shakai chōsa-shi I*. Tokyo: Keiō tsūshin, 1989.

Kawashima Takeyoshi. *Kawashima Takeyoshi chosakushū dai jū maki*. Tokyo: Iwanami shoten, 1983.

———. *Kekkon*. Tokyo: Iwanami shoten, 1954.

Keizai kikaku chō. *Kokumin seikatsu hakusho*. Tokyo: Ōkurashō insatsu kyoku, various years.

Kelly, William W. "At the Limits of New Middle-Class Japan: Beyond ' 'Mainstream Consciousness.'" In *Social Contracts Under Stress: The Middle Classes of America, Europe and Japan at the Turn of the Century*. Edited by Olivier Zunz, Leonard Schoppa, Nobuhiro Hiwatari, 232-253. New York: Russell Sage Foundation, 2002.

———. "Finding a Place in Metropolitan Japan: Ideologies, Institutions, and Everyday Life." In *Postwar Japan as History*. Edited by Andrew Gordon, 189-216. Berkeley: University of California Press, 1993.

———. "Rationalization and Nostalgia: Cultural Dynamics of New Middle-Class Japan." In *American Ethnologist* 13. 4 (November 1986), 603-618.

Kensetsu kōhō kyōgikai, ed. *Kensetsushō jūnen shōshi*. Kensetsu hōkō kyōgikai, 1963.

Kensetsushō, ed. *Ashita no jūtaku to toshi*. Tokyo: Shōkokusha, 1949.

Kensetsushō nijū nenshi henshū iinkai, ed. *Kensetsushō nijū nenshi*. Tokyo: Kensetsu hōkō kyōgikai, 1968.

Kiefer, Christie. "The *Danchi Zoku* and the Evolution of Metropolitan Mind." In *Japan: The Paradox of Progress*. Edited by Lewis Austin, 279-300. New Haven: Yale University Press, 1976.

Kōdo seichō o kangaeru-kai, ed. *Kōdo seichō to nihonjin: Part 2: kazoku-hen: kazoku no seikatsu no monogatari*. Tokyo: Nihon edeitā sukūru shuppan-bu, 1985.

Kōei jūtaku nijū nenshi kankō iinkai, ed. *Kōei jūtaku nijū nenshi*. Tokyo: Nihon jūtaku kyōkai, 1973.

Kon Wajirō. *Jūkyo-ron: Kon Wajirō shū, dai 4 maki*. Tokyo: Domesu shuppan, 1971.

———. *Kasei-ron: Kon Wajirō-shū dai 6 maki*. Tokyo: Domesu shuppan, 1971.

———. *Seikatsu-gaku: Kon Wajirō shū dai 5 maki*. Tokyo: Domesu shuppan, 1971.

Koschmann, J. Victor. *Revolution and Subjectivity in Postwar Japan*. Chicago: The University of Chicago Press, 1996.

Leary, John Patrick. "Detroitism." In *Guernica: A Magazine of Art and Politics* (January 15, 2011). http://guernicamag.com/. Accessed August 1, 2014.

Lefebvre, Henri. *The Production of Space*. Cambridge, MA: Blackwell, 1991.

———. *Writings on Cities*. Cambridge, MA: Blackwell Publishers, 1996.

Maruyama Masao. "8/15 and 5/19." In *Sources of Japanese Tradition, Volume II*. Edited by Wm. Theodore deBary, Carol Gluck, Arthur Tiedeman. New York: Columbia University Press (2005), 1094-1097.

Massey, Doreen. *Space, Place and Gender*. Minneapolis: University of Minnesota Press, 1994.

May, Elaine Tyler. *Homeward Bound: American Families in the Cold War Era*. New York: Basic Books, 1988.

McClain, Yoko. "Ariyoshi Sawako: Creative Social Critic." *Journal of the Association of Teachers of Japanese* XII: 2 and 3 (May and September, 1977): 211-228.

Mills, C. Wright. *White Collar: The American Middle Classes*. New York: Oxford University Press, 1951.

Minami Hiroshi. *Zoku: Shōwa bunka*. Tokyo: Keisō shobō, 1990.

Minerbi Luciano, Peter Nakamura et al., eds. *Land Readjustment: The Japanese System*. Boston: Oelgaschlager, Gun and Hain, Publishers, Inc., 1986.

Miura Shigekazu, Takabayashi Naoki et al. eds. *Chiba-ken no hyakunen*. Tokyo: Yamakawa shuppankyoku, 1990.

Murakami Yasusuke. "The Age of New Middle Mass Politics: The Case of Japan." *The Journal of Japanese Studies* 8:1 (1982): 29-72.

Nelson, Deborah. *Pursuing Privacy in Cold War America*. New York: Columbia University Press, 2002.

Nihon jūtaku kōdan jū nenshi kankō iinkai, ed. *Nihon jūtaku kōdan jū nenshi*. Tokyo: Nihon jūtaku kōdan, 1965.

Nihon jūtaku kōdan nijū nenshi kankō iinkai, ed. *Nihon jūtaku kōdan nijū nenshi*. Tokyo: Nihon jūtaku kōdan, 1975.

Nihon jūtaku sōgō sentā, ed. *Nihon ni okeru shūgō jūtaku no fukyū katei*. Tokyo: Nihon jūtaku sōgō sentā, 1997.

Nishibe Susumu. "A Denunciation of Mass Society and Its Apologists." *Japan Echo* 13:1 (1986): 39-43.

Nishikawa Yūko. "The Changing Form of Dwellings and the Establishment of the *Katei* in Modern Japan." *U.S.-Japan Women's Journal English Supplement: Nichibei josei jānaru* 8 (1995): 3-36.

———. *Kariya to mochiya no bungaku-shi*. Tokyo: Sanseidō, 1998.

———. "Otoko no ie, onna no ie, seibetsu no nai heya." In *Jendā to nihonshi, ge*. Edited by Wakita Haruko and S.B. Hanley. Tokyo: Tokyo daigaku shuppankai, 1995, 609-643.

Nishiyama Uzō. *Chiiki kūkan ron: Nishiyama Uzō chosaku shū 3*. Tokyo: Keisō shobō, 1968.

———. *Jūkyo ron: Nishiyama Uzō chosaku shū 2*. Tokyo: Keisō shobō, 1968.

———. *Jūtaku keikaku: Nishiyama Uzō chosaku shū 1*. Tokyo: Keisō shobō, 1967.

———. *Kore kara no sumai: jūyōshiki no hanashi*. Tokyo: Sagami shobō, 1947.

———. "Modan ribingu." *Asahi shūkan* (February 28, 1960): 43.

———. *Nihon no jūtaku mondai*. Tokyo: Iwanami shinsho, 1952.

———. *Nihon no sumai I*. Tokyo: Keisō shobō, 1975.

———. *Nihon no sumai II*. Tokyo: Keisō shobō, 1976.

———. *Sensō to jūtaku: seikatsu kūkan no tankyū–ge*. Tokyo: Keisō shobō, 1983.

———. *Sumikata no ki*. Tokyo: Bungei shunjū, 1965.

———. "Tokushū: Shin nihon no jūtaku kenchiku." *Shin kenchiku*1.XXI (January 1946).

Ochiai, Emiko. *The Japanese Family System in Transition: A Sociological Analysis of Family Change in Postwar Japan*. Tokyo: Simul Press, Inc., 1997.

Oda Mitsuo. "*Kōgai" no tanjō to shi*. Tokyo: Seikyū-sha, 1997.

Okamoto Kohei. "Suburbanization of Tokyo and the Daily Lives of Suburban People." In *The Japanese City*. Edited by P.P. Karan and Kristin Stapleton, 79-105. Lexington: The University Press of Kentucky, 1997.

Ōkōchi Kazuo. *Nihonteki chūsankai-kyū*. Tokyo: Bungei shunjū, 1960.

Oldenziel, Ruth, and Karin Zachmann. "Kitchens as Technology and Politics: An Introduction." In *Cold War Kitchen: Americanization, Technology, and European Users*. Edited by Ruth Oldenziel and Karin Zachmann, 1-29, Cambridge, MA: The MIT Press, 2009.

Ōmoto Keinō. "*Shōgen:"nihon no jūtaku seisaku*. Tokyo: Nihon hyōronsha, 1991.

Osawa, Mari. "Twelve Million Full-Time Housewives: The Gender Consequences of Japan's Postwar Social Contract." In *Social Contracts Under Stress: The Middle Classes of America, Europe and Japan at the Turn of the Century*. Edited by Olivier Zunz, Leonard Schoppa, Nobuhiro Hiwatari, 255-277. New York: Russell Sage Foundation, 2002.

Oshima, Ken Tadashi. "Denenchofū: Building the Garden City in Japan." *Journal of the Society of Architectural Historians* (June 1996): 140-51.

Ōyama Ken, Satō Dai, and Hayazumi Kenrō. *Danchi-dan*. Tokyo: Kinema Junposha, 2012.

Ōyama Ken. *Danchi-san*. Tokyo: Intāburein, 2008.

Partner, Simon. *Assembled in Japan: Electrical Goods and the Making of the Japanese Consumer*. Berkeley: University of California Press, 1999.

Pawley, Martin. *Architecture versus Housing*. New York: Praeger Publishers, 1971.

Reynolds, Jonathan M. *Maekawa Kunio and the Emergence of Japanese Modernist Architecture*. Berkeley: University of California Press, 2001.

Riesman, David, and Evelyn Thompson Riesman. *Conversations in Japan: Modernization, Politics, and Culture*. New York: Basic Books, 1967.

Rōdō tōkei kenkyūkai, "Sengo nihon on 'chūkanso' ni tsuite: sono tōkei ni yoru bunseki." *Keizai hyōron* (November 1957): 64-83.

Ronald, Richard. "Home Ownership, Ideology and Diversity: Re-evaluating Concepts of Housing Ideology in the Case of Japan." *In Housing, Theory and Society* (2004. Vol. 21): 49-64.

———. "The Japanese Home in Transition: Housing, Consumption, and Modernization."

In *Housing and Social Transition in Japan*. Edited by Yosuke Hirahama and Richard Ronald, 165-192. New York: Routledge, 2007.

Ross, Kristin. *Fast Cars, Clean Bodies: Decolonization and the Reordering of French Culture*. Cambridge, MA: The MIT Press, 1996.

Ruoff, Kenneth J. *The People's Emperor: Democracy and the Japanese Monarchy, 1945–1995*. Cambridge, MA: Harvard University Asia Center, 2003.

Sand, Jordan. "The Ambivalence of the New Breed: Nostalgic Consumerism in 1980s and 1990s Japan." In *The Ambivalent Consumer: Questioning Consumption in East Asia and the West*. Edited by Sheldon Garon and Patricia L. Maclachlan. Ithaca: Cornell University, 2006, 85-108.

——. "At Home in the Meiji Period: Inventing Japanese Domesticity." In *Mirror of Modernity: Invented Traditions of Modern Japan*. Edited by Stephen Vlastos, 191-207. Berkeley: University of California Press, 1998.

——. "The Cultured Life as Contested Space: Dwelling and Discourse in the 1920s." In *Being Modern in Japan: Culture and Society from the 1910s to the 1930s*. Edited by Elise K. Tipton and John Clark, 99-118. Honolulu: University of Hawaii Press, 2000.

——. *House and Home in Modern Japan: Architecture, Domestic Space, and Bourgeois Culture, 1880–1930*. Cambridge, MA: Harvard University Asia Center, 2003.

Sakamoto Kazue. *"Kazoku" imēji no tanjō: nihon eiga ni miru "hōmu dorama" no keisei*. Tokyo: Shiyōsha, 1997.

Sanuki Toshio. *Seichō suru toshi suitai suru toshi*. Tokyo: Jijitsūshinsha, 1983.

Sayare, Scott. "Razing a Neighborhood and a Social Engineering Idea." *The New York Times* (September 7, 2011): A8.

Schaller, Michael. *The American Occupation of Japan: The Origins of the Cold War in Asia*. New York: Oxford University Press, 1985.

Schissler, Hanna, ed. *The Miracle Years: A Cultural History of West Germany, 1949–1968*. Princeton: Princeton University Press, 2001.

Scott, James. *Seeing Like a State: How Certain Schemes to Improve the Human Condition Have Failed*. New Haven: Yale University Press, 1998.

Seikatsu kagaku chōsakai, ed. *Danchi no subete*. Tokyo: Seikatsu kagaku chōsakai, 1963.

Shiki Yūichi, Uchida Seizō, et al.. *Sekai-ichi utsukushii danchi zukan*. Tokyo: Ekusunareggi, 2012.

Shinkeisei dentetsu kabushiki kaisha shashi hensan jimukyoku, ed. *Shinkeisei dentetsu gojū nenshi*. Tokyo: Shinkeisei kabushiki kaisha, 1997.

Shioda Maruo. *Danchi seikatsu jutsu*. Tokyo: Orion shuppansha, 1968.

——. *Sumai no sengo-shi*. Tokyo: Saimaru shuppan-kai, 1975.

——. *Sumeba danchi*. Tokyo: Kōbundō, 1963.

Sorensen, André. *The Making of Urban Japan: Cities and Planning from Edo to the Twenty-first Century*. New York: Routledge, 2002.

———. "Post-Suburban Tokyo? Urbanization, Suburbanization, Reurbanization." In Nicholas Phelps and Fulong Wu, *International Perspectives on Suburbanization*, 210-224. New York: Palgrave, 2011.

Spigel, Lynn. *Make Room for T.V.: Television and the Family Ideal in Postwar America*. Chicago: The University of Chicago Press, 1992.

Steven, Rob. *Classes in Contemporary Japan*. New York: Cambridge University Press, 1983.

Suzuki Hitoshi. *Kinkō toshi: aru chihō toshi no sengo shakai-shi*. Tokyo: Nihon keizai shimbun-sha, 1973.

Suzuki Shigebumi. *Gendai nihon jūkyo ron: sumai o yomu*. Tokyo: Kenchiku shiryō kenkyūsha, 1999.

Suzuki Shigebumi. *Suzuki Shigebumi jūkyo ronshū: sumai no keikaku, sumai no bunka*. Tokyo: Shōkokusha, 1988.

Swingewood, Alan. *A Short History of Sociological Thought*. New York: St. Martin's Press, 1984.

Tada, Michitarō. "The Glory and Misery of 'My Home.'" In *Authority and the Individual in Japan: Citizen Protest in Historical Perspective*. Edited by J. Victor Koschmann, 207-217. Tokyo: University of Tokyo Press, 1978.

Taira, Koji. "Dialectics of Economic Growth, National Power, and Distributive Struggles." In *Postwar Japan as History*. Edited by Andrew Gordon, 167-186. Berkeley: University of California Press, 1993.

Tanaka Kakuei. *Building a New Japan: Remodeling the Japanese Archipelago*. Tokyo: Simul Press, 1972.

Tanizaki, Junichirō. *Naomi*. Translated by Anthony H. Chambers. New York: North Point Press, 1990.

Tatematsu, Wahei. *Distant Thunder: A Novel of Contemporary Japan*. Translated by Lawrence J. Howell and Hikaru Morimoto. Rutland, Vermont: Charles E. Tuttle Company, 1999.

Takenaka Tsutomu. *Danchi no nanatsu no daizai*. Tokyo: Kōbundō, 1964.

Terade Kōji. *Seikatsu bunka-ron e no shōtai*. Tokyo: Kōbundō, 1994.

"Tokushū: shin kōdan (sono 1): nihon jūtaku kōdan jūtaku kyōkyū no ayumi." *Jūtaku* (September 1981): 2-83.

"Tokushū: yuragi no naka no kazoku to nLDK: sengo nihon no kazoku to jūtaku." *Kenchiku zasshi* 110. No. 1371 (April 1995): 15-67.

Twitchell, James. "Two Cheers for Materialism." In *The Consumer Society Reader*. Edited by Juliet B. Schor and Douglas B. Holt, 281-290. New York: The New Press, 2000.

Ueno Chizuko, ed. *Shufu ronsō o yomu I*. Tokyo: Keisō shobō, 1989.

Urban, Florian. *Tower and Slab: Histories of Global Mass Housing*. New York: Routledge, 2012.

Vogel, Ezra. *Japan's New Middle Class: The Salaryman and His Family in a Tokyo Suburb*. Berkeley: University of California Press, 1963.

Wakuda Yasuo. *Nihon no shitetsu*. Tokyo: Iwanami shoten, 1981.

Walker, Richard A. "A Theory of Suburbanization: Capitalism and the Construction of Urban Space in the United States." In *Urbanization and Urban Planning in Capitalist Society*. Edited by Michael Dear and Allen J. Scott, 383-429. New York: Methuen, 1981.

Waswo, Ann. *Housing in Postwar Japan: A Social History*. New York: RoutledgeCurzon, 2002.

———. "Urban Housing Policy in 20th-Century Japan." *ISS Discussion Paper Series No. F-82*. Tokyo: University of Tokyo Institute of Social Science.

Watanabe Hiroyuki. *Kisha jūtaku monogatari: norimono ni sumu to iu koto*. Tokyo: INAX shuppan, 1993.

Watanabe Shunichi. *"Toshi keikaku" no tanjō: kokusai hikaku kara mita nihon kindai toshi keikaku*. Tokyo: Kashiwa shobō, 1996.

Wildt, Michael. "Continuities and Discontinuities of Consumer Mentality in West Germany in the 1950s." In *Life after Death: Approaches to the Cultural and Social History of Europe During the 1940s and 1950s*. Edited by Richard Bessel and Kirk Schumann. Cambridge UK: Cambridge University Press, 2003, 211-229.

Yamada Kōichi, Takahashi Akiko, and Baba Masako. *Monogo / mono no kenchiku-shi: daidokoro no hanashi*. Tokyo: Shikajima shuppankai, 1995.

Yamakawa Masao. "Omamori." In *Yamakawa Masao zenshū 3*. Tokyo: Chikuma shobō, 2000, 263-273.

Yanagida Kunio. *Danchi bunmei-ron*. Tokyo: Sanpō, 1963.

Yasuda Munemutsu. *Anpo to kōdo seichō*. Tokyo: Heibonsha, 1975.

Yoda, Tomiko, "The Rise and Fall of Maternal Society: Gender, Labor, and Capital in Contemporary Japan." In *Japan After Japan: Social and Cultural Life From the Recessionary 1990s to the Present*. Edited by Tomiko Yoda and Harry Harootunian. Durham: Duke University Press, 2006, 239-274.

Yomiuri shimbun shakai-bu, ed. *Warera sarariiman*. Tokyo: Yomiuri shimbun-sha, 1961.

Yoshimoto, Takaaki. "The End of a Fictitious System." In *Sources of Japanese Tradition, Volume II*. Edited by Wm. Theodore deBary, Carol Gluck, Arthur Tiedeman. New York: Columbia University Press, 2005, 1097-1100.

Young, Louise. "Marketing the Modern: Department Stores, Consumer Culture, and the New Middle Class in Interwar Japan." *International Labor and Working-Class History* 55 (1999): 52-70.

Zunz, Olivier. "Introduction: Social Contracts Under Stress." In *Social Contracts Under Stress: The Middle Classes of America, Europe, and Japan at the Turn of the Century*. Edited by Olivier Zunz, Leonard Schoppa, and Nobuhiro Hiwatari. New York: Russell Sage Foundation, 2002,

Index

(Page numbers in *italics* indicate illustrations)

About the Author

Laura Neitzel lived and worked in Japan for many years before pursuing a Ph.D. in Japanese History at Columbia University. She has made her career at Brookdale Community College in Lincroft, New Jersey where she teaches East Asian and world history.

Professor Neitzel is deeply involved in community and international education and travels frequently with her students to Asia and other destinations. She has found her home on the Jersey Shore with her husband Tom.

Weatherhead
East Asian Institute

Studies of the Weatherhead East Asian Institute
Columbia University

Selected Titles
(Complete list at: http://www.columbia.edu/cu/weai/weatherhead-studies.html)

Chinese Law in Imperial Eyes: Sovereignty, Justice, and Transcultural Politics, by Li Chen. Columbia University Press, 2015.

The Age of Irreverence: A New History of Laughter in China, by Christopher Rea. University of California Press, 2015

The Nature of Knowledge and the Knowledge of Nature in Early Modern Japan, by Federico Marcon. University of Chicago Press, 2015

The Fascist Effect: Japan and Italy, 1915-1952, by Reto Hoffman. Cornell University Press, 2015

The International Minimum: Creativity and Contradiction in Japan's Global Engagement, 1933-1964, by Jessamyn R. Abel. University of Hawai'i Press, 2015

Empires of Coal: Fueling China's Entry into the Modern World Order, 1860-1920, by Shellen Xiao Wu. Stanford University Press, 2015

Casualties of History: Wounded Japanese Servicemen and the Second World War, by Lee K. Pennington. Cornell University Press, 2015

City of Virtues: Nanjing in an Age of Utopian Visions, by Chuck Wooldridge. University of Washington Press, 2015

The Proletarian Wave: Literature and Leftist Culture in Colonial Korea, 1910-1945, by Sunyoung Park. Harvard University Asia Center, 2015.

Neither Donkey Nor Horse: Medicine in the Struggle Over China's Modernity, by Sean Hsiang-lin Lei. University of Chicago Press, 2014.

When the Future Disappears: The Modernist Imagination in Late Colonial Korea, by Janet Poole. Columbia University Press, 2014.

Bad Water: Nature, Pollution, & Politics in Japan, 1870-1950, by Robert Stolz. Duke University Press, 2014.

Rise of a Japanese Chinatown: Yokohama, 1894-1972, by Eric C. Han. Harvard University Asia Center, 2014.

Beyond the Metropolis: Second Cities and Modern Life in Interwar Japan, by Louise Young. University of California Press, 2013.

From Cultures of War to Cultures of Peace: War and Peace Museums in Japan, China, and South Korea, by Takashi Yoshida. MerwinAsia, 2013.

Imperial Eclipse: Japan's Strategic Thinking about Continental Asia before August 1945, by Yukiko Koshiro. Cornell University Press, 2013.

The Nature of the Beasts: Empire and Exhibition at the Tokyo Imperial Zoo, by Ian J. Miller. University of California Press, 2013.

Public Properties: Museums in Imperial Japan, by Noriko Aso. Duke University Press, 2013.

Reconstructing Bodies: Biomedicine, Health, and Nation-Building in South Korea Since 1945, by John P. DiMoia. Stanford University Press, 2013.

Taming Tibet: Landscape Transformation and the Gift of Chinese Development, by Emily T. Yeh. Cornell University Press, 2013.

Tyranny of the Weak: North Korea and the World, 1950–1992, by Charles K. Armstrong. Cornell University Press, 2013.

The Art of Censorship in Postwar Japan, by Kirsten Cather. University of Hawai'i Press, 2012.

Asia for the Asians: China in the Lives of Five Meiji Japanese, by Paula Harrell. MerwinAsia, 2012.

Lin Shu, Inc.: Translation and the Making of Modern Chinese Culture, by Michael Gibbs Hill. Oxford University Press, 2012.

Occupying Power: Sex Workers and Servicemen in Postwar Japan, by Sarah Kovner. Stanford University Press, 2012.

Redacted: The Archives of Censorship in Postwar Japan, by Jonathan E. Abel. University of California Press, 2012.

Empire of Dogs: Canines, Japan, and the Making of the Modern Imperial World, by Aaron Herald Skabelund. Cornell University Press, 2011.

Planning for Empire: Reform Bureaucrats and the Japanese Wartime State, by Janis Mimura. Cornell University Press, 2011.

Realms of Literacy: Early Japan and the History of Writing, by David Lurie. Harvard University Asia Center, 2011.

Russo-Japanese Relations, 1905–17: From Enemies to Allies, by Peter Berton. Routledge, 2011.

Behind the Gate: Inventing Students in Beijing, by Fabio Lanza. Columbia University Press, 2010.

Imperial Japan at Its Zenith: The Wartime Celebration of the Empire's 2,600th Anniversary, by Kenneth J. Ruoff. Cornell University Press, 2010.